100 Great American Novels
You've (Probably) Never Read

Karl Bridges

UNLIMITED

A Member of the Greenwood Publishing Group

Westport, Connecticut • London

Library of Congress Cataloging-in-Publication Data

Bridges, Karl, 1964–
  100 great American novels you've (probably) never read / Karl Bridges.
    p. cm.
  Includes bibliographical references and index.
    ISBN-13: 978-1-59158-165-9 (alk. paper)
1. American fiction—Stories, plots, etc. 2. American fiction—20th century—Stories,
plots, etc. 3. American fiction—Bio-bibliography. 4. American fiction—20th century—
Bio-bibliography. 5. American fiction—History and criticism—Handbooks, manuals, etc.
6. American fiction—20th century—History and criticism—Handbooks, manuals, etc.
I. Title. II. Title: One hundred American novels you've (probably) never read.
PS373.B75 2007
813.01'0873—dc22   2007018666

British Library Cataloguing in Publication Data is available.

Library of Congress Catalog Card Number: 2007018666
ISBN-13: 978-1-59158-165-9

First published in 2007

Libraries Unlimited, 88 Post Road West, Westport, CT 06881
A Member of the Greenwood Publishing Group, Inc.
www.lu.com

Printed in the United States of America

The paper used in this book complies with the
Permanent Paper Standard issued by the National
Information Standards Organization (Z39.48–1984).

10 9 8 7 6 5 4 3 2 1

Contents

Preface

What makes a book popular? Why does one book soar to the top of the best-seller list while another, published at the same time and of equal merit, languishes, eventually to be consigned to the remainder bin? Some of the greatest novels ever written never receive the acclaim, accolades, and recognition they deserve—in fact, it's likely you've never even heard of them. Whether it's because of lack of marketing, the wrong publisher, or one of many other possible reasons, there are hundreds of literary masterpieces sitting on library shelves gathering dust.

One of the most important elements in answering this question is what could be termed "resonance," which can be defined as how well a book fits into the social and political framework of its era. How well does a particular piece of writing reflect the anxieties and hopes of the time?

The Harry Potter books provide us with a perfect example of this. When one thinks about it, the whole Harry Potter series seems almost perfectly created for the current era of terror and war we find ourselves in. Harry lives in a traditional society, England, with a very definite class structure. After becoming a member of a secret society, he goes to a school where he wears a uniform and gets merits and demerits depending on his behavior. The school trains him, under the supervision of a pseudo-governmental agency—the Ministry of Magic—to fight a war against an evil menace that is threatening society. What does Harry want to do after graduation? Become an Auror—join what amounts to, in wizard society, the secret police. All in all, one would have been surprised if, given current levels of societal anxiety, Harry Potter hadn't become immensely successful.

Popularity can also kill. The fact is, many critics don't especially like popular works. A book that sells a lot of copies is probably, on average, not going to be as well reviewed or have as long-term a reputation as a smaller-selling book that appeals to the intellectual class of critics—the group that makes or breaks literary reputations. One of the greater publishing successes of the past decade has been the Left Behind series by Tim LaHaye and Jerry Jenkins—a set of novels dealing with the Tribulation and the Second Coming of Christ. These millenarian novels are immensely popular with large segments of the American population—their sales figures and prominent position in the bookracks at every Wal-Mart are testimony to this. These books are not taken seriously by intellectuals and critics, many of whom have no religious views or are actively hostile to religion. Critics consider it a bad sign that sales are huge for books promoting a strident, militant millenarianism announcing that God is coming back next Tuesday and that boy is he mad—they believe that the writing somehow isn't good and that they are bad books.

Genre drives popularity. Product placement in bookstores drives sales. An author identified with a popular genre is more likely not only to get published, but also to have his or her books placed and marketed in a way that ensures their commercial success and their enduring popularity. Consider the placement of books in any popular chain bookstore. The popular books, especially the techno/military novels, such as those by Tom Clancy or Dale Brown, are prominent, front and center. If you want to read something like Dickens or P. G. Wodehouse, you'll find it pushed to the side or upstairs. And sadly, a great deal of good writing you won't find at all because it just isn't there.

Most people buying books don't realize how many of the books available for purchase are dictated by the tax code. There's simply no financial incentive for publishers to keep books in print for a long time and allow them to develop an audience. If it doesn't sell immediately, a book is remaindered. The other culprit in this scenario is discounting. Allowing bookstores to discount means that larger stores have an inordinate advantage over smaller bookstores in terms of influencing not only what gets sold, but even what gets published. This reduces the number of venues in which books can be available and, over time, develop an audience. This American practice is in marked contrast to other countries, such as France, where discounting is banned, and thus, smaller bookstores thrive.

Commercial issues aside, there remains the question of what elements make a book popular. Books enjoyed by people in power will be more successful than books that don't. Why, for example, has everyone heard of Shakespeare, whereas playwright Thomas Middleton is largely forgotten? They were contemporaries who wrote about similar subjects. One major difference is that Shakespeare was popular with the king, and Middleton was not. We have the same phenomenon today. Oprah's Book Club can catapult an unknown author to fame overnight—even if the book, in the view of some, is of subpar quality. Exposure drives popularity.

Education is another thing that greatly affects the popularity of books. English classes tend to focus on a few works by a few major authors—Shakespeare (*Romeo and Juliet*), Dickens (*Tale of Two Cities*), and Hemingway (*The Sun Also Rises*) being typical examples. Omission of the vast majority of English literature—for reasons of time, lack of interest (of either students or teachers), or, sadly in some communities, local censorship—means that students aren't exposed to many excellent writers. Also, unfortunately, many schools are now teaching to the test rather than teaching their students what they might need to know to be truly literate readers. No child may be left behind, but Chaucer is.

In spite of all of these obstacles to reading and to the success of specific titles, what really impressed me as I developed this book was the depth and breadth of the American writing and reading culture. I rejected many good books, probably more than I actually included, just because there was no space. The quality of American writers, especially younger ones, is simply astounding. Additionally, in the course of writing this book, I routinely haunted bookstores in a variety of cities. I was never in a bookstore, either independent or chain, that was not packed with people—all enjoying themselves immensely. The people who go on about the death of reading are wrong. Hopefully, this guide will provide readers with even more avenues for enjoying American literature.

Acknowledgments

I'd like to acknowledge the administration and staff of the University of Vermont, especially my colleagues in the Bailey/Howe Library who were most helpful and supportive, especially during the half-year sabbatical I was granted to complete this work.

I would also thank the staffs of the various bookstores and libraries that I frequented, in Vermont and elsewhere, while I sought books for this project. They were universally helpful, even with the most obscure requests. You are all a credit to your respective professions. In addition, I received helpful advice from a variety of librarians across the country who suggested titles, advised me on the issues relating to indexing, or otherwise supported my search for obscure titles. I would name you individually if not for the fear I would leave someone out. You know who you are.

And finally, I would like to thank my family. My father, William Bridges, read the draft manuscript and made helpful suggestions. My mother, along with my father, gave me house-room during the writing and helpfully suggested it would be a good thing not to work on this project for a week. To my cats, Ryan, Heather, and Benny, who enjoyed having Daddy home all the time, but were confused by why he would rather sit in front of a small box than play with them—sorry, guys. I'll make it up to you.

And last, but always first in my heart, thank you to my wife Rita, who tolerated my writing this book in the small confines of our apartment—dear, you can have the dining room table back now.

Introduction

Reading should always begin with questions. In most pleasure reading, these questions are simple. Do I like this kind of book? Did I like it the first time I read it? Do I like the writer? Has he or she, in the past, had something to say that I found useful or enjoyable? Is there something in this book that I want to know about? This is a relatively easy and painless process, and if we answer ourselves falsely, the worst that can happen is that we waste an afternoon of leisure. With luck, this will be in winter or when it's raining or at some other time or place, such as on the train or in an airport, where we don't feel the loss too greatly.

The book in your hands is somewhat different from a book one might read for recreation in that it is a reference book—a book about books, a book you might expect to find in the library. For such a book, one applies longer and more difficult questions. The first questions that any intelligent reader should ask in reading a book of this kind are the following: How were the titles featured in this book selected? What criteria were used? What are the qualifications of the selector, and what biases does that person bring to the process? To some extent, you may be disappointed in the answers, for book selection is always, to a lesser or greater degree, a subjective act of art—whether it is selecting books for one's own pleasure or, as in the present author's case, selecting books for (he hopes) the pleasure of others. To the extent that I can, I answer the questions just posed in the following section.

Scope and Selection Criteria

This guide covers only novels, and not nonfiction works and alternate literary formats, such as short stories. As this book's title suggests, the works covered are meant to be "great American novels," as well as novels not widely read by today's readers. So the selection is limited to books written by American authors. There has been a deliberate decision not to include books by foreign authors—mostly in the interest of simplicity and focus. That being said, the definition of "American" is left somewhat broad—Sax Rohmer, for instance, although a British writer, is included because of the popularity of his works in the United States and because, at the time of his death, he was living in America with intentions of staying. There are other writers, such as Robert McAlmon, who, although American by nationality, spent much of their writing careers abroad.

One goal of this book is to represent a wide time span—one equaling the length of American history. Although this book ends up heavily weighted toward books of the twentieth century, there are earlier works as well—the oldest from the eighteenth century. This choice was made partly because fewer nineteenth-century novels that were available during that century are still available to modern readers; and those that are available are often already identified as "classics." There are plenty of sources for people who want to know about Melville's *Moby Dick*. Many of the more obscure nineteenth-century writers are too didactic, too archaic in style or content, or simply too tedious to sustain contemporary interest, but some were included to give people a sense of the period and to suggest some novels that have stood the test of time.

There was also the consideration of availability. Many authors from earlier times are obscure—or at least not well known, which often makes obtaining the books more difficult. With the selection or books weighted toward the twentieth century, the readers' chance of obtaining copies of the books—in either original or reprinted editions—is improved for readers, especially ones who don't happen to live near large libraries. However, librarians, especially those in smaller libraries, do wonders in locating almost any book regardless of how obscure it may be.

A guide to books that no one can get seemed a fairly pointless exercise in regard to increasing the reading pleasure of general readers. Not all of the authors and books covered in this collection qualify as "obscure"; in fact, some authors, such as Thornton Wilder and Conrad Richter, are among the more well known of American authors. But the works represented here are their lesser-known works, rather than signature titles, even though these books may have won awards or hit best-seller lists when originally released.

The year 1997 was used as a cutoff publication date for books covered in this work. Although many wonderful novels have appeared since then, a certain amount of time is needed to determine whether a book has indeed been overlooked or forgotten. How can one tell whether a book published in 2003 has become obscure? Or is important? Or worthwhile?

The definition of what constitutes an "obscure" book has been forever changed by the advent of Google (and its text-digitizing efforts), as well as by online bookstores, especially the giants Amazon.com and eBay, which, like it or not, now represent two of the world's great book marketplaces. Books, now more than ever, keep being sold, circulated, read, and rediscovered long after they leave the shelves of brick-and-mortar bookstores. Unlike many librarians, I don't distrust Google. Anything that gets good books (and good ideas) into the hands of readers is okay by me. Just because the song has changed doesn't mean we can't keep dancing.

There was thoughtful intention in selecting books that offer diversity in both subjects and authors. As a result, there are books on a wide range of subjects (e.g., immigration, farming, factory workers, academia) by a wide range of authors (e.g., women, gay and lesbian, immigrants) in many genres, ranging from fantasy and science fiction to murder mysteries to war novels. As an author, I sought a range of books that would reflect the widest possible breadth of American writing. It wasn't an attempt to make a collection that was "politically correct" in the modern sense of the phrase, but rather to illustrate how deep and vibrant our writing culture actually is.

A wide range of resources was used to identify "great" novels—best-seller lists, contemporary reviews, library catalogs, book-sale lists, and advertisements. I also consulted with other readers, particularly my colleagues. The question "Have you heard of this book?" has often been heard from my cubicle in the last year. Some acquaintances now cringe when they see me and hear the words "Have you read . . . ?" My colleagues, family, and friends, I think, represent a well-educated cross section of the American reading public, so I found them to be useful in testing particular cases.

Methodology

I read every book in this work in its entirety. I made a deliberate choice not to consult secondary sources and criticisms because I wanted the opinions expressed to be my own rather than simply repetitions of the words of others. In some cases, such as for the author Sax Rohmer, there were few critical works available to consult anyway. The opinions in this book are my own, and I take responsibility for any omissions or errors of fact. I realize that some people may object to this lack of reference to critics. However, I thought it was important to see what the reaction of a typically, or reasonably, well-educated contemporary reader—myself—was to books rather than to simply restate the words of critics. I'm sure that some professional critics will disagree with both my choice of books and my opinions. Such is life. I did research each author for the biographical section as well as locate other works by the authors and suggest readings.

Organization and Format

Titles in this guide are arranged alphabetically by author name. For each book, you will find

- a brief extract to give you a sense of the writer's style;
- a synopsis of the work;
- a short biography;
- a list of selected works by the writer; and
- a brief list of suggested works to consult for more information about the author, the novel, and related subjects.

The lists of suggested works are not intended to be comprehensive bibliographies. They are designed, rather, to give readers starting points for finding more works by the author or for finding books that provide background for the novel. For example, in the case of Marianne Wiggins's *John Dollar*, suggestions include several works on life in the British Empire and the Raj—such as James Morris's excellent *Pax Britannica*. Whenever possible, I have tried to suggest readings that are readily available in libraries or bookstores and that are of interest to the general reader. The book cited at the start of each entry is the edition actually used by me. I have generally tried to use editions that are currently available rather than tracking down the original first editions.

The careful reader may note that the biographies differ in length. Although every effort was made to find background information on these authors and create balanced biographical profiles, the amount of material available differs widely. In the case of lesser-known authors, sometimes little or nothing is available. Writers often live through their works and leave a paucity of biographical material behind. In the cases of famous authors, there is generally an overflow of materials, with plenty of biographies and other materials available for those interested; so long biographical entries for such authors would be redundant.

Although this book is designed as a professional resource for librarians, especially those engaged in advising readers, it is, I hope, also—and more importantly—a resource for general readers. One of my colleagues, Trina Magi, offered an insightful comment when I was writing this book: although there are plenty of "Top 100" lists of great novels, there is little or nothing available for the people who have worked themselves through those lists. My hope is that individuals dip into this and find something worthwhile to fill that gap.

Selections are based on the criteria discussed previously, but they also reflect my own biases based on a lifetime of reading. By my estimate, I have spent the equivalent of about 50,000 hours of my life reading. For the past 15 years, I have also worked as a professional academic reference librarian, with over 10,000 hours at a reference desk (and counting!). And finally, although, this is a matter of luck rather than any deliberate intention on my part, I had the good fortune to grow up in a family of professional writers, so I have had lifelong experience with discussions of what makes a good book.

Admittedly, a few selections may strike some readers as somewhat old-fashioned, which is probably a result of my education—which has been primarily historical and classical—and my personal literary tastes, which are, admittedly, conservative, but I've made a conscious effort to broaden my thinking (and my reading) in the course of this project to create a wider appeal. I will leave it to the reader as to whether I have been successful in this regard. I hope I have been.

I think that I have read enough (and have had enough experience in advising others about their reading) to express a reasonably informed opinion about a book. I make no pretense to being a professional literary scholar. In some sense, this book is a more traditional, almost Victorian, mode of criticism as opposed to the modern techniques of textual interpretation and the like. To literary scholars and specialists, I again offer my apologies for treading in your sacred groves, but in my effort to encourage people to read, I hope I will have your indulgence.

Horatio Alger

Mark, The Match Boy

New York: Scribner Paperback Fiction, 1998

Originally published: 1869

Genre: Young Adult Fiction

Quote

> While the boys, — for the elder of the two is but eighteen — are making preparations to go
> out, a few explanations may be required by the reader. Those who have read "Ragged
> Dick" and "Fame and Fortune," — the preceding volumes of this series, — will understand
> that less than three years ago Richard Hunter was an ignorant and ragged bootblack about
> the streets, and Fosdick, although possessing a better education, was in the same busi-
> ness. By a series of upward steps, partly due to good fortune, but largely due to his own
> determination to improve, and hopeful energy, Dick had now become a book-keeper in the
> establishment of Rockwell & Cooper, on Pearl Street, and possessed the confidence and
> good wishes of the firm in a high degree.[1]

Synopsis

Richard Hunter, a young man on the rise, meets a Mr. Bates, who engages him to find his
missing grandson, Mark. As it turns out, Mark is living the life of a street urchin—begging,
bootblacking, and otherwise doing what he needs to do to survive. Unlike his companions,
however, Mark maintains his moral values of honesty, refusing to engage in thievery or other
crimes. He gets a place in the Newsboy's Lodging House—a hostel for abandoned children.
After collapsing on the street, he comes into the care of Richard Hunter and gets himself a job
in a bookstore. Mark is then framed by a fellow employee for stealing from the cash drawer. Of
course, everything is eventually sorted out, and the book comes to a happy conclusion.

Critical Commentary

The idea of the Horatio Alger story, characterized by the poor boy who, through hard work
and diligence, makes something of himself, has been enshrined in American mythology to the
point of being a cliché. Most people use the phrase "Horatio Alger story" without ever having
read any of the novels that inspired the term. *Mark, The Match Boy* is an excellent example
of Alger's work, worth considering in view of Alger's continuing influence on the American
psyche. Alger's novels are more than simply pieces of Americana; they reveal important and
continuing truths about American psychology—as relevant today as when they were written.

This book is worth a closer look by modern readers for its engaging storyline and for what
it reveals about the times in which it was written. Granted, it's difficult to get interested at first
in a novel in which the beginning pages discuss how to collect a debt, and Richard Hunter,

the grown-up and successful protagonist of Alger's earlier novel *Ragged Dick*, is, basically, something of a prig. However, in the context in which Alger wrote the novel, especially given the prevailing exploitation of child labor and the increasing abuses of Gilded Age capitalism, Alger's characterization is more understandable. As the story continues, you may find yourself becoming more interested and involved in the plot until, predictably, the novel comes to its happy conclusion.

Philosophically, the novel delves much deeper than a mere surface reading would indicate. In an age of increasing business development and devaluing of the individual (not unlike contemporary times), Alger used his novel to celebrate the role of the individual. Ironically, he defined success almost entirely in a material way—celebrating the acquisition of property—which is how the mythos of Alger has come down to the present. Leaving that aside, Alger's characters are defined by their moral beliefs, which embrace an obvious Puritan Christianity. A humanitarian ethos is evident in Alger's characters, requiring them, as a condition of their success, to have a sense of helpfulness and charity toward their fellow man—an obvious slap at the emerging industrial society, which was marked by its lack of consideration of human values, as evidenced by such abuses as child labor and lack of social welfare legislation. Filled with positive role models and examples of ethical behavior, this novel is suitable for both younger children and teenagers.

Author Sketch

Born in Revere, Massachusetts, on January 13, 1832, Alger was educated at Harvard, graduating in 1854. He was subsequently a journalist, teacher, and Unitarian minister. In 1866 he moved to New York City and devoted himself to literature. He wrote more than 40 novels, which were well received upon publication. He died July 18, 1899, in Natick, Massachusetts.[2]

Other Works by the Author

John Maynard: A Ballad of Lake Erie. N.p., 1850.
Nothing to Do: A Tilt at Our Best Society. Boston: James French, 1857.
Nothing to Eat. Not by the Author of "Nothing to Wear." New York: Dick and Fitzgerald, 1857.
Timothy Crump's Ward: A Story of American Life. Boston: Loring, 1866, microform.
Rough and Ready; Or, Life among the New York Newsboys. Boston: Loring, 1869.
Paul the Peddler, or, the Adventures of a Young Street Merchant. Boston: Loring, 1871.
Slow and Sure: Or from Street to the Shop. Boston: Loring, 1872.
Julius, or, the Street Boy out West, Tattered Tom Books. Second Series. Boston: Loring, 1874.
Grand'ther Baldwin's Thanksgiving: With Other Ballads and Poems. Boston: Loring, 1875.
Wait and Hope; or, Ben Bradford's Motto. Philadelphia: H. T. Coates, 1877.
The Young Adventurer, or, Tom's Trip across the Plains. Pacific Series. Philadelphia: Porter & Coates, 1878.
The Young Miner, or, Tom Nelson in California. Pacific Series. Philadelphia: Porter & Coates, 1879.
Ben's Nugget, or, a Boy's Search for a Fortune: A Story of the Pacific Coast. Philadelphia: Porter & Coates, 1882.
The Train Boy. New York: G.W. Carleton, 1883.
Frank Fowler, the Cash Boy. Alger Series for Boys. New York: A. L. Burt, 1887.
Joe's Luck, or, a Boy's Adventures in California. Boys' Home Series. New York: A. L. Burt, 1887.
Bob Burton, or, the Young Ranchman of the Missouri. Philadelphia, Chicago, Toronto: John C. Winston, 1888.

The Errand Boy, or, How Phil Brent Won Success. New York: A. L. Burt, 1888.

Struggling Upward; or, Luke Larkin's Luck. New York: Hurst, 1890.

Ralph Raymond's Heir. A Novel. New York: F. M. Lupton, 1892.

Digging for Gold: A Story of California. Philadelphia, Chicago, Toronto: John C. Winston, 1892.

Dean Dunham: Or, the Waterford Mystery. New York: Street & Smith, 1900.

The Backwoods Boys; Or, the Boyhood and Manhood of Abraham Lincoln. New York: Street and Smith, 1904.

Herbert Carter's Legacy; Or, the Inventor's Son. New York: New York Book, 1909.

Tony the Tramp, or, Right Is Might, Best of the Famous Alger Stories for Boys. New York: New York Book, 1909.

Ragged Dick, and Mark, the Match Boy. New York: Collier Books, 1962.

Silas Snobden's Office Boy. Garden City, NY: Doubleday, 1973.

Cast Upon the Breakers. Garden City, NY: Doubleday, 1974.

Suggestions for Further Reading

Hoyt, Edwin Palmer. *Horatio's Boys; The Life and Works of Horatio Alger, Jr.* Radnor, PA: Chilton Book, 1974.

Klein, Marcus. *Easterns, Westerns, and Private Eyes: American Matters, 1870–1900.* Madison: University of Wisconsin Press, 1994.

Nackenoff, Carol. *The Fictional Republic: Horatio Alger and American Political Discourse.* New York: Oxford University Press, 1994.

Scharnhorst, Gary, and Jack Bales. *Horatio Alger, Jr.: An Annotated Bibliography of Comment and Criticism, Scarecrow Author Bibliographies; No. 54.* Metuchen, NJ: Scarecrow Press, 1981.

———. *The Lost Life of Horatio Alger, Jr.* Bloomington: Indiana University Press, 1985.

Notes

1. Horatio Alger, *Mark, The Match Boy* (New York: Scribner Paperback Fiction, 1998), p. 221.
2. http://www.lib.rochester.edu/camelot/cinder/bio.htm

Edward Anderson

Hungry Men

New York: Penguin, 1985

Originally published: 1935

Genre: Mainstream/Literary Fiction

Quote

> I'm going to walk clear to the end of this street. I like this street. I like New Orleans. It's kind of like a girl you have met two or three times and didn't think so much of and then all of a sudden you see her again and you want to hold her.[1]

Synopsis

Acel Stecker is a hobo, an unemployed musician who travels Depression-era America taking odd jobs—although more often than not, he is turned away. His travels range from New York to Washington to New Orleans to Chicago. He experiences all the good and bad that the Depression has to offer the unemployed. Acel makes friends along the way with Lungren and with Boats, a socialist who challenges Acel's belief in democracy. Eventually, Acel forms a small street band in Chicago, the members of which are arrested after they get into a fight for refusing to play the Communist anthem, the "International." Freed by the judge who applauds the band's patriotism, Acel sees that playing patriotic songs is an angle they can use to become successful.

Critical Commentary

In *Hungry Men,* Edward Anderson creates a compelling, character-driven novel that provides a realistic and sensitive view of life among the down-and-out during the Great Depression. Making outstanding use of plot and dialogue in a fast-moving episodic style, *Hungry Men* vividly describes life at the time, while probing underlying causes and possible solutions for the era's economic crisis. Although set in an era remote from our own, this novel's concern with issues of economic justice and survival are still relevant to modern audiences.

Today, it's easy to consider the Depression as a time of inactivity—of locked factory doors and the unemployed slowly shuffling forward in breadlines. Anderson effectively dispels this perception. His characters live lives of action, focusing primarily on basic issues of survival. They are constantly in motion, moving from town to town in search of a toehold back to not even prosperity, but just some kind of struggling normalcy. Anderson creates a portrait of modern pioneers—forced by circumstances into an almost frontier-like existence, with all the nobility and rawness that one would expect to find in that environment.

While engaged in the day-to-day struggle for life, Anderson's characters take part in an ongoing dialogue about how they came to their situations. Doctrines of Christianity, democracy, Communism, and capitalism are all examined and found wanting. In the end Anderson concedes that the only real solution is for people to depend on their individual initiative and the support of their neighbors.

This novel reflects the era's disenchantment with the existing economic system. Interesting plot devices, compelling characters, and Anderson's excellent use of language combine with the universality of the central theme—an individual's struggle against crushing economic forces—to make this a thought-provoking read. Although it is a period piece, which may help account for its obscurity, the novel's honesty could be painful (and unnecessary) for anyone who actually lived through this difficult era. For today's reader, however, the sometimes-harsh realism gives the work its power, resulting in a novel that is brief yet has a heavy emotional impact. The themes of economics and the role of the individual within the economic system still ring true with the contemporary reader.

Author Sketch

Born in Weatherford, Texas, on June 19, 1905, Anderson worked on newspapers in Oklahoma and Texas before publishing *Hungry Men* in 1935. After publishing another novel, *Thieves Like Us* (1937), he went to California and did screenwriting for various movie studios while continuing work for newspapers. Later, he returned to Texas, where he worked as a newspaper editor at Brownsville until his death on September 5, 1969.[2]

Other Works by the Author

Thieves Like Us: A Novel. New York: Frederick A. Stokes, 1937.

Suggestions for Further Reading

Bremer, William W. *Depression Winters: New York Social Workers and the New Deal, American Civilization.* Philadelphia: Temple University Press, 1984.

Casey, Janet Galligani. *The Novel and the American Left: Critical Essays on Depression-Era Fiction.* Iowa City: University of Iowa Press, 2004.

Crouse, Joan M. *The Homeless Transient in the Great Depression: New York State, 1929–1941.* Albany: State University of New York Press, 1986.

Knepper, Cathy D., and Eleanor Roosevelt. *Dear Mrs. Roosevelt: Letters to Eleanor Roosevelt through Depression and War.* New York: Carroll & Graf, 2004.

Notes

1. Edward Anderson, *Hungry Men* (New York: Penguin, 1985), p. 133.
2. http://www.tsha.utexas.edu/handbook/online/articles/AA/fan38.html

Mariano Azuela

The Underdogs

New York: Penguin Books/Signet Classics, 1996

Originally published: 1915

Genre: Military Fiction

Quote

> The sierra is clad in gala colors. Over its inaccessible peaks the opalescent fog settles like
> a snowy veil on the forehead of a bride.
>   At the foot of a hollow, sumptuous and huge as the portico of an old cathedral, Demetrio
> Macias, his eyes leveled in an eternal glance, continues to point the barrel of his gun.[1]

Synopsis

Demetrio Macias is an Indian peasant who lives in a small village in Mexico. When the
Mexican Revolution comes to his village, he is forced, in order to save his own life and the lives
of his family, to join the rebel army. Although he takes this step out of necessity, he quickly
finds that he has a talent for the military life and becomes a successful general in the army of
Pancho Villa. However, as time goes on, Macias sees the poverty and corruption that surround
him, and this undermines the revolutionary zeal of both him and his compatriots.

Critical Commentary

The importance of the relationship between Mexico and the United States is being
underscored daily by current debates over immigration, trade, crime, and other topics. Yet for
the most part, Americans remain woefully ignorant of the history of Mexico. Mariano Azuela's
The Underdogs, which was first published in an El Paso newspaper, goes some way to bridge
that gap by giving readers a soldier's view of the events of the Mexican Revolution. Thus, it is
an important part of American literature, especially that of the transborder region. Some may
disagree with the inclusion here of a novel by a writer who is primarily recognized as a Mexican
writer. However, this work reveals the interconnected nature of the two countries, especially
along the border region, and as such, it deserves inclusion. This relates to American history
because the Mexican Revolution, which this novel concerns itself with, often spilled over into
a number of border states, such as Texas and Arizona, to the point that an American
expeditionary force, under General Pershing, was actually sent into Mexico to deal with the
instability.

Fundamentally, *The Underdogs* is a character study that contrasts the views of two main
characters, the student Luis Cervantes and the soldier Demetrio Macias, who, largely by accident, ends up being a successful officer in Pancho Villa's army. Cervantes seeks philosophical justification for the evil that he sees as resulting from the war, whereas Macias, more of a

realist, simply sees the conflict as an another opportunity for the rich to fatten themselves at the expense of the poor.

Azuela depicts the misery of daily life for combatants on both sides, as well as for the civilian population. Rather than being a story of grand battles, this is a novel about the treachery, deceit, and lies that exist at the ground level of every war—where the participants are less interested in ideology than in simply surviving the day and, if possible, getting some little piece of loot for themselves. The story is filled with short descriptions of everyday life at war—which sometimes includes battles, but more often features the participants fighting boredom or each other or simply looking for an excuse to ditch the whole exercise in favor of a drunken evening at the nearest cantina.

The Underdogs can be seen as a classic antiwar novel in the same philosophical vein as Erich Maria Remarque's *All Quiet on the Western Front.* It provides an action-packed and colorful read that clearly shows the environment and peasant society of revolutionary Mexico. However, Azuela's descriptions resemble less the story of a grand social revolution or some modern war story than a medieval tale of the Crusades, such as the works by Joinville and Villehardouin, or even the first book of the Iliad where the concern is less defeating the Trojans than securing loot. The story itself is rather circular: in the end the characters seem no better off—and victory of the revolution seems no closer—than at the beginning. Regardless, in a gripping and emotional story of men at war, Azuela has written a classic work that should be of interest to anyone who cares about Mexican history or wishes to better understand U.S. history.

Author Sketch

Born January 1, 1873, in Jalisco, Mexico, Mariano Azuela was educated and worked as doctor. He combined his vocation as a physician with a noted and successful career as a writer and man of letters, publishing numerous novels. He died March 1, 1952, in Mexico City.[2]

Other Works by the Author

Two Novels of the Mexican Revolution: The Trials of a Respectable Family and the Underdogs. San Antonio: Principia Press of Trinity University, 1963.

Azuela, Mariano, Frances Kellam Hendricks, and Beatrice Berler. *Three Novels.* San Antonio: Trinity University Press, 1979.

Suggestions for Further Reading

Gilly, Adolfo. *The Mexican Revolution.* Expanded and rev. ed. New York: New Press, distributed by Norton, 2005.

Gonzales, Michael J. *The Mexican Revolution, 1910–1940.* Albuquerque: University of New Mexico Press, 2002.

Hart, John M. *Revolutionary Mexico: The Coming and Process of the Mexican Revolution.* 10th anniversary ed. Berkeley: University of California Press, 1997.

Martinez, Eliud. *The Art of Mariano Azuela: Modernism in La Malhora, El Desquite, La Luciernaga.* Pittsburgh: Latin American Literary Review Press, 1980.

Robe, Stanley Linn, and Mariano Azuela. *Azuela and the Mexican Underdogs.* UCLA Latin American Studies, Vol. 48. Berkeley: University of California Press, 1979.

Notes

1. Mariano Azuela, *The Underdogs* (New York: Penguin Books/Signet Classics, 1996), p. 161.

2. *Contemporary Authors Online,* Gale, 2003; http://www.colegionacional.org.mx/Azuela.htm; http://www.farmworkers.org/azuela1.html

Thomas Bell

Out of This Furnace

Pittsburgh: University of Pittsburgh, 1976

Originally published: 1941

Genre: Mainstream Fiction

Quote

> Everybody knew everybody else in those days. . . . It's not like that now anywhere, North
> Braddock or East Pittsburgh or anywhere. There was more friendliness. . . . Nobody was
> a stranger. At first, when there were still a lot of Irish living here, we kept together because
> we had to. But when the Irish got out it was all our own people. It was good then.[1]

Synopsis

Djuro Kracha emigrates from Slovakia to the steel mills of Braddock, Pennsylvania, in the
latter part of the nineteenth century. After initial success in opening his own small store, he
eventually comes to a bad end by losing his money in real estate speculation. His daughter,
Mary, marries a steel worker named Mike Dobrejcak and raises a family with him in circumstances that, although poor economically, are filled with love and hope for the future. In the
1920s, Mary and Mike's son, Dobie Dobrejcak, becomes involved with a successful effort to
unionize the steel mills.

Critical Commentary

In *Out of This Furnace* Thomas Bell has created a dynamic, compelling portrayal of immigrant life at the turn of the last century. This multigenerational novel focuses on the development
of the labor movement in the steel industry in a realistic, and at times almost documentary,
examination of issues of acculturation and social mobility. The issues of adapting to a changing
economy are still relevant to modern readers in this well-written and engaging story.

Bell's writing style reflects the diverse natures of his characters. The story is told episodically,
beginning with the arrival of Djuro Kracha, and the death of Dubik. The next section, focusing
on Djuro's daughter Mary and her husband, Mike, is warmer and more intimate, reflecting the
couple's relationship. The last section, which focuses on Dobie, carries an aura of reportage, reflecting the confidence of the native-born American and documenting the climaxes in the establishment of a viable union. Although the focus is on a particular ethnic group, the Slovaks,
during a specific historical period, the issues raised here are timeless and universal, important
in understanding the problems and concerns of immigrants past and present.

Vivid and realistic descriptions with an almost photographic level of detail contribute to the
strength of this novel, and today's readers may enjoy the book as historical fiction. The city of
Pittsburgh could be considered a character in this book, with the sights and smells of the city,

from the mills to the stores and saloons and churches, permeating the work. Bell spends a great deal of time and effort on creating a realistic and accurate portrait of immigrant life during the early twentieth century. Not only does he discuss life in the steel mill, but he also devotes equal effort to depicting the lives of women and showing the hardships of urban poverty without the social supports and services we have come to expect.

Obviously, there is a certain amount of historical background to be introduced; this is not done in a heavy-handed, polemical manner, but through the use of dialogue that is engaging, vigorous, and clear. This depiction of immigrant life is fascinating and would be useful for anyone, including students, seeking a better understanding of the everyday life of people in the last years of the nineteenth century and the first years of the twentieth. Effective pacing holds the reader's interest, with the plot building in a logical and thoughtful way straight through to the conclusion. In the process, the novel raises important and central issues about the role of the citizen that are worth considering perhaps now more than ever, especially for teenagers developing their own conceptions of their role in society and their civic responsibilities. It is a book well recommended for all readers, and particularly young adults.

Author Sketch

Born March 7, 1903, in Braddock, Pennsylvania, Thomas Bell worked in the steel mills as an electrician before becoming a writer in the 1920s. From 1933 onward, he completed five novels. He died of cancer in Santa Cruz, California, on January 17, 1961.[2]

Other Works by the Author

The Second Prince. New York: G.P. Putnam's Sons, 1935.
All Brides Are Beautiful. Boston: Little, Brown, 1936.
Till I Come Back to You. Boston: Little, Brown, 1943.
There Comes a Time. Boston: Little, Brown, 1946.

Suggestions for Further Reading

Hall, Christopher. *Steel Phoenix: The Fall and Rise of the U.S. Steel Industry*. New York: St. Martin's Press, 1997.
Metzgar, Jack. *Striking Steel: Solidarity Remembered, Critical Perspectives on the Past*. Philadelphia: Temple University Press, 2000.
Stolarik, M. Mark. *Immigration and Urbanization: The Slovak Experience, 1870–1918*. New York: AMS Press, 1989.

Notes

1. Thomas Bell, *Out of This Furnace* (Pittsburgh: University of Pittsburgh, 1976), p. 330.
2. *New York Times*, January 18, 1961, p. 33.

Anne Bernays

Professor Romeo

New York: Penguin, 1990

Originally published: 1989

Genre: Mainstream/Literary Fiction

Quote

> When Barker joined the Harvard faculty, Von Stampler had assured him that he would thenceforth be considered, both by those within it and those not so fortunate, to be a member of the Upper Class. Barker wondered first whether this was true, and secondly whether it was, per se, a good thing to be a member of the Upper Class.[1]

Synopsis

Jacob Barker, a successful academic at Harvard, has from his earliest days used his position as professor to take sexual advantage of his students and colleagues—he sees sleeping with them as a perk that comes with the job. This novel tracks Barker's career and life through the decades, which include several marriages and numerous affairs. Ultimately, he runs afoul of new female administrators on his campus with disastrous results.

Critical Commentary

Anne Bernays has created one of the more compelling portraits of a loveable cad in recent memory. Aside from being a penetrating study of individual character, this is also an engaging, humorous satire about a professor and university administrators, all of whom are abusing the system for their own ends. *Professor Romeo* may not please people in the Harvard public relations office—Harvard is fairly well roasted throughout—but anyone else should enjoy this book immensely.

This novel tells the story of the life of Jacob Barker as a Harvard academic from the 1960s through the 1980s. Bernays follows Barker as he moves through the academic ranks while taking advantage of almost every female (student or other) he can. This is a story of a foolish man who feels that his superior intellect justifies his immoral behavior. Barker's relationships with his various wives, his students, and his colleagues and, perhaps most poignantly, his son, are described and comically dissected.

Rather than depicting Barker as an evil and menacing character, Bernays portrays him as a bumbler, an aging Lucky Jim, who manages to ruin his marriages, his extramarital relationships, and eventually his career. This is the story of a man who plays with fire for much too long and finally gets his comeuppance. Bernays's descriptions of university life and the interactions of faculty members with each other and with students are both authentic and articulately written.

Through Barker, Bernays creates a savage piece of satire about the politics of university life, especially the abuses of power when university administrators run amok. Barker's eventual ruin is brought about by the efforts of university administrators to enforce new policies of political correctness and zero tolerance—instituted, it is made clear, not for purposes of justice or truth, but to promote a specific social agenda.

Bernays's description of the Kafkaesque kangaroo court into which Barker is finally brought if not to justice, then at least to account, provides a hilarious account of university life—where truth is seen to matter less than appearance, and procedures are bent, supposedly toward fairness, but resulting in quite the opposite for everyone concerned. There's a delicious irony in the portrayal of how the mechanisms of an institution supposedly devoted to truth are used for the exact opposite.

Ultimately, *Professor Romeo* is a novel about becoming an adult. Barker is not an evil person, just someone who has never grown up, justifying his behavior with the juvenile rationale that everyone else is doing the same thing and that he never forced anyone to do anything. Through the events of the novel, Barker is finally forced to confront himself and is ejected into the "real world."

Bernays has taken the more frequently used story of a careless student who won't take responsibility for his actions and has cleverly adapted it by making a professor that central character. Barker is Holden Caulfield with tenure. Rather than cast him as a tragic figure, Bernays depicts him as someone who has figured out his true nature—that of a skirt-chasing lecher—and is comfortable with that. That doesn't make him a good person, but he's at least more honest than many people in his institution. Bernays raises some interesting and thought-provoking questions about how modern universities are run and about the people who run them—all worth considering.

All in all, the book is a thought-provoking read, especially for those who think that places such as Harvard and Yale are filled with people better than themselves. Those people may be smarter (or not) than the rest of us, but as this novel illustrates, they share the same common human failings as everyone else—a fact worth remembering as society discusses the future of higher education. Anyone interested in a good humorous story, and in the values and morals that are running modern higher education, particularly those working in academia, will find this well worth their time.

Author Sketch

Bernays was born September 14, 1930, in New York City and was educated at Wellesley College and Barnard College (BA 1952). She has worked in publishing and in academia, including Emerson College and Harvard.[2]

Other Works by the Author

Growing Up Rich. Boston: Little, Brown, 1975.
The School Book: A Novel. New York: Harper & Row, 1980.
The Address Book: A Novel. Boston: Little, Brown, 1983.
Trophy House. New York: Simon & Schuster, 2005.
Bernays, Anne, and Justin Kaplan. *Back Then: Two Lives in 1950s New York.* New York: Morrow, 2002.

Bernays, Anne, and Pamela Painter. *What If? Writing Exercises for Fiction Writers.* New York: Harper Collins, 1990.

Kaplan, Justin, and Anne Bernays. *The Language of Names.* New York: Simon & Schuster, 1997.

Twain, Mark, Anne Bernays, Forrest G. Robinson, and Shelley Fisher Fishkin. *Merry Tales.* New York: Oxford University Press, 1996.

Suggestions for Further Reading

Herman, Deborah M., and Julie M. Schmid. *Cogs in the Classroom Factory: The Changing Identity of Academic Labor.* Westport, CT: Praeger, 2003.

Notes

1. *Professor Romeo* (New York: Penguin, 1990), p. 141.
2. *Contemporary Authors Online,* Gale, 2006.

Roark Bradford

John Henry

New York: The Literary Guild, 1931

Originally published: 1931

Genre: Historical Fiction/Folklore

Quote

> "Well," says John Henry, "I b'lieve I'll be gitting around. I've got an eetch on my heel and a run-around on my weary mind. I've got to scratch my feet on strange ground and rest my weary mind on a strange pillow. So fix up my bundle, old woman, and gimme my hat. 'Cause I'm fixin' to git around some."[1]

Synopsis

Bradford tells the story of John Henry, a mythical character and a Mississippi River roustabout. Famous for his strength and speed, Henry travels around performing prodigious feats of endurance—moving massive amounts of cotton bales as well as romancing women. He eventually becomes involved in a cotton-moving race with a steam winch, which kills him.

Critical Commentary

Mythology is a central element in the cultural cohesiveness of a civilization—thus the enduring popularity of such works as Homer's Iliad and more modern myths, such as the Star Wars saga. One important element of mythology is folklore—stories of mythic characters in common everyday life that develop important ideas about society and individuals. In modern America, folklore has been too often discounted, seen as either simply children's stories or as being only of interest to academic specialists. Roark Bradford's *John Henry* takes a classic folktale and recasts it as a novel, illustrating that folklore is much more than an oral tradition and can be a compelling and interesting read for adults.

This fascinating character study of John Henry is based, in part, on the experiences of a real person, John William Henry, who died while working as a contract laborer while imprisoned in West Virginia in the 1860s. Over time, the life story of this real person evolved into a series of stories that provided inspiration for generations of laborers and other unskilled workers. Bradford's novel exemplifies how these oral traditions, kept largely by the poor, were reimagined and redeveloped for a more literate and upscale audience.

Distinctive use of African American dialect is the most defining characteristic of *John Henry*. Throughout the book, the voices of the characters, thick with traditional Southern patois, create an atmosphere charged with a humanistic vision of the Old South. It might be said that this novel promotes stereotypes, which may in part account for this book's (and its author's) drop into obscurity during the 1950s and 1960s; but Bradford's portrayal of blacks is filled with affection and good sense. He may ignore the harsh realities of race relations, but he is, after all, writing fantasy.

Bradford may be one of the more unappreciated satirists in American literature. Although the use of dialect, which some readers see as patronizing toward the African American characters, may cause this work to be dismissed as politically incorrect, to dismiss the book is to overlook a wonderfully effective writer working in one of the oldest traditions of literature. In this novel, readers can find a compelling and almost musical story that takes traditional elements of Southern folklore and oral tradition and melds them into a well-written and interesting story with excellent pacing and fantastic characters—a book that echoes the descriptions of Southern life by better-known and more accepted writers such as Mark Twain and William Faulkner.

Author Sketch

Bradford, a novelist, short-story writer, and journalist, was born in Lauderdale County, Tennessee. He was educated at the University of California, where he earned an LLB degree shortly before the United States entered World War I. After serving in the army, he became a reporter, leaving in 1926 to become a full-time writer of stories and plays, including *Ol' Man Adam an' His Chillun* (1928), adapted into the 1930 Broadway play *The Green Pastures*, which ran for 73 weeks in New York and earned a Pulitzer Prize for its playwright, Marc Connelly. Bradford died in New Orleans in 1948.[2]

Other Works by the Author

Ol' Man Adam an' His Chillun; Being the Tales They Tell about the Time When the Lord Walked the Earth Like a Natural Man. New York: Harper & Brothers, 1928.

This Side of Jordan. New York: Harper & Brothers, 1929.

Ol' King David and the Philistine Boys. New York: Harper & Brothers, 1930.

Kingdom Coming. New York: Harper & Brothers, 1933.

Let the Band Play Dixie, and Other Stories. New York: Harper, 1934.

The Three-Headed Angel. New York: Harper & Brothers, 1937.

How Come Christmas; A Modern Morality. New York: Harper, 1948.

The Green Roller. New York: Harper, 1949.

Connelly, Marc, and Roark Bradford. *Little David, Play in One Act.* New York: Dramatists Play Service, 1937.

Connelly, Marc, Robert Edmond Jones, and Roark Bradford. *The Green Pastures.* New York: Farrar & Rinehart, 1930.

Suggestions for Further Reading

Cobb, James C. *Away Down South: A History of Southern Identity.* New York: Oxford University Press, 2005.

Keats, Ezra Jack. *John Henry, an American Legend.* New York: Pantheon Books, 1965.

Osborne, Mary Pope, and Michael McCurdy. *American Tall Tales.* New York: Knopf, 1991.

Notes

1. Roark Bradford, *John Henry* (New York: The Literary Guild, 1931), p. 5.

2. http://tennesseeencyclopedia.net/imagegallery.php?EntryID=B076; http://www.ibiblio.org/john_henry/; http://www.wm.edu/news/?id=6082

Charles Brockden Brown

Edgar Huntly, or, Memoirs of a Sleep-Walker

New York: Penguin Books, 1988

Originally published: 1797

Genre: Mainstream Fiction

Quote

> The incapacity of sound sleep denotes a mind sorely wounded. It is thus that atrocious criminals denote the possession of some dreadful secret. The thoughts, which considerations of safety enables them to suppress or disguise during wakefulness, operate without impediment, and exhibit their genuine effects, when the notices of sense are partly excluded, and they are shut out from a knowledge of their entire condition.[1]

Synopsis

This story of murder and mystery in the wilderness of the American frontier relates the adventures of a young man, Edgar Huntly, who becomes involved with the sleepwalking Clithero Weymouth. Weymouth is in search of missing money and Queen Deb—a mysterious Indian woman living in the wild. Murders, shipwrecks, and American Indian hostages all mix together in a terrifying tale of darkness and intrigue.

Critical Commentary

Horror novels, such as those written by Dean Koontz, remain one of the most popular genres in American popular literature year after year. What many readers don't realize is that the modern horror novel has a precedent in the early days of the nation: Charles Brockden Brown's *Edgar Huntly* is a forerunner to these modern fictions. In this novel, which can be considered America's first real contribution to the tradition of Gothic fiction, we see the precursor to such later writers as Edgar Allan Poe and Stephen King. Although the genre of horror was not recognized as such when this book was written, contemporary horror fans, as well as readers who enjoy historical fiction and even Gothic romances, will find this novel fits their interests.

Characterized by intellectualism, Brown was truly an Atlantic writer, influenced by the sensibilities of the eighteenth-century European intellectual tradition in which early America partook. Like Benjamin Franklin in the scientific field, Brown, as a writer, participated in a wider trans-Atlantic intellectual movement. Brown's interest was in developing the idea of an unknown force hiding behind the mundane. A novel of contrasts, *Edgar Huntly* begins in a vividly portrayed wilderness before shifting to the civilized world of Dublin society—and even there, Brown finds darkness, murder, and evil hiding in the shadows, along with a poignant love story.

Adept at plotting and pacing, Brown makes excellent use of the characters' written correspondence as framing devices to supplement the narration and to create internal spaces within the novel, where he develops several storylines—all of which seem to revolve around the theme of captivity. Each of the characters is confined or limited by various elements in his or her life. This confinement contrasts with elements of wildness and otherness symbolized by the American Indians and the implicit threat they both pose. Brown traded in the conventional Gothic use of the castle—a building that confines—and made the open space of the wilderness the threatening element.

Various aspects of the story—most notably Edgar Huntly's sleepwalking and the use of his double, Clithero Edny—create psychological suspense. Brown enhances the suspense by writing in the first person, allowing the reader to follow the narrator into madness. *Edgar Huntly* is a psychological novel written before the practice of psychiatry or even modern conceptions of the conscious and subconscious were clearly articulated. This makes Brown's achievement even more amazing in that he was able to convey his ideas without the vocabulary and common knowledge that a modern reader of horror fiction takes for granted.

Modern readers approach horror stories with a built-in vocabulary of images and literary conventions. Brown wrote for an audience without these preconceived notions or expectations—which would have made this, for the reader at the time, an even more striking and frightening story. The contrast between the psychology of the late eighteenth-century reader and the more sophisticated readers of the early twenty-first century makes this a provocative novel for the thoughtful student of literature. *Edgar Huntly* deftly reflects underlying issues of identity and, considered in context, provides a powerful psychological portrait of a new nation. This is a useful and engaging book for anyone who has an interest either in the development of historical fiction or in history generally—as well as anyone who enjoys a good spooky story.

Author Sketch

Born in Philadelphia on January 17, 1771, Brown was educated at the Friends Latin School before studying law, although he never practiced. From the late 1790s onward, he was generally a full-time writer, although he had brief stints as a magazine editor and an import trader. He died on February 22, 1810.[2]

Other Works by the Author

The Novels and Related Works of Charles Brockden Brown. Bicentennial ed. 6 vols. Kent, Ohio: Kent State University Press, 1977.

Clara Howard: In a Series of Letters; Jane Talbot: A Novel. Bicentennial ed. Kent, Ohio: Kent State University Press, 1986.

Three Gothic Novels, The Library of America; 103. New York: Library of America, 1998.

Suggestions for Further Reading

Barnard, Philip, Mark Kamrath, and Stephen Shapiro. *Revising Charles Brockden Brown: Culture, Politics, and Sexuality in the Early Republic.* Knoxville: University of Tennessee Press, 2004.

Cody, Michael. *Charles Brockden Brown and the Literary Magazine: Cultural Journalism in the Early American Republic.* Jefferson, NC: McFarland, 2004.

Hinds, Elizabeth Jane Wall. *Private Property: Charles Brockden Brown's Gendered Economics of Virtue.* Newark: University of Delaware Press, 1997.

Kafer, Peter. *Charles Brockden Brown's Revolution and the Birth of American Gothic.* Philadelphia: University of Pennsylvania Press, 2004.

Stern, Julia A. *The Plight of Feeling: Sympathy and Dissent in the Early American Novel.* Chicago: University of Chicago Press, 1997.

Notes

1. Charles Brockden Brown, *Edgar Huntly, or, Memoirs of a Sleep-Walker* (New York: Penguin Books, 1988), p. 13.

2. *Dictionary of Literary Biography,* Vol. 37: *American Writers of the Early Republic,* ed. Emory Elliot (Detroit: Gale, 1985), pp. 69–81.

Frederick Buechner

Godric

San Francisco: HarperSanFrancisco, 1980

Originally published: 1980

Genre: Historical Fiction/Christian Fiction

Quote

> Why did we weep? I asked myself. We wept for all that grandeur gone. We wept for martyrs cruelly slain. We wept for Christ, who suffered death upon a tree and suffers still to see our suffering. But more than anything, I think, we wept for us, and so it ever is with tears.[1]

Synopsis

Godric is the fictional autobiography of a real-life twelfth-century English Christian saint. It follows his adventures as a youth—abandoning his life as a peasant to peddle holy relics, working as an estate manager and as a pirate with his partner Roger Mouse, preying on travelers to the Holy Land, and conducting a pilgrimage to Rome to see the Pope—and his eventual conversion, which results in his becoming a revered holy hermit.

Critical Commentary

One trend in the teaching of English literature is a focus on a small number of writers, usually starting with Chaucer or Shakespeare and ending, if the student is fortunate, with modern poets such as Pound and Eliot. This is, one hopes, a function of the short amount of time available in the classroom rather than any malicious intent on the part of English teachers.

Discussion of written English as a much older language—dating back to the seventh century—and of literature produced prior to Chaucer is passed over quickly, if such discussion happens at all. As a result, a large corpus of interesting material remains unknown to students, although in some schools some may read a modern translation of *Beowulf*. *Godric,* a retelling of the ancient story of an English saint, is important both because it is a good story and because it reminds modern readers that the history of their literature is longer and richer than they may have realized.

Stylistically, *Godric* uses the language and conventions of ancient literature. By writing the novel in the first person, Buechner makes active use of historical Anglo-Saxon language conventions while rooting the story in the domestic reality of early England—a dirty, loud, brawling place. At the start of the story, Godric is clearly no saint, but an active participant in the events of his time. He is a hustler, a con man, an enforcer—in many respects not a likeable character and an unlikely candidate for sainthood. Yet as the story moves backward and forward in time, the readers witnesses an evolution of character, with Godric as an old holy man telling a story, looking backward to his younger sinful self. Godric is also a mystic, seeing visions of saints and striving for a better way of life, in spite of his sins. A reluctant, bad-tempered, sometimes back-sliding convert, Godric is a genuine, believing Christian nevertheless.

As a historical tale of ancient England, *Godric* shines. This is a portrait of a society in the midst of change, in which the invasion of William the Conqueror in 1066 is a real event and not simply a distant historical abstraction. Other characters, loud and colorful, live, love, eat, and die. Buechner's book captures the artistic quality of Chaucer and other early English authors in depicting a lively and diverse society where a great deal is happening. Readers will walk away from this book with a much greater appreciation of the complexity and depth of medieval society than they might have had previously.

On a spiritual level, we have in *Godric* a story of Christian revelation and how it can lead to redemption. It illustrates the fundamental Christian idea of the sinner who can be redeemed, even at the last moment. The text argues that holiness is where God wants it to be, not necessarily where we as humans might place it. More to the point, Buechner shows us the real depth and beauty of English literature at the moment of its origins. For both these reasons, this is a wonderful and rich book worthy of notice. Readers who are entranced by stories and history of medieval life or who have an interest in religion, especially the history of Christianity, will find this book worthwhile. A fascinating work that may usefully encourage further exploration of earlier and neglected parts of English literature, it is an interesting complement to conventional material about the Middle Ages, such as *The Canterbury Tales* or *Sir Gawain and the Green Knight,* that students may have already been exposed to. Thus, this novel is recommended to adolescent readers as well as adults interested in medieval life.

Author Sketch

Buechner, born July 11, 1926, graduated from Princeton in 1947 and published his first novel, *A Long Day's Dying,* in 1950. In 1953 he moved to New York to become a full-time writer. Buechner received his bachelor of divinity degree from Union Theological Seminary in 1958. He then served as the school chaplain at Philips Exeter Academy from 1958 to 1967 before quitting to move to Vermont and return to writing as a profession.[2]

Other Works by the Author

A Long Day's Dying. New York: Knopf, 1950.
The Season's Difference. New York: Knopf, 1951.
The Return of Ansel Gibbs. New York: Knopf, 1958.
The Hungering Dark. New York: Seabury Press, 1968.
The Alphabet of Grace. New York: Seabury Press, 1970.
The Entrance to Porlock. New York: Atheneum, 1970.
Lion Country. New York: Atheneum, 1971.
Open Heart. New York: Atheneum, 1972.
Love Feast. New York: Atheneum, 1974.
Telling the Truth: The Gospel as Tragedy, Comedy, and Fairy Tale. San Francisco: Harper & Row, 1977.
Treasure Hunt. New York: Atheneum, 1977.
The Book of Bebb. New York: Atheneum, 1979.
Peculiar Treasures: A Biblical Who's Who. San Francisco: Harper & Row, 1979.
The Final Beast. San Francisco: Harper & Row, 1982.

The Sacred Journey. San Francisco: Harper & Row, 1982.

Now and Then. Cambridge: Harper & Row, 1983.

A Room Called Remember: Uncollected Pieces. San Francisco: Harper & Row, 1984.

Hungering Dark. San Francisco: Harper & Row, 1985.

The Magnificent Defeat. San Francisco: Harper & Row, 1985.

Brendan. New York: Atheneum, 1987.

Whistling in the Dark: An ABC Theologized. San Francisco: Harper & Row, 1988.

The Wizard's Tide: A Story. San Francisco: Harper & Row, 1990.

Telling Secrets. San Francisco: HarperSanFrancisco, 1991.

The Clown in the Belfry: Writings on Faith and Fiction. San Francisco: HarperSanFrancisco, 1992.

The Son of Laughter. San Francisco: HarperSanFrancisco, 1993.

Wishful Thinking: A Seeker's ABC. Rev. and expanded ed. San Francisco: HarperSanFrancisco, 1993.

The Longing for Home: Recollections and Reflections. San Francisco: HarperSanFrancisco, 1996.

On the Road with the Archangel: A Novel. San Francisco: HarperSanFrancisco, 1997.

The Storm: A Novel. San Francisco: HarperSanFrancisco, 1998.

The Eyes of the Heart: A Memoir of the Lost and Found. San Francisco: HarperSanFrancisco, 1999.

Speak What We Feel (Not What We Ought to Say): Reflections on Literature and Faith. San Francisco: HarperSanFrancisco, 2001.

Suggestions for Further Reading

Dean, Trevor. *Crime in Medieval Europe, 1200–1550.* Harlow, England, and New York: Longman, 2001.

Loyn, H. R. *The English Church, 940–1154, The Medieval World.* Harlow, England, and New York: Longman, 2000.

Rice, Francis. *The Hermit of Finchale: The Life of Saint Godric.* Edinburgh: Pentland Press, 1994.

Schofield, Phillip R. *Peasant and Community in Medieval England, 1200–1500, Medieval Culture and Society.* Basingstoke, Hampshire, and New York: Palgrave-Macmillan, 2003.

Notes

1. Frederick Buechner, *Godric* (New York: HarperCollins, 1980), p. 64.
2. http://www.wheaton.edu/learnres/ARCSC/collects/sc05/bio.htm

Edward Bunker

No Beast So Fierce

New York: Random House, 1993

Originally published: 1973

Genre: Crime Fiction

Quote

> I was going to war with society, or perhaps I would only be renewing it. Now there were no misgivings. I declared myself free from all rules except those I wanted to accept—and I'd change those as I felt the whim. I would take whatever I wanted. I'd be what I was with a vengeance: a criminal.[1]

Synopsis

Released from prison after eight years, Max Dembo resolves to go straight. However, he finds that prison has marked him permanently, making it almost impossible for him to have a normal life. After slipping back into the criminal life simply to survive, he becomes involved with a jewel heist that goes wrong, leaving a police officer dead, which forces him to leave the country. At the novel's conclusion, Dembo is planning to return to America. He knows this will probably get him killed, but at least he will die on his own terms and as what he is—a criminal.

Critical Commentary

The crime novel is a staple of American fiction—often full of stereotypes, poor plotting, bad characterizations, and inadequate endings. In *No Beast So Fierce*, Edward Bunker deftly avoids these pitfalls in a book that is as honest and unsparing a look at the American underworld as has ever been written. In this novel the reader sees the true face of crime and its victims.

Bunker's adept use of dialogue is a joy. The characters speak authentically, as one would expect real people and actual criminals to. The protagonist, Max Dembo, is portrayed without clichés as a fully realized individual, who longs for freedom. Dembo first wants to be a part of society, but after society rejects him, he accepts what he really is—a career criminal. Thus, in a sense, this novel can be described as a meditation on free will. The effects of crime—on both the victims and the perpetrators—are presented honestly and realistically.

Bunker also ably describes California, not the false media image of the state familiar to everyone, but the raw and dirty California, the backstreets and working-class ghettos that exist in the shadows of the freeways and the American Dream. Some of the characters who inhabit this world may not be likeable, but seeing their hot, ugly, and dirty environment, the reader can understand why they are the way they are. The novel exudes a film-noir atmospheric quality without becoming derivative or falling into cliché. It's like taking a mental walk on a Saturday night through the poor neighborhoods of south-central Los Angeles where the only sound is that of gunshots, lit by the hovering spotlight of the police helicopter.

Bunker avoids the happy ending often found in crime novels, with the criminal riding away into the sunset with his ill-gotten gains. Max Dembo doesn't get the girl or the loot. He spends all his money and by the end is looking to return to America, where he will probably meet either a police bullet or a long imprisonment—if he's lucky enough to avoid death row. The author makes no moral judgment. Neither an evil person nor some kind of antihero, Max simply is what he is. Readers are left to make their own evaluations.

By taking this challenging path, Bunker raises serious questions about the responsibility of the state toward the individual—especially prisoners and former prisoners—who are shut out of society even after their debt supposedly has been paid. What do we do with a permanent underclass that is uneducated and without opportunity and for which being a criminal is really the only option? Is it right to restrict the liberty of prisoners on parole in ways that are demeaning to the point of being humiliating? In a country that has one of the highest incarceration rates in the world, these are questions worth considering. This book will appeal to anyone interested in issues of social justice, and it is especially recommended for college-age readers studying sociology or criminal justice or those working in social services. Of course, it is also an engaging read for anyone who enjoys a solid and realistic crime novel filled with action.

Author Sketch

Edward Bunker, born in Hollywood, California, in 1933, had a transient, impoverished childhood and became involved with crime as teenager, eventually ending up in San Quentin prison at age 17. In prison he decided to become a writer. After many rejections, *No Beast So Fierce* was published in 1973, while Booker was incarcerated. Bunker continued writing and, upon his release from prison, became a full-time writer, film technical adviser, and character actor, appearing in such movies as *Reservoir Dogs*. He died on July 23, 2005.[2]

Other Works by the Author

The Animal Factory. New York: Viking Press, 1977.
Little Boy Blue. New York: Viking Press, 1981.
Dog Eat Dog. New York: St. Martin's Press, 1996.
Education of a Felon: A Memoir. New York: St. Martin's Press, 2000.
Mr. Blue: Memoirs of a Renegade. Harpenden, England: No Exit Press, 2000.

Suggestions for Further Reading

Blomberg, Thomas G., and Karol Lucken. *American Penology: A History of Control, New Lines in Criminology.* New York: Aldine de Gruyter, 2000.
Hassine, Victor, Thomas J. Bernard, and Richard McCleary. *Life without Parole: Living in Prison Today.* Los Angeles: Roxbury, 1996.
Tonry, Michael H. *The Future of Imprisonment.* Oxford and New York: Oxford University Press, 2004.

Notes

1. Edward Bunker, *No Beast So Fierce* (New York: Random House, 1993), p. 105.
2. http://www.timesonline.co.uk/article/0,,60-1707974,00.html

Abraham Cahan

The Rise of David Levinsky

New York: Harper & Row, 1960

Originally published: 1917

Genre: Historical Fiction

Quote

> Sometimes, when I think of my past in a superficial, casual way, the metamorphosis I have
> gone through strikes me as nothing short of a miracle. I was born and raised in the depths
> of poverty and I arrived in America—in 1885—with four cents in my pocket. I am now worth
> more than 2 million dollars and recognized as one of the two or three leading men in the
> cloak-and-suit trade in the United States. And yet when I take a look at my inner identity it
> impresses me as being precisely the same as it was thirty or forty years ago. My present
> station, power, the amount of worldly happiness at my command, and the rest of it, seem
> to be devoid of significance.[1]

Synopsis

David Levinsky is a young Hasidic Jewish immigrant to America. He wants to study the
Talmud, but to survive he turns to making money in the garment district of New York's Lower
East Side. This novel traces his life as he becomes increasingly assimilated as well as more and
more divorced from both his Jewish heritage and his authentic self. Although he is ultimately
successful in business, he pays a high personal and spiritual cost for his success.

Critical Commentary

Abraham Cahan creates, in *The Rise of David Levinsky,* a vivid portrait of the immigrant
experience. In first-person narrative voice, couched within a traditional linear, episodic narrative structure, he traces the experiences of a single Jewish immigrant moving from poverty to
the achievement of wealth. Cahan's effective use of language and his moving detailed portraits
of the challenges and opportunities facing David Levinsky make this a distinctive and provocative work. The writer vividly describes the lives of his characters, who, despite their material
success, remain essentially alienated from both the larger society and themselves.

Through dramatic imagery, an interesting narrative structure, and compelling dialogue,
Cahan produced a classic work describing the joys and tragedies of the immigrant experience.
Especially memorable are his descriptions of Levinsky's experiences in relation to his religious
views and the assimilations, both large and small, he is required to make in order to succeed in
American society. Cahan echoes the themes of earlier works, such as William Dean Howell's
The Rise of Silas Lapham, that question the role and emphasis on material success in American
culture in the emerging economy of the late nineteenth century and early twentieth century.

All in all, this is a fascinating observation of the price paid by an individual compromising his values as he grows into adulthood.

The voice of the author comes through clearly in this novel, with a lyrical autobiographical tone. It would be wrong, however, to simply see this work as a fictionalized version of Cahan's own immigrant experience. Cahan seriously engages with the larger issues of the emerging socialist realism of twentieth-century literature, heavily influenced by the social ideals of the Progressive movement.

Cahan's effective depiction of David Levinsky's tortured psychological life, his material success, and his personal failure is riveting and dramatic. In our own consumerist culture, with its de-emphasis of spiritual values, this work retains its relevance. *The Rise of David Levinsky* is a novel especially recommended for those interested in the history of the Jewish immigrant experience, but is suitable for anyone interested in a well-written and engaging biographical novel, and it is an appropriate selection for almost any high school or college American history course.

Author Sketch

Cahan came to America from Russia in 1882. In 1897 he gained employment with the prominent Jewish newspaper *The Forward*, where he stayed for most of his professional life. Cahan was a prolific novelist and short-story writer, contributing to many magazines, such as *Harper's* and *Scribner's*. He was also active in Jewish social and political causes as well as Socialist politics. Cahan died in 1951.[2]

Other Works by the Author

None

Suggestions for Further Reading

Harap, Louis. *The Image of the Jew in American Literature: From Early Republic to Mass Immigration.* 2nd ed. Philadelphia: Jewish Publication Society of America, 1978.

Hopkinson, Deborah. *Shutting out the Sky: Life in the Tenements of New York, 1880–1924.* New York: Orchard Books, 2003.

Kosak, Hadassa. *Cultures of Opposition: Jewish Immigrant Workers, New York City, 1881–1905.* SUNY Series in American Labor History. Albany: State University of New York Press, 2000.

Soyer, Daniel. *A Coat of Many Colors: Immigration, Globalism, and Reform in the New York City Garment Industry.* New York: Fordham University Press, 2005.

Notes

1. Abraham Cahan, *The Rise of David Levinsky* (New York: Harper & Row, 1960), p. 1.
2. *New York Times,* July 13, 1930, p. 27.

Ernest Callenbach

Ecotopia

New York: Bantam Books, 1990

Originally published: 1975

Genre: Speculative Fiction

Quote

> Video sets are everywhere, but strangely enough I have seldom seen people sitting before
> them blotted out in the American manner. Whether this is because of some mysterious
> national traits, or because of programming being markedly different, or both, I cannot yet
> tell. But Ecotopians seem to use TV, rather than letting it use them.[1]

Synopsis

Several years after the state of California has seceded from the United States and has
become isolated in a North Korean–esque way from the rest of the world, a journalist is
granted permission to visit the country. What he finds is a collaborative sustainable community built on sensible principles of ecology and the appropriate use of some technologies (and
rejection of others) to create a better world—so much better that the journalist decides to
stay.

Critical Commentary

America is currently in what could be considered a "green renaissance," in which interest in
all things environmental has become popular—from the construction of ecologically friendly
buildings to the development of hybrid fuel-saving cars. Although these events and changes
have many causes, concern for the environment has been expressed in popular literature for
a long time, andpresumably, this has had some role in the development of present events and
trends regarding the environment. Ernest Callenbach's *Ecotopia* is a wonderful early example
of ecological fiction that combines a striking story about the environment within the age old
tradition of utopian fiction—echoing Edward Bellamy's *Looking Backwards* (1888), which also
depicted the use of appropriate technologies to meet human needs, and even earlier works dating from Phillip Stubs's *The Anatomie of Abuses* (1585).

Callenbach takes what are now commonly accepted ecological practices—use of compost-
ing, vegetarianism, and recycling—to create a vision of an ecologically and socially stable society, a positive vision of a community where diversity and difference are celebrated and people
work together in harmony. The author is somewhat vague about what effect the isolation of
California has had on the rest of the world, but this vagueness adds to the charm of the novel.
The reader is left to wonder for themselves what the effects, large and small, would be of no
California in the world economy and political landscape. It's a fine example for all writers of

how leaving some things to the reader's imagination rather than spelling everything out in detail can be a useful and effective writing technique.

Ecotopia is marked by striking descriptions of a landscape transformed by proper ecological practice. Callenbach takes the conventional narrative device of a "stranger in a strange land" and uses it in a manner that is neither moralizing nor preachy. True, the narrator spends much of his time listening to the citizens of Ecotopia rather than being engaged in action, but this creates a thoughtful and peaceful flow to the novel. This is a novel about ideas, almost epistolary in manner, which makes it highly effective by forcing the reader to think about the ideas being presented.

The pacing of the novel is adequate, and the characters are thoughtfully and carefully drawn. To be sure, the author is trying to make an ideological point. However, he makes the point with a light touch. This book is sure to appeal to anyone who is interested in ecology and the environment and to those who find novels of alternative history to be appealing. *Ecotopia* is a recommended book also for students and teachers interested in a gentle introduction to, and spurring of discussion on, ecological issues.

Author Sketch

Born April 3, 1929, in Williamsport, Pennsylvania, Callenbach attended the University of Chicago before moving to California and joining the staff of the University of California Press. Besides working as a book editor on award-winning works of film, art, and natural history, he founded the journal *Film Quarterly* and taught film at UC-Berkeley and San Francisco State. He founded Banyan Tree Books in 1975.[2]

Other Works by the Author

Ecotopia Emerging. Berkeley: Banyan Tree Books, 1981.

Bring Back the Buffalo! A Sustainable Future for America's Great Plains. Berkeley and London: University of California Press, 2000.

Callenbach, Ernest, and Elmwood Institute. *Ecomanagement: The Elmwood Guide to Ecological Auditing and Sustainable Business.* San Francisco: Berrett-Koehler, 1993.

Notes

1. Ernest Callenbach, *Ecotopia* (New York: Bantam Books, 1990), p. 42.
2. http://www.ernestcallenbach.com/biography.htm

Vera Caspery

Laura

New York: Ibooks, 2000

Originally published: 1942

Genre: Crime Fiction/Mystery-Detection

Quote

> Then, as the final contradiction, there remains the truth that she made a man of him as fully
> as man could be made of that stubborn clay. And when that frail manhood is threatened,
> when her own womanliness demands more than he can give, his malice seeks her destruc-
> tion. But she is carved from Adam's rib, indestructible as legend, and no man will ever aim
> his malice with sufficient accuracy to destroy her.[1]

Synopsis

Laura Hunt has been murdered—a female body, the face destroyed by a shotgun blast, has
been found in her apartment. The police detective on the case, Mark McPherson, has three
suspects: Waldo Lydecker, an older (and, it is implied, somewhat destitute) journalist who
had a relationship with Laura; Shelby Carpenter, a playboy; and Ann Treadwell, Laura's aunt.
Through his sleuthing, McPherson becomes fascinated by Laura and is surprised by his investigation, which is filled with twists and turns to its ultimate surprising conclusion.

Critical Commentary

Laura is a story that almost everyone (at least everyone who is of a certain age or who has a
serious interest in film) knows, although few have read the book. This is a fascinating example
of a novel that achieved its real success as a movie, while sinking into obscurity in its original
written incarnation. The novel provides fascinating insights into the social mores of the World
War II era, especially the tensions and ambiguity people felt about sexual roles in a changing
society under threat. It retains relevance for the modern reader—especially those interested in
a good old-fashioned crime novel. Fans of television shows such as *CSI* or *Law & Order* will
find much in this novel to their liking.

On first consideration, this book can be seen as a traditional 1940s detective thriller in the
style of Hammett's *The Maltese Falcon* and similar works. Caspery, however, developed her
story using the interesting narrative device of having the same story told from four different
perspectives, which adds to the interest and drama of the story. The characters of this novel
are its other striking feature. The most interesting and possibly the most sinister character is
Waldo Lydecker. He appears refined and elegant, and there is an implication that he is homosexual—which, in this time period, had definite negative social connotations. He seems to be
a person with secrets and a hidden agenda. Perhaps the book reflects the prejudices of author

Caspery's time against homosexuality, but it could also be said that Lydecker fits into the literary tradition of the aesthete, harking back to Oscar Wilde's *The Picture of Dorian Gray.*

The hero of the story is the practical detective Mark McPherson, who is assigned the case while preferring to be at Ebbets Field. A man of action, he is a distinct contrast to Lydecker, who is depicted almost from the start as a pseudo-intellectual, the writer of a gossip column, a collector, a man about town, a gourmand—in short, a social parasite who is initially (and increasingly) suspect. Countries fighting wars, this novel says, need doers, not thinkers.

The theme of women in the workplace also predominates. This was an especially sensitive topic during the early 1940s, with the entry of large numbers of women into the job market. Laura is a proto-modern woman with a job, a gloriously appointed apartment, and an active, independent life. She is a woman who has the option of choosing marriage or not. The plotline used by Caspery expresses the ambiguity that many people felt about working women. To many readers, the other prominent female character, Diane Redfern, could be seen as the epitome of the small-town girl who goes to the big city and becomes a "fast woman," reflecting the ambiguity that many Americans of the period felt about urbanization and the decline of the rural majority.

This novel reflects society's distrust of the other, in whatever form that takes—whether in the sexual otherness of Lydecker or in the female independence of Laura. Intellectual issues aside, it is a wonderfully written and exciting murder mystery, full of twists and turns, that will appeal to fans of that genre. It features swift pacing, crisp dialogue, and a dramatic conclusion. It also, when read carefully, is a useful and thought-provoking book for both students of World War II and those who are interested in the development of film noir as a genre. It is recommended for a general readership—and, perhaps, as a gift, with a DVD of the film included.

Author Sketch

Born in Chicago in 1899, Caspery began working in advertising in 1916 and quickly became a respected writer of short stories, plays, and novels. Beginning with her adaptation of her novel *Laura* for the screen in 1943, Caspery became a well-known screenwriter with a wide range of credits, including *I Can Get It for You Wholesale, The Blue Gardenia, Les Girls,* and *Bachelor in Paradise.* She retired from the movie business in 1961 and died in 1987.[2]

Other Works by the Author

None

Suggestions for Further Reading

Biesen, Sheri Chinen. *Blackout: World War II and the Origins of Film Noir.* Baltimore: Johns Hopkins University Press, 2005.

Ehrenstein, David. *Open Secret: Gay Hollywood, 1928–1998.* New York: William Morrow, 1998.

Silver, Alain, and Elizabeth Ward. *Film Noir: An Encyclopedic Reference to the American Style.* Rev. & expanded ed. Woodstock, NY: Overlook Press, 1988.

Wager, Jans B. *Dames in the Driver's Seat: Rereading Film Noir.* Austin: University of Texas Press, 2005.

Notes

1. Vera Caspery, *Laura* (New York: Ibooks, 2000), p. 233.
2. http://movies2.nytimes.com/gst/movies/filmography.html?p_id=84406&mod=bio

Charles Waddell Chesnutt

The Quarry

Princeton: Princeton University Press, 1999

Originally published: 1928

Genre: Mainstream Fiction

Quote

"And I," inquired Donald, looking at himself in the mirror, "am I—a Negro?"

"Yes, my darling," she returned sadly, as she clasped him in her arms, "you share the blood of a despised race and so are one of them. But don't you worry about it, honey. God made us all and He'll not forsake us. And when you grow up and become the leader of our people, we'll prove to the white folks that we're just as good as they are."[1]

Synopsis

This is a novel of dramatic changes in identity and circumstances. Adopted by the Seatons, a white family in Cleveland, Ohio, Donald is lovingly raised as the Seatons' own child. Later, it is discovered that Donald's natural father is a mulatto—Donald is black; this was unknown to Seatons before now because of a clerical error at the orphanage. So the Seatons give toddler Donald up to a black family in Memphis, the Glovers. Raised by the Glovers, Donald grows up intelligent and talented, chafing at the indignities of living in the Jim Crow South. Eventually, Donald relocates to New York and becomes involved with progressive elements of the urban black community while pursuing his higher education. He then moves to England, where he has a love affair with a rich white woman and is offered the opportunity to live permanently in England as part of the aristocracy, on a wonderfully appointed and lush English estate, free from the concerns and indignities associated with his race.

However, Donald decides to return to America. After the discovery of another clerical error, Donald finds out he is actually white. Rejecting this, Donald chooses to live as a black man and live in the black community, working to improve race relations.

Critical Commentary

What does being "white" or "black" mean? In *The Quarry* Charles Chesnutt raises this compelling question. The result is a novel that will interest many readers, especially students of history and race relations. Chesnutt follows his primary character over a lifetime, examining the consequences that the decision to classify a baby as "black" have on his development and future. Through a carefully constructed narrative, Chesnutt shows Donald's evolution as he goes from being a character acted upon—by his family's expectations—to becoming a self-aware and thoughtful human being. Ultimately, Donald rejects life as a white person to live as black, being authentic to his true moral and spiritual self.

The story moves from the Deep South to the industrial Northeast and then to Europe, where Donald rejects the opportunity to live the life of an English aristocrat, free from the shackles of racism. Through these transitions, the author highlights contrasts in attitude about race and class. In particular, the reader sees the difference between the American and European views on class. Europeans are portrayed as feeling no particular shame in wealth and status or in the race of the person possessing either wealth or status being an issue. This view is contrary to the traditional American morality that often makes judgments about wealth and status on the basis of how it is acquired, with race often being an issue..

Chesnutt avoids the easy and simplistic option of simply leaving his character in Europe. By returning Donald to America, he forces both Donald and the reader to confront the ugly realities of American racism. This makes this novel more than a period piece. Chesnutt explores the meaning of race and the relationships between races, which are still as relevant to modern life as they were when Chesnutt was writing, which was an era dominated by the modernism and progressive social ethics of the Harlem Renaissance.

Author Sketch

Born June 20, 1858, in Cleveland, Ohio, Charles W. Chesnutt was educated at the Howard University, and he worked as a teacher in South and North Carolina from 1872 to 1883. After 1883 he supported himself as a stenographer and court reporter, although he was trained as a lawyer and passed up several lucrative offers of employment in that field. Beginning in the late 1890s, he published several pieces of fiction, short and long, to an indifferent public, although with good critical approval. He died November 15, 1932.[2]

Other Works by the Author

Stories, Novels, & Essays. New York: Library of America, 2002.

Evelyn's Husband. Jackson: University Press of Mississippi, 2005.

Brown, William Wells, Frances Ellen Watkins Harper, and Charles Waddell Chesnutt. *Three Classic African-American Novels*. Vintage Classics. New York: Vintage Books, 1990.

Chesnutt, Charles Waddell, and Richard H. Brodhead. *The Conjure Woman, and Other Conjure Tales*. Durham, NC: Duke University Press, 1993.

Chesnutt, Charles Waddell, and Charles Duncan. *The Northern Stories of Charles W. Chesnutt*. Athens: Ohio University Press, 2004.

Suggestions for Further Reading

Petrie, Paul R. *Conscience and Purpose: Fiction and Social Consciousness in Howells, Jewett, Chesnutt, and Cather, Studies in American Literary Realism and Naturalism*. Tuscaloosa: University of Alabama Press, 2005.

Wilson, Matthew. *Whiteness in the Novels of Charles W. Chesnutt*. Jackson: University Press of Mississippi, 2004.

Wonham, Henry B. *Charles W. Chesnutt: A Study of the Short Fiction*. Twayne's Studies in Short Fiction. New York: Twayne, 1998.

Notes

1. Charles W. Chesnutt, *The Quarry* (Princeton: Princeton University Press, 1999), p. 56.

2. "Charles W. Chesnutt," in the *Dictionary of Literary Biography,* Vol. 50: *Afro-American Writers before the Harlem Renaissance,* ed. Trudier Harris (Detroit: Gale, 1986), pp. 36–51.

Christopher Coe

I Look Divine

New York: Vintage Contemporaries, 1989

Originally published: 1987

Genre: Mainstream/Literary Fiction

Quote

> For a few years Nicholas's favorite place in the world was the bar off the lobby of the Ritz in Madrid. He was partial especially to the skylight ceiling and to the light he said came through it in the summer between seven-thirty and nine o'clock in the evening. He said that was the best light for bone structure, and he appreciated, too, that men were not admitted without jackets and ties.[1]

Synopsis

The unnamed brother of the deceased Nicholas, informed of his death, visits Nicholas's residence, and as he sits among his brother's belongings, he reviews the life of his brother and his relationship to him. Nicholas was a brilliant and selfish man who lived basically for his own pleasure while, it is suggested, he was kept by a variety of men as a kind of gigolo—roaming the world from hotel to hotel without ever really making authentic connections with other people.

Critical Commentary

A fascinating and revealing meditation on the nature of truth, this stunning novel by Christopher Coe examines the relationship between two brothers through the lens of outward appearance. The result is an intriguing piece of fiction that, though modern in setting, discusses issues of life and death in a way that gives *I Look Divine* at least broad if not quite universal appeal.

Coe has made a challenging stylistic choice in presenting this book in almost total flashback through the perspective of the surviving brother. By placing the scene of the novel within the apartment of the dead brother, Nicholas, Coe gives the story an almost stage-like quality, as the surviving sibling moves through various rooms, picking up and handling objects that become a silent chorus of testimony to the life of the deceased. At the same time, Coe reveals the tragically damaged relationship between the two brothers that developed over a lifetime.

The length of this book, 109 pages, makes it almost a novelette, but Coe packs in an enormous amount of content. His use of language and his ability to create interesting dialogue as well as narrative make this novel engaging. In fact, Coe has created the literary equivalent of the portrait miniature, with details packed into a tiny frame, like the smaller paintings of William Payne.

There is ample use of symbolism in this novel. Coe's use of hotel bars, for example, mostly in foreign cities such as Rome, becomes an ongoing background motif, contrasted at one point with the characters' slumming visit to a much seedier bar. The hotel bar becomes a symbol both of the emptiness of Nicholas's life and of its gradual disintegration.

The significant question raised by this novel is not new: what constitutes a well-lived life? In the case of Nicholas, the reader may be left with a profound sense of ambiguity, unsure about the real facts of his life—was he a gigolo? Was the kind of life he led—artificial, posed, calculated—a good life? Coe has created one of the more selfish characters in recent literature, a kind of modern Dorian Gray. Like Wilde's character, Nicholas lives without any real human contact—he is a person without authenticity whose energy is spent in artifice rather than honesty. Nicholas's brother, who remains unnamed throughout the book, seems to have an equally sterile life, although his details are vague or missing. Is it possible to draw some larger symbolic meaning from the character of Nicholas? Does he represent the decadence of America and its ultimate moral decline? Perhaps. Who, really, is his brother? What is the character of Nicholas's brother? These are important questions that make this book appealing to the thoughtful reader. More significant and important are the sadly beautiful descriptions of the destruction of the human spirit. As in a classic Greek tragedy—where we see that one's character is one's fate—that quality of predestination permeates the novel and makes it memorable. Coe has created a captivating memoir of his deceased character in this fascinating examination of an individual's life as told by his brother, written in a style that is original and creative. This is a wonderful book for anyone interested in the eternal question of what makes a life well lived—this novel would be highly appropriate for a university course in philosophy or ethics or a book discussion group.

Author Sketch

Coe was born in 1953 and died on September 6, 1994, at his home in Manhattan. He was 41. A family member gave the cause of death as AIDS. A few months before, Coe had published his second novel, *Such Times,* which describes an affair between two men, one of whom dies of AIDS, leaving the other to tell their story. A *New York Times* reviewer, Andrea Barnet, called Coe "a daring writer, as unflinchingly honest about his characters' affectations and fatuous desires, their treacheries and small self-deceptions, as he is about the truth of their hearts."[2]

Other Works by the Author

Such Times. New York: Harcourt and Brace, 1993.

Suggestions for Further Reading

Canning, Richard. *Gay Fiction Speaks: Conversations with Gay Novelists.* Between Men—Between Women series. New York: Columbia University Press, 2000.

Levin, James. *The Gay Novel in America.* New York: Garland, 1991.

Nelson, Emmanuel S. *Contemporary Gay American Novelists: A Bio-Bibliographical Critical Sourcebook.* Westport, CT: Greenwood Press, 1993.

Summers, Claude J. *Gay Fictions: Wilde to Stonewall: Studies in a Male Homosexual Literary Tradition.* New York: Continuum, 1990.

Notes

1. Christopher Coe, *I Look Divine* (New York: Vintage Contemporaries, 1989), p. 37.
2. *New York Times,* September 12, 1993, p. 471.

Laurie Colwin

Shine On, Bright & Dangerous Object

New York: Penguin Books, 1984

Originally published: 1975

Genre: Mainstream/Literary Fiction

Quote

> Sam was my risk. He was the biggest emotional risk I had ever taken, and it seemed to me
> that it was in love and friendship that risk is real. A broken bone is a broken bone, but a
> broken heart is quite another thing. Sam's risks were risks of the bone, and they did drive
> us apart, since he died as a result of one. His risks were only dares.[1]

Synopsis

Elizabeth Bax's life is turned upside down when her husband, Sam, a daredevil Boston lawyer, pushes his luck one time too many and drowns sailing his boat off the coast of Maine—with
a certain degree of ambiguity about whether it was an accident or suicide. Elizabeth moves
from Boston to New York, drifting through a few jobs and an affair, before becoming engaged
to Sam's brother. All the while, she is mentally reviewing her life with Sam to see what went
wrong. Uncertain and unresolved, she retreats to a music camp in the Berkshires where she
has a brief affair with a man from Memphis named Charlie who helps her move forward in
her life.

Critical Commentary

In *Shine On, Bright & Dangerous Object,* Laurie Colwin provides one of the most poignant
pictures of the mourning process in recent literature. Colwin traces the trajectory of Elizabeth
Bax on a rocketing ride through tragedy, grief, fumbling at life, and eventual happiness. Written with wit and intelligence, this novel shows a wonderful sense of style and grace in dealing
with what, in clumsier hands, would have been a difficult and awkward subject. Grief is an
inevitable part of the human experience. This novel, suitable for adolescents on up, deals with
the topic in a sensitive and thoughtful manner.

With a keen ear for the lifestyle and manners of upper-class New Yorkers, Colwin describes
a reserved family and its reaction to death. The contrast between the open world of New York
and the cloistered world of Boston is delivered with brightness and verve. Colwin also contrasts
the personality of the reserved Elizabeth and that of her reckless husband, Sam. As Elizabeth
reviews their life together while trying to make a new one for herself, Colwin's use of flashback
and forward motion in the narrative effectively balances the story.

The strength of this novel lies in Colwin's ability to take an ordinary occasion and endow it
with a sense of the miraculous. The death of Sam Bax is seen through the clear lens of Colwin's

vision beyond its tragedy—to be something that Elizabeth can take strength from as she finds her way, perhaps not into the life she wanted or expected, but into a life she can accept nevertheless. For anyone who grieves (or for those who wonder how to approach someone who is grieving), this book will be not only entertaining, but also thought-provoking and useful.

Author Sketch

A Manhattan native, Colwin attended Bard College and Columbia University. She published many short stories and four novels, some of which were adapted for stage and television. She also worked for literary agents and publishers as a food columnist and as a translator. She won a Guggenheim Fellowship in 1987. Colwin was married and had one daughter. She died on October 24, 1992, at the age of 48.[2]

Other Works by the Author

Home Cooking. New York: Knopf, 1988.
Family Happiness: A Novel. New York: Perennial Library, 1990.
Goodbye without Leaving. New York: Poseidon Press, 1990.
The Lone Pilgrim: Stories. New York: Perennial Library, 1990.
A Big Storm Knocked It Over: A Novel. New York: HarperCollins, 1993.
Happy All the Time: A Novel. New York: HarperPerennial, 1993.
Another Marvelous Thing. New York: HarperPerennial, 1995.
Passion and Affect. New York: HarperPerennial, 1995.

Suggestions for Further Reading

Didion, Joan. *The Year of Magical Thinking.* New York: Knopf, 2005.
Gilbert, Sandra M. *Death's Door: Modern Dying and the Ways We Grieve.* New York: Norton, 2006.
Silverman, Phyllis R. *Widow to Widow: How the Bereaved Help One Another.* 2nd ed. Series in Death, Dying, and Bereavement. New York: Brunner-Routledge, 2004.

Notes

1. Laurie Colwin, *Shine On, Bright & Dangerous Object* (New York: Penguin Books, 1984), p. 68.
2. *New York Times,* October 25, 1992, p. 44.

Robert Coover

The Origin of the Brunists

New York: Norton, 1966

Originally published: 1966

Genre: Historical Fiction

Quote

The white bird: images of light and grace and the Holy Spirit, signal, as Eleanor Norton
learned upon asking the One to Come, of a new life, another age. Has so radical a wonder
ever happened before? Have mortals before been invaded by beings from higher aspected
spheres?[1]

Synopsis

A mine disaster in the small American town of West Condon kills 97 people. The only sur-
vivor, Giovanni Bruno, subsequently experiences religious visions that rapidly influence people
in the town and across the country, leading to a millenarian cult, the Brunists, whose members
gather on a local mountainside waiting for the apocalypse. There are varying reactions within
the town. Preacher Abner Baxter declares that the followers are devils, and banker Ted Cava-
naugh and other locals forms a booster-like Common Sense Society to preserve the town as it
was, while local reporter Justin Miller uses the situation to sell newspapers. Townspeople, who
have been using the mine disaster as an excuse for their own drinking, promiscuity, or worse,
are hostile to the Brunists and eventually riot to stop them. When all is over, dozens of people
have been killed or injured.

Critical Commentary

In this engaging cautionary tale, Coover traces the origins of a religious movement and
its effects on a small eastern U.S. mining town. The story is especially poignant in that a
central event in the novel and the catalyst for the religious revival is a massive mine disaster
that kills almost 100 people. Coover deftly traces the rise of the Brunists' religious zealotry and
the community's reactions to it, contrasting this with various other responses of community
members to the tragedy, to provide a remarkable psychological portrait of a community in
crisis.

Through his use of multiple points of view, Coover switches rapidly from various members
of the religious group to other community members, including the mayor, the newspaper editor, local teenagers, and even children. The narrative is further enriched by the author's use of
flashbacks and well-developed characters. As a result, the book reads with an almost cinematic
quality as it makes use of pans, fades, and internal monologue, which serve as a kind of underlying narration.

In the mine-disaster sequences, Coover shows a sophisticated command of language, particularly the language of miners. He fits the language and diction appropriately to the various characters and makes careful use of words. For example, he avoids the use of the word "cult" until well into the book, recognizing the implications and effect on the reader of such a word. In other instances, his word choices are colorful, if more obscure. (The average reader presumably will not know the meaning of such phrases as "a hot mole"—referring to a hot iron mold.)

The reactions to disaster in this story range from the strange theology of the Brunists, a group in some ways as creepy as anything envisioned by H. P. Lovecraft, to the materialistic contemporary civic boosterism of the Babbitt-like mayor. There is also the ultimately pointless spiritualism of Eleanor Norton. All of these responses are artfully contrasted with the spiritual bankruptcy of many of the other characters who simply descend into frivolity, violence, and self-loathing. Although Christianity is invoked by all the characters, ultimately it is understood (and practiced) by almost no one—not even by the priests and ministers who do a remarkably poor job of promoting their doctrines.

Coover has created a wonderful portrait of people in general and mindsets they can develop that can lead them into a cult—and, surprisingly, how they are usually distinguished by their "normalcy" more than by their strangeness. They are us. We are them. In our present age of disaster and violence, with its strong religious undercurrents, this book takes on new importance. People interested in the response of a community to tragedy or in the origins of religious fanaticism, which given events of recent years likely includes everyone, should find this an good read.

Author Sketch

Coover was born February 4, 1932, in Charles City, Iowa, and educated at Southern Illinois University, Indiana University, and the University of Chicago. He has been employed at several universities, including Bard College (1966–67), the University of Iowa (1967–69), Princeton University (1972–73), Columbia University (1972), Virginia Military Institute (1976), Brandeis University (1981), and Brown University (1981–present). His honors include a Guggenheim fellowship, 1971; a National Book Award nomination, 1977, for *The Public Burning;* a National Endowment for the Humanities award, 1985; a Rea Award from the Dungannon Foundation, 1987, for *A Night at the Movies;* and a DAAD fellowship, 1991.[2]

Other Works by the Author

The Universal Baseball Association, Inc.: J. Henry Waugh, Prop. New York: Random House, 1968.
Pricksongs & Descants; Fictions. New York: Dutton, 1969.
A Theological Position; Plays. New York: Dutton, 1972.
The Water Pourer; An Unpublished Chapter from "The Origin of the Brunists." Bloomfield Hills, MI: Bruccoli-Clark, 1972.
The Public Burning. New York: Viking Press, 1977.
A Political Fable. New York: Viking Press, 1980.
Spanking the Maid: A Novel. New York: Grove Press, 1982.
In Bed One Night & Other Brief Encounters. Providence: Burning Deck, 1983.
Gerald's Party: A Novel. New York: Linden Press, 1986.

A Night at the Movies, or, You Must Remember This. New York: Linden Press, Simon & Schuster, 1987.

Whatever Happened to Gloomy Gus of the Chicago Bears? New York: Linden Press, 1987.

Pinocchio in Venice. New York: Linden Press, Simon & Schuster, 1991.

Briar Rose. New York: Grove Press, 1996.

John's Wife: A Novel. New York: Simon & Schuster, 1996.

Ghost Town: A Novel. New York: Henry Holt, 1998.

Grand Hotels (of Joseph Cornell). Providence: Burning Deck, 2001.

The Adventures of Lucky Pierre: Directors' Cut. New York: Grove Press, 2002.

The Grand Hotels (of Joseph Cornell). Providence: Burning Deck, 2002.

A Child Again. San Francisco: McSweeney's Books, 2005.

Coover, Robert, and Kent Dixon. *The Stone Wall Book of Short Fictions.* Iowa City: Stone Wall Press, 1973.

Coover, Robert, Jerome Kaplan, and Michael McCurdy. *Charlie in the House of Rue.* Lincoln, MA: Penmaen Press, 1980.

Coover, Robert, and Michael Kupperman. *Stepmother.* San Francisco: McSweeney's Books, 2004.

Hawkes, John, Robert Coover, and Patrick McGrath. *The Lime Twig; Second Skin; Travesty,* Penguin Twentieth-Century Classics. New York: Penguin Books, 1996.

Suggestions for Further Reading

Chaplin, James Patrick. *Rumor, Fear, and the Madness of Crowds.* New York: Ballantine Books, 1959.

Garrett, Clarke. *Spirit Possession and Popular Religion: From the Camisards to the Shakers.* Baltimore: Johns Hopkins University Press, 1987.

Stein, Stephen J. *The Shaker Experience in America: A History of the United Society of Believers.* New Haven: Yale University Press, 1992.

Trompf, G. W. *Cargo Cults and Millenarian Movements: Transoceanic Comparisons of New Religious Movements.* Berlin and New York: Mouton de Gruyter, 1990.

Notes

1. Robert Coover, *The Origin of the Brunists* (New York: Norton, 1966), p. 334.

2. *Dictionary of Literary Biography,* Vol. 2: *American Novelists Since World War II, First Series,* ed. Jeffrey Helterman and Richard Layman (Detroit: Gale, 1978), pp. 106–121.

John Cramer

Twistor

New York: Avon Books, 1991

Originally published: 1989

Genre: Speculative Fiction/Science Fiction

Quote

> The towers and battlements of Physics Hall shone wetly in the morning light filtering through the Seattle drizzle. The structure would have been well suited for shooting arrows and pouring boiling oil down upon some horde of barbarians, were any so foolish as to venture onto the campus of the University of Washington to besiege Physics Hall.[1]

Synopsis

David Harrison, a young physicist at the University of Washington, accidentally discovers the "twistor effect," which opens a gateway to alternate universes. Threatened by thugs hired by corporate spies who want to exploit his discovery, David, along with two young children of one of his colleagues, jumps into another world. Once there, he must use his wits and scientific skills, like a modern Robinson Crusoe, to save the children and himself and to get home.

Critical Commentary

Science fiction doesn't get a great deal of critical respect. However, science fiction novels can be entertaining and can also lead thoughtful readers to become better informed about science. John Cramer's *Twistor* is one of those novels that informs and inspires. It's written by a working scientist who knows his subject—and knows how to write well. The result is a compelling and thought-provoking novel that engages readers in learning more about the real world.

The story is interesting not so much for the science—based on reality but stretched for dramatic effect—as for Cramer's thoughtful and effective exposition of how the business of science works. He ably describes university life and procedures, the politics of scientific funding, and the fuzzy (and often messy) intersection between pure research and commercial application. Readers may wonder how much of this story is, or could be, true. To answer that question, Cramer provides a useful appendix that outlines the basic science and scientific assumptions he used in developing the novel.

Cramer's strong, believable characters successfully embody the various types one would expect to find in a university setting: David Harrison, the practical yet rather unworldly physicist; his overworked graduate student Victoria; and the scheming scientist/businessman Allan Saxon. David Harrison makes a fantastic discovery, but that doesn't get him out of teaching his nine o'clock class in basic physics (and making it interesting!) to a bored group of students. Victoria is a good role model for girls who see themselves as aspiring scientists—she is by turns clever, thoughtful, and, in a word, curious, which is an essential quality for a good scientist (or, indeed, for anyone wanting to have an interesting life).

The fantastic plot, in which the heroes escape their enemies by fleeing to an alternate universe, makes the story move along faster. Cramer's depictions of late 1980s Seattle are accurate and beautiful, but what's really great about this novel is how it depicts a fascinating world—of the university and the even more closed world of professional scientists—that most people know little about. The book shows readers that science can be fun.

Although almost 20 years old at the time of this writing, *Twistor* is prescient in depicting the way the Internet has changed the nature of scholarly communication. Especially interesting is how the novel depicts the Internet before the World Wide Web, when it was just e-mail and a few specialists connecting to large computer centers. This novel beautifully captures this pre-browser world.

In short, *Twistor* is a well-crafted and thoughtful novel that provides a fast-moving and entertaining story—and one that promotes science. It is a great read not only for fans of science fiction, but also for anyone who is interested in science and how it is actually practiced. Leaving aside the technology, this is a rollicking, fast-moving adventure story suitable for readers of all ages.

Author Sketch

Born in Houston, Texas, Cramer has a BA, MA, and PhD in physics from Rice University. Since 1964 he has been a faculty member at the University of Washington, where he researches ultra-relativistic heavy ion physics, pion and kaon HBT interferometry, silicon drift detectors, and time projection chamber detection techniques. He is also an active writer and science columnist.[2]

Other Works by the Author

Einstein's Bridge. Eos, 1998.
Siege of Haven. E-published by PublishAmerica, 2006.

Suggestions for Further Reading

Greene, B. *The Elegant Universe: Superstrings, Hidden Dimensions, and the Quest for the Ultimate Theory.* New York: Norton, 2003.
Hartwell, David G., and Kathryn Cramer. *The Ascent of Wonder: The Evolution of Hard SF.* London: Orbit, 1994.
Hawking, S. W., and Leonard Mlodinow. *A Briefer History of Time.* New York: Bantam Books, 2005.
Stenger, Victor J. *Timeless Reality: Symmetry, Simplicity, and Multiple Universes.* Amherst, NY: Prometheus Books, 2000.

Notes

1. John Cramer, *Twistor* (New York: Avon Books, 1991), p. 1.
2. http://faculty.washington.edu/jcramer/faculty.html

Harry Crews

A Feast of Snakes

New York: Atheneum, 1976

Originally Published: 1976

Genre: Mainstream/Literary Fiction

Quote

> The rattlesnake roundup had been going on now as long as anybody in town could remember, but until twelve years ago it had been a local thing, a few townspeople, a few farmers. They'd have a picnic, maybe a sack race or a horsepulling contest and then everybody would go out into the woods and see how many diamondbacks they could pull out of the ground.[1]

Synopsis

Mystic, Georgia, is the home of the annual Rattlesnake Roundup, which turns this isolated rural hamlet into a mini-city of thousands—all there for drinking, dog fights, and, of course, catching rattlesnakes. The central character, Joe Lon Mackey, a former local high-school football hero turned bootlegger, is fed up with his awful boring life. He decides to get attention and ultimately goes berserk, but not before inciting a strange series of events that turn the community upside down.

Critical Commentary

Almost every caricature of Southern personality found in literature—the corrupt sheriff, the dog-fighting redneck, the failed football star—can be found here. That being said, the author has written them with such care and such insight into their personalities that one forgives him his conventions. He has twisted the stereotypes to such an extreme that, finally, they become caricatures of themselves in a Southern grotesque that both repels and intrigues. Sure to fascinate any reader interested in well-developed characters, this book also features a twisting and turning plotline that ends in utter mayhem.

The characters exist largely without any hope of redemption or change. Life for them is what it is. With colorful imagery, the author creates a world of utter brutality and ugliness, in what might be described as the written equivalent of an auto crash—one doesn't want to look while driving past, but ends up compelled to view the carnage. The author writes with enthusiasm for his subject in an engrossing narrative style.

The story centers on the annual community rattlesnake festival. The snake serves as a symbol for the internal moral ugliness of the characters, who, without exception, lack hope of redemption and, more troubling, are without any real awareness or desire to be redeemed. They have abandoned their hopes of living in a more conventional world for a perverted festival of violence.

Set in the American South, the story could be that of any dispossessed people anywhere. Denied any chance to be successful in the outer world and, indeed, lacking both the abilities and the courage that would be required even to try, the characters end up wallowing in their own moral despair. This book shouldn't be compared in either style or quality to Dante's *Inferno,* but the reader has the same sense of moral outrage in viewing these characters that the reader experiences in Dante's deepest circles of hell—the sense that they somehow got what they deserved. Creepy, weird, and wonderful, this is a book not to be missed by any fan of Southern literature or those interested in a book that is, by turns, scary and wacky. Most fans of dark comedy will find this a book to their liking, although the subject matter probably makes this unsuitable for younger readers below high school age.

Author Sketch

Crews was born June 7, 1935, in Georgia, and he moved to Florida in the 1940s. After service in the Marine Corps during the Korean War, Crews enrolled at the University of Florida, where he later became a faculty member in the English Department. Since the 1960s, Crews has produced stories, essays, magazine articles, screenplays, and an autobiography. In 1997 he retired from the University of Florida to devote himself to writing.[2]

Other Works by the Author

The Gospel Singer. New York: Morrow, 1968.
Naked in Garden Hills. New York: Morrow, 1969.
This Thing Don't Lead to Heaven. New York: Morrow, 1970.
Karate Is a Thing of the Spirit; A Novel. New York: Morrow, 1971.
Car; A Novel. New York: Morrow, 1972.
The Hawk Is Dying. New York: Knopf, 1973.
The Gypsy's Curse; A Novel. New York: Knopf, 1974.
Blood and Grits. New York: Harper & Row, 1978.
A Childhood, the Biography of a Place. New York: Harper & Row, 1978.
All We Need of Hell. New York: Harper & Row, 1987.
The Knockout Artist. New York: Harper & Row, 1988.
Body. New York: Poseidon Press, 1990.
Scar Lover. New York: Poseidon Press, 1992.
The Mulching of America: A Novel. New York: Simon & Schuster, 1995.
Celebration: A Novel. New York: Simon & Schuster, 1998.
Crews, Harry, and Erik Bledsoe. *Getting Naked with Harry Crews: Interviews.* Gainesville: University Press of Florida, 1999.

Suggestions for Further Reading

Elie, Lolis Eric, ed. *Cornbread Nation 2: The United States of Barbecue.* Chapel Hill: University of North Carolina Press, 2004.
Kimbrough, David L. *Taking Up Serpents: Snake Handlers of Eastern Kentucky.* Macon, GA: Mercer University Press, 2002.
Martinez, J. Michael, William D. Richardson, and Ron McNinch-Su. *Confederate Symbols in the Contemporary South.* Gainesville: University Press of Florida, 2000.

Wyatt-Brown, Bertram. *The Shaping of Southern Culture: Honor, Grace, and War, 1760s–1890s*. Chapel Hill: University of North Carolina Press, 2001.

Notes

1. Harry Crews, *A Feast of Snakes* (New York: Atheneum, 1976), p. 17.
2. http://www.harrycrews.com

James Crumley

The Wrong Case

New York: Vintage Contemporaries, 1986

Originally published: 1975

Genre: Crime Fiction/Mystery-Detection

Quote

> Since I assumed dissolutions of marriage would arrange themselves without my profes-
> sional assistance, my prospects were several and unseemly. I could take up repossession
> full time, taking back the used cars and cheap appliances so sweetly promised by the
> installment loan, pursuing bad debtors as if I were a hound from some financially respon-
> sible hell.[1]

Synopsis

Milo Milodragovitch, an ex-cop, makes a meager living as a private detective in his small
northwestern U.S. hometown. He is hired by a mysterious woman to find her missing brother.
This doesn't fit his usual line of work, but he takes the job in hopes of being able to pick up the
woman. In the course of his investigation, he runs into a strange group of people, ranging from
vicious bikers to drug dealers, none of whom—including his client, it turns out—are who they
seem to be. After becoming embroiled in a series of arsons and murders and a heroin-dealing
ring run by the local mafia, Milo brings everyone to justice—sort of.

Critical Commentary

What happened to "the cowboy" after the closing of the American West? In *The Wrong
Case*, James Crumley posits one possible answer. In Milo Milodragovitch, Crumley conjures
a complex character in a novel that combines elements of the classic Western novel and the
modern detective story. Writing in the first person, Crumley quickly develops the persona of
Milo, a down-on-his-luck detective. Drawing on the traditional elements of film noir—the
seedy downtown office and the woman in distress—Crumley reinvents them within the context of the modern Pacific Northwest. Readers are drawn into the story, which evolves in a
dramatic manner, while gaining insights into the past of the town and of Milo—both of whom
have seen better days.

Intriguing characters add to the interest of the story, including the mysterious Helen Duffy
who becomes Milo's client, her missing brother, and the assorted malcontents and ne'er-do-
wells who make up Milo's friends and acquaintances. Crumley has a great ear for dialogue,
especially that of Milo, who comes off as alternately witty and cynical; he is hardened by life,
yet vulnerable and emotionally involved in the case. The plot moves quickly, with twists and
turns that keep the pages turning.

While examining the sordid reality of modern life, hemmed in by development and restrictions, *The Wrong Case* also echoes the classic Western genre dominated by the idea of the single lone man standing for justice. Milo, with his hard drinking habits and situational ethics—as well as an office hideaway in the back of a seedy bar—is hardly Gary Cooper in *High Noon,* but Crumley effectively develops the theme of the pursuit of justice to create a novel that will appeal to a wide range of readers, a novel with a compelling human story that transcends the murder mystery genre.

Author Sketch

Born October 12, 1939, in Three Rivers, Texas, Crumley was educated at Georgia Tech and Texas A&I University, after which he studied at Iowa State University under novelist Richard Yates. Since 1966, Crumley has worked as a writer and academic, including stints at the University of Arkansas at Fayetteville (1969–1970), at Colorado State University (1971–1974), at Reed College (1976–1977), and as a visiting professor at Carnegie-Mellon University. Since the mid-1980s, he has lived in Missoula, Montana.[2]

Other Works by the Author

One to Count Cadence. New York: Random House, 1969.
The Last Good Kiss: A Novel. New York: Random House, 1978.
Dancing Bear. New York: Random House, 1983.
Muddy Fork and Other Things. Livingston, MT: Clark City Press, 1991.
The Mexican Tree Duck. New York: Mysterious Press, 1993.
Bordersnakes. New York: Mysterious Press, 1996.
The Final Country. New York: Mysterious Press, 2001.
The Right Madness. New York: Viking Penguin, 2005.

Suggestions for Further Reading

Hillerman, Tony, and Otto Penzler. *The Best American Mystery Stories of the Century.* Boston: Houghton Mifflin, 2000.
Kittredge, William, and Annick Smith. *The Last Best Place: A Montana Anthology.* A Montana Centennial Book. Helena: Montana Historical Society Press, 1988.
Mysterious Press. *The Mysterious Press Anniversary Anthology: Celebrating 25 Years.* New York: Mysterious Press, 2001.
Penzler, Otto. *The Mighty Johns: 1 Novella & 13 Superstar Short Stories from the Finest in Mystery & Suspense.* Beverly Hills, CA: New Millennium Press, 2002.

Notes

1. James Crumley, *The Wrong Case* (New York: Vintage Contemporaries, 1986), p. 4.
2. "James Crumley," in *Dictionary of Literary Biography,* Vol. 226: *American Hard-Boiled Crime Writers,* ed. George Parker Anderson (Detroit: Gale, 2000), pp. 92–99.

Don DeLillo

Players

New York: Vintage, 1991

Originally published: 1977

Genre: Mainstream/Literary Fiction

Quote

It was her original view that the World Trade Center was an unlikely headquarters for an
outfit such as this. But she changed her mind as time passed. Where else would you stack
all this grief?[1]

Synopsis

Pammy and Lyle Wynant are a typical New York power couple. He has a job on Wall Street,
and she works for a grief counseling firm. A shooting on the floor of the stock exchange at
first seems to have nothing to do with them, other than involving a man, George, they knew
slightly. But as time goes on, through a combination of boredom and happenstance, the couple
becomes involved with a group of terrorists linked to the killing. Who these terrorists represent or what they hope to accomplish is vague, but Pammy and Lyle are increasingly drawn
into the shadowy world of terror to the surprising conclusion.

Critical Commentary

The complicity of Americans with terrorism provides the central theme in this elegant and
witty novel. DeLillo indirectly criticizes the moral degeneracy of American culture that esteems
material things over moral values. The two main characters, Pammy and Lyle Wynant, seem to
be the typical New York couple, with high-paying professional jobs. Yet over the course of the
novel, their ordinary upper-class life becomes increasingly unhinged as they become more and
more involved in a terrorist plot.

The plotting is tight, but DeLillo leaves the motivations of the terrorists vague. What are
they protesting? What is their cause? In this very ambiguity, they become symbolic of a climate
of violence that permeates modern society. The result is a novel that should engage readers
who are concerned with world events as well as those who simply like a story with a roller
coaster ride and mysterious characters filled with ambiguity.

As the story moves forward, it becomes obvious that mirrors reflect mirrors and that no one is
who they seem to be. The state of modern political life is also examined. Government no longer
expresses a fixed philosophical position, but rather only the politics of opportunity. DeLillo explores his theme with verve, creating a plot with various twists that keep the reader guessing. The
result is an artful psychological portrait of how ordinary persons come to accept and participate in
violence, as well as a meditation on the nature of the state and the role of order in a just society.

For some people, this novel may be unreadable for emotional reasons. It was published in 1977, and real events have since overtaken fiction. The idea of a terrorist plot on New York City may repel some readers, especially when, ironically, one of the characters works at a grief counseling service based in the World Trade Center. However, this thoughtful reflection on the nature of terrorism should be welcomed as a balance to many current novels—such as those of Dale Brown or Tom Clancy, for example—that promote a kind of American triumphalism over terror. There is irony here given the plotting of the novel, but the author should not be faulted for his prescience in setting his novel where he did. Art often has a strange way of becoming coincident with life. *Players* remains a well-developed reflection on the issue of violence and its relationship to the individual—a classic theme of many excellent novels (*The Brothers Karamazov* comes to mind)—so *Players* should be of interest to almost any reader of fiction.

Author Sketch

DeLillo was born November 20, 1936, and was educated at Fordham University (BA 1958). He has been a professional writer since the 1960s. His professional recognitions have included a Guggenheim fellowship, 1979; an American Academy of Arts and Letters Award in Literature, 1984; and a PEN/Faulkner Award, 1992, and a Pulitzer Prize nomination, both for *Mao II*. For *Underworld,* he received a National Book Award nomination and a National Book Critics Circle Award nomination, both in 1997, and a Pulitzer Prize nomination and the William Dean Howells Medal of the American Academy of Arts and Letters, in 2000. He also received the Jerusalem Prize in 2000. He is widely considered one of the great postmodernist writers of the late twentieth century.[2]

Other Works by the Author

Americana. Boston: Houghton Mifflin, 1971.
End Zone. Boston: Houghton Mifflin, 1972.
Great Jones Street. Boston: Houghton Mifflin, 1973.
Ratner's Star. New York: Knopf, 1976.
Running Dog. New York: Knopf, 1978.
Amazons: An Intimate Memoir by the First Woman Ever to Play in the National Hockey League. New York: Holt, Rinehart, and Winston, 1980.
The Names. New York: Knopf, 1982.
White Noise. New York: Viking, 1985.
The Day Room: A Play. New York: Knopf, 1986.
Libra. New York: Viking, 1988.
Mao II. New York: Viking, 1991.
Underworld. New York: Scribner, 1997.
Valparaiso: A Play in Two Acts. New York: Scribner, 1999.
The Body Artist: A Novel. New York: Scribner, 2001.
Cosmopolis: A Novel. New York: Scribner, 2003.
Love-Lies-Bleeding: A Play. New York: Scribner, 2005.
DeLillo, Don, and Thomas DePietro. *Conversations with Don DeLillo.* Literary Conversations Series. Jackson: University of Mississippi, 2005.

Suggestions for Further Reading

Donovan, Christopher. *Postmodern Counternarratives: Irony and Audience in the Novels of Paul Auster, Don DeLillo, Charles Johnson, and Tim O'Brien.* Literary Criticism and Cultural Theory Series. New York: Routledge, 2004.

Engles, Tim, and John N. Duvall. *Approaches to Teaching DeLillo's White Noise, Approaches to Teaching World Literature.* New York: Modern Language Association of America, 2006.

Kavadlo, Jesse. *Don DeLillo: Balance at the Edge of Belief.* New York: Peter Lang, 2004.

LeClair, Tom. *In the Loop: Don DeLillo and the Systems Novel.* Urbana: University of Illinois Press, 1987.

Osteen, Mark. *American Magic and Dread: Don DeLillo's Dialogue with Culture.* Penn Studies in Contemporary American Fiction. Philadelphia: University of Pennsylvania Press, 2000.

Yuknavitch, Lidia. *Allegories of Violence: Tracing the Writing of War in Twentieth-Century Fiction.* New York: Routledge, 2001.

Notes

1. Don DeLillo, *Players* (New York: Vintage, 1991), p. 18.
2. "Don DeLillo," in *Dictionary of Literary Biography,* Vol. 173: *American Novelists Since World War II, Fifth Series,* ed. James R. Giles and Wanda H. Giles (Detroit: Gale, 1996), pp. 14–36.

Philip K. Dick

Lies, Inc.

New York : Vintage Books/Random House, 2004

Originally published: 1965

Genre: Speculative Fiction/Science Fiction

Quote

> The SubInfo computers owned by Lies Incorporated had been caught in an unnatural act by a service mechanic. SubInfo computer Five had transmitted information which was not a lie. It would have to be taken apart to see why. And to whom the correct information had gone.[1]

Synopsis

Rachmael Ben Applebaum's life is in turmoil. His family business of spaceship freighting has been destroyed by the development of a teleportation machine that is rapidly moving people from an overcrowded Earth on a one-way trip to a utopian planet named Whale's Mouth. Suspicious of this project, especially the universally upbeat propaganda depicting the planet, Applebaum decides to take his last remaining spaceship on an 18-year journey to Whale's Mouth to find out the truth and transport back to Earth anyone who wants to return.

At the same time, Matson Glazer-Holliday, owner of Lies, Inc., a large international security company, and his mistress, Freya Holm, also decide to go to Whale's Mouth, along with 2,000 soldiers, to see what the story actually is. What they find is a German industrial combine, Trails of Hoffman, which has created a police state and is preparing to take over Earth. The plot is eventually crushed with the help of the United Nations, which may or may not have been in on the scheme from the outset.

Critical Commentary

In *Lies, Inc.*, Philip K. Dick creates a wry commentary on the excesses and awful possibilities of the emerging security state. He works within the science fiction genre, twisting the story into a bizarre and fascinating shape that causes the reader to reflect on the relationship between humans and their governments.

Dick starts with a fairly straightforward plot premise, a simple mystery: people are teleporting to the planet Whale's Mouth, but none of them come back. However, he combines this thread with long, convoluted (and sometimes incomprehensible) sequences in which he describes fantastic LSD trips to altered para-realities. The reader is emotionally jerked in different directions as what had been, more or less, a standard science fiction novel quickly morphs into strange, hallucinogenic ramblings, which serve to unsettle and confuse.

Everyone at Whale's Mouth is overwhelmed by the sheer size and scale of the corporate police state and the technology that dominates their lives. The idea of "creditor balloons," which
hound people for payment, anticipates the idea of e-mail spam, with its unrelenting, unwanted
solicitations. Other elements in the story provide fascinating pieces of exposition, as when
characters are given a book—a copy of a novel—which misleads the characters about what will
happens next.

Lies, Inc. is a precursor to the modern genre of alternative history, popularized by writers
such as Harry Turtledove. Dick's description of an overpopulated future dominated by international mega-corporations fits the literary tradition of dystopian fiction, of which Orwell's
1984 is the best-known example. To this scenario Dick melds postwar paranoia, making the
Germans the dominant evil figures. With tacit criticism of the entire industrial and governmental state that has developed since the late 1940s, the story explores the idea that accepting
a technology implies accepting the ideology that goes along with it. An additional underlying
theme highlights the ability of governments and corporations to manipulate information. The
neurotic central character, Rachmael Ben Applebaum, discovers the truth in part because he
looks at old records that could not be tampered with.

Ultimately, in this creative examination of how people cope with chaos and change, the
reader is left with a number of disturbing questions. How does one make meaning of a universe
that, for all practical purposes, cannot be understood or influenced in any meaningful way?
How do we, as a society, create a common grammar for recording and explaining our existence
in the world? The result is a complicated book that is deeply thought-provoking.

Author Sketch

Born December 16, 1928, in Chicago, Illinois, Dick was, from 1952 on, a prolific science-
fiction author with some commercial success, although he had only limited mainstream recognition. He wrote more than 150 short stories and 36 novels, including many books now
recognized as science-fiction classics, including *Do Androids Dream of Electric Sheep* (1968),
The Three Stigmata of Palmer Eldritch (1965), *Time Out Of Joint* (1959), and the Hugo Award–
winning *The Man in the High Castle* (1962). Dick died of a heart attack in 1982. His greatest
fame has been posthumous; his work has found mass appeal, and many of his books have been
adapted to film, including *Blade Runner* and *Total Recall*, which were both box-office hits.[2]

Other Works by the Author

The Man in the High Castle: A Novel. New York: G. P. Putnam's Sons, 1962.
The Preserving Machine. New York: Ace Books, 1969.
Solar Lottery. Boston: Gregg Press, 1976.
Dr. Bloodmoney: Or, How We Got Along after the Bomb. Boston: Gregg Press, 1977.
A Handful of Darkness. Boston: Gregg Press, 1978.
The Divine Invasion. New York: Timescape Books, 1981.
The Transmigration of Timothy Archer. New York: Timescape Books, 1982.
Puttering About in a Small Land. Chicago: Academy Chicago Publishers, 1985.
Radio Free Albemuth. New York: Arbor House, 1985.
Mary and the Giant. New York: Arbor House, 1987.
The Broken Bubble. New York: Arbor House/Morrow, 1988.

The Three Stigmata of Palmer Eldritch. New York: Vintage Books, 1991.

The Man Who Japed. New York: Vintage Books, 2002.

The Minority Report. New York: Pantheon Books, 2002.

Dick, Philip K., Andy Hopkins, and Joc Potter. *Do Androids Dream of Electric Sheep?* Simplified ed. Oxford: Oxford University Press, 1995.

Martin, Les, and Philip K. Dick. *Blade Runner.* New York: Ballantine Books, 1982.

Suggestions for Further Reading

Carrère, Emmanuel, and Timothy Bent. *I Am Alive and You Are Dead: A Journey into the Mind of Philip K. Dick.* New York: Henry Holt, 2004.

McKee, Gabriel. *Pink Beams of Light from the God in the Gutter: The Science-Fictional Religion of Philip K. Dick.* Dallas: University Press of America, 2004.

Palmer, Christopher. *Philip K. Dick: Exhilaration and Terror of the Postmodern, Liverpool Science Fiction Texts and Studies.* Liverpool: Liverpool University Press, 2003.

Sutin, Lawrence. *Divine Invasions: A Life of Philip K. Dick.* New York: Harmony Books, 1989.

Umland, Samuel J. *Philip K. Dick: Contemporary Critical Interpretations.* Contributions to the Study of Science Fiction and Fantasy, no. 63. Westport, CT: Greenwood Press, 1995.

Notes

1. Philip K. Dick, *Lies, Inc.* (New York: Vintage Books/Random House, 2004), p. 1.

2. "Philip K. Dick," in *Dictionary of Literary Biography,* Vol. 8: *Twentieth-Century American Science-Fiction Writers,* ed. David Cowart and Thomas L. Wyner (Detroit: Gale, 1981), pp. 134–140.

Harriett Doerr

Stones for Ibarra

New York: Viking Penguin, 1984

Originally published: 1984

Genre: Mainstream/Literary Fiction

Quote

> Through the gates she watched trees lose their green and the tile pattern of the driveway disappear. As she stood next to the heap of stones a miner passed her on his bicycle, then two others coasted by. She raised her hand and the riders waved back. But her intention had been to stop them.[1]

Synopsis

Sara and Richard Everton, two middle-aged Americans, decide to chuck their conventional lives for a new one in Mexico—after Richard is diagnosed with cancer. They move to the village of Ibarra and reopen the Everton family copper mine, which was abandoned 40 years earlier during the Mexican Revolution. This novel describes the couple's experiences as they learn to live with their new neighbors.

Each villager has a different story to tell: Chuy Santos, who sets up a taxi business; the parish priests, who want to convert the Evertons; the brothers Basilio and Domingo, who come to a tragic end. This is a story of mutual observations in which the natives and the Evertons look at each other with wonder, all against the backdrops of the Mexican landscape and Richard Everton's terminal illness.

Critical Commentary

Novels about Americans abroad have become something of a staple in American literature, going back as far as the nineteenth century with Mark Twain's *Innocents Abroad* (1869). Harriett Doerr's *Stones for Ibarra* is a charming and original contribution to this genre, with the twist that it isn't so much about the foreigners observing the lives of the natives as it is the natives watching the foreigners in their midst, using their observations as a lens to understand their own community and themselves.

Strong characterizations in this novel are dominated by the well-drawn and sensitive portraits of the various Mexican villagers and their reactions to the Americans as the natives try to integrate them into their community while getting on with their own lives. The characters range from the town drunk to an ambitious young university student to an aging priest. These people appear in vignettes within the main course of the story, as the Evertons try to reopen an old copper mine while dealing with Richard Everton's increasingly serious cancer.

Doerr has created a lifelike and believable village placed, somewhat mysteriously, in an un-named Mexican state—presumably in northern Mexico—five days' drive from San Francisco. In this story of contrasts and misunderstandings, the Evertons' religion (or lack of it) contrasts with the villagers' beliefs—a mixture of devout Catholicism and native superstition. In a won-derfully funny scene, Sara Everton plants maguey cacti, for their looks; meanwhile, the sensible (and hopeful) villagers assume she is doing it to make mescal.

The real appeal of this novel is how it shows the differing views of people from two cultures about history and change. To the Evertons, the history of the village and of Mexico is somewhat glorious, whereas the natives would like to forget most of it. The villagers, unlike the Evertons, blend past and present—they hunger for progress, at least as reflected in the neighboring town, which has a movie house. But they also respect their traditions, such as the use of witch doctors and folk magic, which the Evertons find silly.

There are plenty of humorous novels about people moving abroad (e.g., Peter Mayle's *A Good Year*), but Doerr goes beyond the typical "fish out of water" story to create a mean-ingful meditation on the nature of progress and the interaction between cultures. This is a delightful book that should appeal to anyone interested in a good story with well-developed characters.

Author Sketch

Doerr was born in Pasadena, California, in 1910, the granddaughter of railway tycoon Henry Edwards Huntington. After attending Smith College in 1927, she transferred to Stan-ford. She dropped out of Stanford in 1930 to marry her husband, Albert. In 1977 she reentered Stanford and developed her writing skills while earning a degree in European history. Doerr's second book, *Consider This, Señora*, was published in 1993 and became a best seller. *The Tiger in the Grass*, a collection of essays and short stories, was published in 1995. She died in 2002 at the age of 92.[2]

Other Works by the Author

Under an Aztec Sun. Covelo, CA: Yolla Bolly Press, 1990.
Consider This, Señora. New York: Harcourt Brace, 1993.
The Tiger in the Grass: Stories and Other Inventions. New York: Viking, 1995.
L'Heureux, John, Wallace Earle Stegner, Robert Stone, and Stanford Writing Workshop. *The Uncommon Touch: Fiction and Poetry from the Stanford Writing Workshop.* Stanford, CA: Stanford Alumni As-sociation, 1989.

Suggestions for Further Reading

Archer, Christon I. *The Birth of Modern Mexico, 1780–1824.* Wilmington, DE: Scholarly Resources, 2003.
Gonzales, Michael J. *The Mexican Revolution, 1910–1940.* Albuquerque: University of New Mexico Press, 2002.
Olcott, Jocelyn. *Revolutionary Women in Postrevolutionary Mexico.* Durham, NC: Duke University Press, 2005.
Vaughan, Mary K., and Stephen E. Lewis. *The Eagle and the Virgin: Nation and Cultural Revolution in Mexico, 1920–1940.* Durham, NC: Duke University Press, 2006.

Notes

1. Harriett Doerr, *Stones for Ibarra* (New York: Viking Penguin, 1984), p. 214.

2. http://www-sul.stanford.edu/depts/hasrg/ablit/amerlit/doerr.html; *Contemporary Authors*, vol. 117 (Detroit, MI: Gale Research), p. 104.

Herman Dreer

The Immediate Jewel of His Soul

College Park, MD: McGrath, 1919

Originally published: 1919

Genre: Mainstream/Literary/African American Fiction

Quote

> The months that lay before William were passing slowly, weary months of anxiety. He had
> before him ambitions which would not crystallize, until the long nights had passed away.
> This by no means meant that he was not working; for he well proportioned his time for
> systematic endeavor, interspersed with timely recreation.[1]

Synopsis

William Smith enters adulthood with all the likely prospects of success, seen by his African American community as their great hope for the future. He initially fulfills their dreams, cruising easily through college and divinity school to become a respected preacher with his own church. But he soon runs afoul of his denomination because of his radical views on race relations and religion, which leads to his removal from the pulpit.

Barred from ministry, Smith moves to an isolated rural community where he begins a model farm. Because of its scientific practices (as well as Smith's good advice to local sharecroppers that improves their economic position), the farm prospers. However, this success doesn't sit well with a number of his white racist neighbors, who see him (and his associates) as uppity and as threatening the local status quo of race relations. The tension eventually escalates into a volatile situation, with a mob marching on his farm, intending to burn it (and Smith) to the ground. This impending holocaust is thwarted by Smith's preparedness, most notably his arming of his African American farmers and neighbors, and by a small group of progressive white farmers who talk the mob down, urging them to look beyond issues of race to see the economic and political benefits that Smith's progressive farming and social ideas will bring to their region.

Critical Commentary

In the era following World War I, racial tensions significantly increased within the United States. Black veterans returning from war demanded civil rights, the economy languished, and racist organizations such as the Ku Klux Klan grew. In the midst of this milieu, a progressive African American cultural movement, the Harlem Renaissance, emerged. The Harlem Renaissance countered the prevailing negative views with positive images of black culture—in art, literature, music, and general social awareness. Herman Dreer's *The Immediate Jewel of His Soul* was a part of this trend; and it deserves better recognition both for its command of its subject matter and as the fine piece of writing that it is.

Here is a wonderfully detailed and complete picture of black life in America at the end of World War I. Through his insightful character study of William Smith—who is seen from his high school graduation through his entry into (and subsequent expulsion from) the ministry to his founding of a progressive farm in the South—Dreer documents various issues important to the black community of the time, including the role of the church, the importance of education, and the need for equality with whites. Smith is, in the classic sense of the word, a hero. He never takes the easy way out of his situation, but instead holds to his principles—even when it results in personal risk to himself. This results in a story with a significant number of dramatic moments. For example, in one episode, Smith, carrying a rifle, walks alone through the streets of a hostile white town to demand his rights—as a citizen and as a man—from the mayor.

This novel also features a triangle romance in which Smith becomes involved with two women, Susan and Thelma, who compete for his affection throughout the novel. The dynamic tension between the women (and Smith) adds to the interest of the novel.

Dreer creates a thought-provoking novel that is, in some sense, an extended meditation on the issue of the proper response to violence—whether that is spiritual and emotional violence, as when Smith is thrown out of the ministry, or physical violence, as when he faces an angry mob. It is also a fascinating study of the conflicted views that people had on the issue of race during the period. Contrary to what one might assume given the subject matter, which includes some detailed descriptions of lynchings, not all the Southern whites are depicted as bigoted racists. Indeed, many are portrayed as progressive—perhaps not in the sense of accepting Smith as a social equal, but in recognizing his talent, intelligence, and accomplishments and the benefits he can bring to the development of a "New South." *The Immediate Jewel of His Soul* tells a compelling story that should engage anyone interested in African American history or the history of the American South.

Author Sketch

Herman Dreer was born in 1888 in Washington, D.C. After graduating from Bowdoin College in Brunswick, Maine, in 1910, he taught at Virginia Theological Seminary in Lynchburg, Virginia. In 1914 he moved to Saint Louis, Missouri, where he taught a variety of subjects at the secondary school level. Dreer established Douglas University in 1935 to meet the needs of the underserved African American community. He was active in civil and social affairs, especially those dealing with civil rights. A writer for both popular publications and scholarly journals, he received his PhD in sociology in 1955 from the University of Chicago with a dissertation titled "Negro Leadership in St. Louis: A Study in Race Relations." From 1950 to 1970, he served as the minister of King's Way Baptist Church. Dreer died in August 1981 at age 92. His home in Saint Louis is now designated as a historical landmark.[2]

Other Works by the Author

American Literature by Negro Authors. New York: Macmillan, 1950.

The History of the Omega Psi Phi Fraternity: A Brotherhood of Negro College Men, 1911 to 1939. Washington, D.C.: The Fraternity.

The Tie that Binds: A Novel of a Youth Who Seeks to Understand Life. Boston: Meador, 1958.

Suggestions for Further Reading

Bayor, R. H. *Race and Ethnicity in America: A Concise History.* New York: Columbia University Press, 2003.

Bryan, G. M. *These Few Also Paid a Price: Southern Whites Who Fought for Civil Rights.* Macon, GA: Mercer University Press, 2001.

Lowery, Charles D., John F. Marszalek, and Thomas Adams Upchurch, eds. *The Greenwood Encyclopedia of African American Civil Rights: From Emancipation to the Twenty-First Century.* Westport, CT: Greenwood Press, 2003.

Theoharis, J., and K. Woodard. *Groundwork: Local Black Freedom Movements in America.* New York: New York University Press, 2005.

Whitt, M. E. *Short Stories of the Civil Rights Movement: An Anthology.* Athens: University of Georgia Press, 2006.

Notes

1. Herman Dreer, *The Immediate Jewel of His Soul* (College Park, MD: McGrath, 1919), p. 22.
2. http://www.umsl.edu/~whmc/guides/whm0167.htm

Edward Eggleston

The Hoosier School Master

New York: Sagamore Press, 1957

Originally published: 1871

Genre: Historical Fiction

Quote

"You see this ere bottom land was all Congress land in them there days, and it sold for a dollar and a quarter, and I says to my ole man, 'Jack,' says I, 'Jack, do you git a plenty while you're a getting,' says I, 'fer 'twon't never be no cheaper'n 'tis now,' and it ha'n't been, I knowed 'twouldn't," and Mrs. Means took the pipe from her mouth to indulge in a good chuckle at the thought of her financial shrewdness.[1]

Synopsis

As the story opens, a speech introduces readers to the regional Hoosier dialect used by all the "locals" in the book. The new schoolmaster, Ralph Hartsook, enters Flat Creek, Indiana, where he must win the hearts and minds of his students. Staying at the home of wealthy old Jack Means, Ralph falls in love with Hannah Thompson, a servant, instead of Mean's daughter, Mirandy. In another situation, a local politician, Pete Jones, and a physician, Dr. Small, try to divert suspicion from themselves by accusing a war veteran, John Pearson, of burglarizing the home of Dutchy Snyder, a toll taker. Ralph and Hannah's brother Shocky save Pearson from being lynched by a mob. Then Ralph is accused of the crime. In the ensuing trial, Ralph successfully defends himself, while events unfold to a happy conclusion.

Critical Commentary

The *Hoosier School Master* is a pioneering work central to the later development of realism in twentieth-century American literature. Eggleston makes skillful use of local dialect as well as highly developed descriptions of local individuals and the activities of their daily lives to depict small-town America. Although the story may seem sentimental to modern readers, it offers lively and interesting character studies of a variety of individuals who, although they can be seen as simple and provincial, are actually quite complex and convey a sense of authenticity to the story.

Eggleston's deft use of dialect is the most compelling aspect of the novel. Eggleston has approached the issue of language from a scholarly, historical, and almost anthropological standpoint, realizing that accuracy in the depiction of language increases the clarity and dramatic effect of the novel. The result is ideally suited for Eggleston's portrayal of rural life. Through this use of authentic language rather than literary wording, Eggleston has created a real sense of connection between the readers and the characters, as well as preserved unique forms of dialect and pronunciation.

Eggleston aptly describes the intricate nuances of a community that outsiders might consider crude and rough, but that in fact is surprisingly sophisticated on a variety of levels—socially, economically, and politically. His sensitive portrayal of country life is characterized by a real respect for the individuality of the characters as well as for the overall social milieu in which they find themselves. He renders in a highly pictorial manner the lifestyles and folkways of a society that, though rooted in traditional social patterns, was also attempting to come to grips with large changes in the social and economic landscape—such as the movement away from a subsistence economy to one more fully involved in the marketplace

The pacing, though more episodic than linear in nature, complements the author's use of language by allowing him to present a diverse group of individuals. The novel displays a true sense of proportion, and although it deals with serious issues, it never takes itself too seriously. It is a thoughtful and charming portrait of a time and place long since lost that is sure to appeal to readers who want not only a gentle nostalgic story, but also one filled with a certain amount of action and mystery.

Author Sketch

Born on December 10, 1837, in Vevay, Indiana, Eggleston was a minister and journalist in the Midwest until 1870. In 1870 he joined the editorial staff of the *Independent* in New York City and began a literary career that included novels, juvenile stories, and two volumes of American history, *The Beginners of a Nation* (1896) and *The Transit of Civilization* (1901). His final years were marked by illness, leading to his death on September 3, 1902, at Lake George, New York.[2]

Other Works by the Author

The Mystery of Metropolisville. New York: O. Judd, 1873.
The Circuit Rider: A Tale of the Heroic Age. New York: Scribner's, 1878.
The Graysons: A Story of Illinois. New York: Century, 1888.
The Hoosier School-Boy. New York: Scribner, 1890.
The Faith Doctor: A Story of New York. New York: Appleton, 1891.
Duffels. New York: Appleton, 1893.
Eggleston, Edward, James Russell Lowell, and William Dean Howells. *Francis Parkman.* Boston: Little, Brown, 1897.

Suggestions for Further Reading

Auringer, O. C., and Josiah Kirby Lilly. *Friendship's Crown of Verse: Being Memorials of Edward Eggleston.* Clinton, NY: G. W. Browning, 1907.
Furlong, Patrick Joseph, and Mary Ellen Gadski. *Indiana: An Illustrated History.* Sun Valley, CA: American Historical Press, 2001.
Gray, Ralph D. *Indiana History: A Book of Readings.* Bloomington: Indiana University Press, 1994.
Peckham, Howard Henry. *Indiana: A History.* Urbana: University of Illinois Press, 2003.
Randel, William Peirce. *Edward Eggleston.* New York: Twayne, 1963.
Shumaker, Arthur Wesley. *A History of Indiana Literature, with Emphasis on the Authors of Imaginative Works Who Commenced Writing Prior to World War II.* Indianapolis: Indiana Historical Bureau, 1962.

Notes

1. Edward Eggleston, *The Hoosier School Master* (New York: Sagamore Press, 1957), p. 15.
2. *Dictionary of Literary Biography*, Vol. 12: *American Realists and Naturalists*, ed. Donald Pizer and Earl N. Harbert (Detroit: Gale, 1982), pp. 165–173.

Richard Elam Jr.

Young Visitor to Mars

New York: Lantern Press, 1953

Originally published: 1953

Genre: Speculative Fiction/Science Fiction

Quote

> A huge waterway cut the landscape in two at the edge of the spaceport. Beyond this stood two large square buildings of transparent plastic substance. Still further out was a sprinkling of houses, one of which the Kentons would occupy. As far as Ted could see, the ground was rust red.[1]

Synopsis

Jill and Ted Kenton are en route to Mars in a rocket ship with their parents. Their scientist father plans to investigate an ancient Martian civilization. After landing on the moon for emergency repairs, the family meets Randy Mathews, whose father has gone missing on Mars. Taking Mathews into their family, the Kentons continue their journey to Mars, but not without misadventure when they have encounters with strange events. In the end, they make an extraordinary discovery that answers all sorts of questions about the past of Mars.

Critical Commentary

Young Visitor to Mars is an engaging science fiction story for children and young adults. Filled with action, vivid descriptions, and an interesting plotline, this is an excellent example of 1950s "space and rockets" science fiction. It combines the optimism of the mid-twentieth century with a fascination with gadgets and science fact and throws in fantasy elements of lost Martian civilizations and exotic extraterrestrial creatures. For the adult reader, this offers an intriguing glimpse into the mindset of the 1950s, which saw science as triumphant, while also maintaining traditional sex roles and the nuclear family. In particular, students of sociology or women's studies should find this novel interesting.

The plot is simple and straightforward. Two children, Ted and Jill Kenton, travel to Mars in 2003 AD with their scientist father and homemaker mother. While there, they have a variety of adventures and discover a lost Martian civilization, before deciding to return to Earth and the United States. What's noteworthy in this story is how science fact and science fiction have been combined. The author ignores known facts about Mars to give the reader water-filled canals, dangerous man-eating plants, and a buried alien city. That said, the story is well written, and it features well-developed characters and has a compelling plot filled with a variety of interesting gadgets and events. The novel mixes fantasy elements with factual didactic digressions—explaining, for example, how plants would be used on a spaceship to provide oxygen.

Issues that might seem problematic, such as why the canals don't freeze, are quickly explained away—they contain a substance we don't understand that keeps them liquid. This reflects the mentality of 1950s America—entertainment should have some "educational" element in it, but without probing too deeply.

Beneath the surface of the story—and this is what makes it interesting for the modern adult reader—the ethos of 1950s America clearly comes through. Despite the technological advances, the social structure is portrayed as unchanged. The father goes to work in an office, and the mom stays home and cleans, while the kids go off to school. Traditional sex roles are fixed, and when challenging events happen, like the air supply in the house going bad, the boys are the ones who save the day. That theme carries through the entire book—with the sister Jill being repeatedly confused by science until her brother Ted sets her straight.

Contemporary readers, especially those knowledgeable about science in general or Mars in particular, may find this a quaint piece of Americana and laugh loudly at the more unbelievable bits. However, for those, especially younger readers, who want an, interesting fast-moving story, this will be a hit. And for thoughtful adults, it also has value as a product of its time. We never got the flying cars we were promised, but this novel is an enjoyable and light reading substitute.

Author Sketch

Born July 16, 1920, Elam was educated at the Richmond Professional Institute (1946–47), Phoenix College (1947–48), and Arizona State University (1948–50). Aside from his writing career, Elam was a successful executive in the printing business in Texas.[2]

Other Works by the Author

Teen-age Science Fiction Stories. New York: Lantern Press, 1952.
Teen-age Super Science Stories. New York: Lantern Press, 1957.
Young Readers Science Fiction Stories. New York: Lantern Press, 1957.
The Cave of Living Treasure. New York: Lantern Press, 1958.
Young Stowaways in Space. New York: Lantern Press, 1960.
Young Visitor to the Moon. New York: Lantern Press, 1965.

Suggestions for Further Reading

Aldiss, B. W., and H. Harrison. *Decade: The 1950s.* New York: St. Martin's Press, 1978.
Elwood, R., and J. Morgan. *Children of Infinity; Original Science Fiction Stories for Young Readers.* New York: Watts, 1973.
Larbalestier, J. *Daughters of Earth: Feminist Science Fiction in the Twentieth Century.* Middletown, CT: Wesleyan University Press, 2006.
Lucanio, P., and G. Coville. *American Science Fiction Television Series of the 1950s: Episode Guides and Casts and Credits for Twenty Shows.* Jefferson, NC: McFarland, 1998.
Prophet, J. *Children's SF: Its History, Literary Development, and Applications in Contemporary Society.* Bloemfontein, South Africa: University of the Free State, 1986.

Notes

1. Richard Elam Jr. *Young Visitor to Mars* (New York: Lantern Press, 1953), p. 84.
2. *Contemporary Authors Online,* Gale, 2002.

Ernest J. Finney

Words of My Roaring

Berkeley and Los Angeles: University of California Press, 1993

Originally published: 1993

Genre: Historical Fiction

Quote

> And Avery had dark eyes, and his hair was black when it was wet. They were the same
> color as both Gladys and Wilma, who they took out of our third-grade class and locked
> up first at the racetrack and then at some prison because they were all spies for Tojo and
> Emperor Hirohito.[1]

Synopsis

The town of San Bruno, California, is transformed by World War II, which brings an influx
of military personnel, factory workers, and others caught up in the war. This novel traces events
in the town by following the lives of interrelated characters, including several children—Mary
Maureen, Avery, and Ruthie—as well as their parents; their grade school teacher Elaine, who
moved there from Nevada; and Chuck, a sailor at the local Navy base who becomes romantically involved with Elaine. The events of the war, air raid warnings, USO dances, and the dis-
ruption of life are masterfully depicted, while at the same time the story moves backward and
forward in time to show what happened to the characters before the war and after.

Critical Commentary

Ernest Finney's *Words of My Roaring* is an absorbing, skillfully written novel about life
in small-town California during World War II. In describing the town of San Bruno, Finney
documents the confusion of a society thrust into war and the resulting psychological disrup-
tion in individual characters. More than a simple period piece or nostalgia, the book is a fine
and inspiring story about humanity and community in a time of crisis.

This book's chapters are written in first person, with stories told from the various viewpoints
of a core set of characters, including a third grader (Mary Maureen) relocated to California
from Tennessee with her sister Ruthie. Other characters are the boy next door, Avery; their
teacher Elaine; and a haunted war veteran, Chuck Sweet, who becomes Elaine's love interest.
This may seem an unlikely mix, but Finney effectively develops each character and endows
them with not only personality, but also fascinating personal histories—in the case of Chuck,
showing his childhood in a Montana orphans' home. As the story moves forward, the reader
develops a great empathy for all of the characters.

Finney also paints a colorful and vivid portrait of California during wartime. From the
war bond drives to the brawling of sailors and soldiers in the streets, this is an atmospheric

novel that captures the essence of a society in rapid transition from depression to world power. Finney gets the details right, mentioning, for example, the confiscation of one woman's radio simply because her dead husband was Italian. Although people today are generally aware of the internment of Japanese Americans in World War II, the government's crackdown on citizens of German and Italian descent is much less known. Finney does a service in reminding readers of this. His details of home-front life are far from sentimental—he also shows the pettiness of life in wartime, filled with shortages and rules and restrictions on regular enjoyments.

Finney deftly avoids falling into syrupy nostalgia or sentimental romanticism, showing us both the joys and pains of World War II California. He has written a fine novel about American life that is historically accurate without being didactic—a book equally valuable and useful as a piece of leisure reading and as informational reading for those interested in the history of the era. This book would be especially suitable for supplemental reading in courses on American history or World War II.

Author Sketch

A native of Northern California, Ernest J. Finney was written a number of novels and works of short fiction, including the novels *Winterchill* and *Lady with an Alligator Purse*.[2]

Other Works by the Author

Birds Landing. Urbana: University of Illinois Press, 1986.
Winterchill. New York: Morrow, 1989.
The Lady with the Alligator Purse: A Novel. Livingston, MT: Clark City Press, 1992.
Flights in the Heavenlies: Stories. Urbana: University of Illinois Press, 1996.
California Time. Western Literature Series. Reno: University of Nevada Press, 1998.

Suggestions for Further Reading

Howe, Russell Warren. *The Hunt for "Tokyo Rose."* Lanham, MD: Madison Books, 1990.
Johnson, Marilynn S. *The Second Gold Rush: Oakland and the East Bay in World War II.* Berkeley: University of California Press, 1993.
Lion Feuchtwanger Memorial Library. *Warners' War: Politics, Pop Culture & Propaganda in Wartime Hollywood.* Los Angeles: The Norman Lear Center Press, 2004.
Lotchin, Roger W. *The Bad City in the Good War: San Francisco, Los Angeles, Oakland, and San Diego.* Bloomington: Indiana University Press, 2003.
Otsuka, Julie. *When the Emperor Was Divine: A Novel.* New York: Anchor Books, 2003.
Starr, Kevin. *Embattled Dreams: California in War and Peace, 1940–1950.* New York: Oxford University Press, 2002.

Notes

1. Ernest J. Finney, *Words of My Roaring* (Berkeley and Los Angeles: University of California Press, 1993), p. 19.
2. http://www.press.uillinois.edu/s96/finney.html

Berry Fleming

The Make-Believers

Sag Harbor, NY: Last Chance Press, 1988

Originally published: 1972

Genre: Historical Fiction

Quote

> One of them was the thought he was going to leave uppermost in the minds of the jury when he summed up. He had no more facts to give them but he did have, this morning, one more thought for them: the trial was a second chance for Sharon County as well as Bondy; a chance to correct an error before it had gone too far.[1]

Synopsis

This is the story of three brothers, Peter, Leonard, and Ike Woodruff, living in Georgia around the turn of the twentieth century before World War I. The novel follows the brothers over the decades as they experience the ups and downs of life, dealing with a variety of events—some extremely troubling. Ike gives up his political career to save a local black man from being lynched and then spends decades trying to figure out who the real killer is. Leonard, an artist, is compelled to a creative life, with movement from place to place—New York, Maine, California, and eventually, home—in the face of a society that doesn't really understand or value his creative impulses. He also must deal with his feelings for Margaret, the wife of a local doctor. And Peter, the businessman, is simply trying to live a peaceful life while being supportive of his brothers' ambitions.

Critical Commentary

The issue of race in America has an ugly history, especially in the judicial system. In *The Make-Believers* Berry Fleming creates a novel that, besides being a wonderful John Grisham–style courtroom thriller, is also a thoughtful and introspective meditation on the issues of truth and race relations.

In the character of Ike Woodruff, Fleming has created one of the more appealing characters in modern fiction. Ike is, seemingly, a paragon of a successful Southern politician. Yet he risks this success to save the life of a black man unjustly accused of murder. The atmosphere and detail of a post–Civil War turn-of-the-century Southern town are accurately and authentically recreated, and the well-paced story has an almost documentary quality.

Fleming also tells a compelling story of a culture in the throes of change. He contrasts the traditional society of the South with the changing and developing world of modern America, especially the world of the arts, showing the artist brother Leonard Woodruff moving between the two cultures, seemingly lost to both.

Fleming goes beyond the traditional story of Southern injustice to say more. The story develops over time, during which he introduces the perspective of several other characters, such as Ike Woodruff's brother and a local doctor, who by accident comes into his own knowledge of the events of the night of the murder. Through these characters, the author creates a riveting psychological study of the effects of violence on a family and community. *The Make-Believers* is a splendid and dramatic portrait of life in the American South in the early twentieth century, as well as a meditation on memory and observation. Readers interested in regional literature, especially that of the American South, or in a compelling murder mystery, should find this a rewarding read.

Author Sketch

Fleming was born November 28, 1931, in St. Mary's, West Virginia. He was educated at West Virginia University (BA and MA, political science, 1953–54) and George Washington University (EdD 1970). He was employed for many years in education, teaching high school in Marietta, Ohio, from 1957 to 1964, and serving as social studies superintendent in the Fairfax County, Virginia, school system from 1964 to 1970. He worked as an assistant professor of education at Virginia Polytechnic Institute from 1970 to 1992.[2]

Other Works by the Author

The Conqueror's Stone. New York: John Day, 1927.

Visa to France. Garden City, NY: Doubleday, Doran, 1930.

Siesta. New York: Harcourt, 1935.

To the Market Place. New York: Harcourt, 1938.

Colonel Effingham's Raid. New York: Duell, 1943.

The Lightwood Tree. Philadelphia: Lippincott, 1947.

The Fortune Tellers. Philadelphia: Lippincott, 1951.

Carnival. Philadelphia: Lippincott, 1953.

Autobiography of a Colony; the First Half-Century of Augusta, Georgia. Athens: University of Georgia Press, 1957.

Captain Bennett's Folly. Sag Harbor, NY: Permanent Press, 1989.

Who Dwelt by a Churchyard: A Novel. Sag Harbor, NY: Permanent Press, 1989.

The Bookman's Tale. Sag Harbor, NY: Permanent Press, 1991.

Family Reunion and Other Stories. Sag Harbor, NY: Permanent Press, 1991.

Suggestions for Further Reading

Abernathy, Jeff. *To Hell and Back: Race and Betrayal in the Southern Novel.* Athens, GA; London: University of Georgia Press, 2003.

Brinkmeyer, Robert H. *Remapping Southern Literature: Contemporary Southern Writers and the West, Mercer University Lamar Memorial Lectures; No. 42.* Athens, GA; London: University of Georgia Press, 2000.

Brundage, W. Fitzhugh. *Lynching in the New South: Georgia and Virginia, 1880–1930, Blacks in the New World.* Urbana: University of Illinois Press, 1993.

Notes

1. Berry Fleming, *The Make-Believers* (Sag Harbor, NY: Last Chance Press, 1988), p. 136.

2. *Contemporary Authors Online,* Gale, 2004.

Ernest J. Gaines

A Gathering of Old Men

New York: Vintage Contemporaries, 1992

Originally published: 1983

Genre: Mainstream/Literary Fiction

Quote

> And I was proud as I could be, til I got back home. The first white man I met, the very first
> one, one of them no-English-speaking things off the river, told me I better not wear that
> uniform or that medal again no matter how long I lived. He told me I was back home now,
> and they didn't cotton to no nigger wearing medals for killing white folks.[1]

Synopsis

A white Cajun landowner in 1970s Louisiana, well known for his meanness, is shot to death.
Eighteen elderly black men take up their shotguns and congregate on the porch of Mathu, the
80-year-old man accused of the murder, all claiming to be the killer. The novel goes on to tell
the story of the murder from different perspectives, as well as the story of each person's individual suffering from racism and poverty.

Critical Commentary

Racism is an open wound in America. Gaines's novel takes a simple and sadly familiar situation—a racially inflamed police standoff after a shooting in 1970s Louisiana—and turns it into
a thoughtful meditation on the state of race relations in the United States. In a novel heavily
tinged by folklore, he shows the generations coming together, dramatically illustrating the idea
that the past is never really over.

Gaines develops the story through 15 different first-person narrators. Louisiana has one
of the more complex U.S. racial histories; beside conflicts between blacks and whites, there
are also tensions between blacks and Cajuns. Gaines displays this vividly. The use of multiple
narrators allows the story to develop from many perspectives and over decades through characters who are realistic and empathetic—even the racist Fix Bouton, despite the ugliness of his
intentions.

The language of this novel captures each character well without falling into caricature. One
may not believe Fix Bouton's rationalizations—he sees his son's death as a matter of honor
requiring retribution rather than as an act of revenge. But one feels that his views are honestly
held, no matter how outdated and ugly they may be.

Each of the narrators—Dirty Red, Clatoo, Rooster Jackson, and the rest—has a unique story
of indignity to tell; their grievances range from simple rudeness by whites to the murder of
a family member. One of the interesting points Gaines makes is that it is not a single awful

incident that cuts deepest, but rather the daily indignities of a lifetime. The whites, for their part, seem genuinely confused by the rebellion of these elderly black men, as if someone had suddenly rescinded some basic natural principle—like gravity. Sheriff Mapes's traditional practice of simply beating any black handy until someone confesses simply doesn't work. At the same time, it's clear that other characters are also out of touch—from the Boutons' son Gil, an LSU football star, to an unnamed college professor who wanders into the local bar and adds his two cents at the risk of a beating by the locals.

In this modern epistolary novel, each of the chapters is written as a letter—either correspondence or a confessional memoir—showing the ground for each man's action in deciding to stand up for himself. Each chapter, in its own way, offers a tribute to the past and reflects the importance of traditional oral culture.

A-well developed sense of community in which everyone knows and understands the various folk stories that hold people together is evident here as well. Everyone has a shared history in which this standoff is just the latest event. These men live in a culture that, unlike our contemporary world, sees little distinction between the living and the dead. One lives one's life for the dead as much as for the living. The old men have never dealt with their own pasts, but this killing gives them one last opportunity to do so. In reality, all of the characters—the old men, Sheriff Mapes, the Cajuns—are being swept away by forces of modernity that really have no interest in history. This novel examines both past and present, each with its own sins and joys.

Author Sketch

Born January 15, 1933, in Oscar, Louisiana, Gaines attended Vallejo Junior College and San Francisco State College (now University), receiving his BA in 1957. He completed graduate studies at Stanford University, 1958–59. Since 1983, he has been a professor of English at the University of Southwestern Louisiana.[2]

Other Works by the Author

Of Love and Dust. New York: Dial Press, 1967.
Bloodline. New York: Dial Press, 1968.
In My Father's House. New York: Knopf, 1978.
Catherine Carmier: A Novel. San Francisco: North Point Press, 1981.
A Lesson Before Dying. New York: Knopf, 1993.
Jefferson Was Sitting on the Bunk. Berkeley: Black Oak Books, 1994.
Conversations with Ernest Gaines. Literary Conversations Series. Jackson: University Press of Mississippi, 1995.
Mozart and Leadbelly: Stories and Essays. New York: Knopf, 2005.
Gaudet, Marcia G., Ernest J. Gaines, and Carl Wooton. *Porch Talk with Ernest Gaines: Conversations on the Writer's Craft.* Southern Literary Studies. Baton Rouge: Louisiana State University Press, 1990.

Suggestions for Further Reading

Bryant, Jerry. "Ernest J. Gaines: Change, Growth, and History." *Southern Review* 10 (1974): 851–864.
Gaudet, Marcia. "Folklore in the Writing of Ernest J. Gaines." *The Griot* 3 (1984): 9–16.

Laney, Ruth. "A Conversation with Ernest Gaines." *Southern Review* 10 (1974): 1–14.

Scholes, Robert, and Robert Kellogg. *The Nature of Narrative.* New York: Oxford University Press, 1966.

Notes

1. Ernest J. Gaines, *A Gathering of Old Men* (New York: Vintage Contemporaries, 1992), p. 104.

2. *Dictionary of Literary Biography,* Vol. 33: *Afro-American Fiction Writers After 1955,* ed. Thadious M. Davis and Trudier Harris (Detroit: Gale, 1984), pp. 84–96.

Leonard Gardner

Fat City

New York: Vintage Contemporaries, 1986

Originally published: 1969

Genre: Mainstream/Literary Fiction

Quote

> Exhausted in the dismal sheets, hearing the coughing, the hawking and spitting in other rooms, he sank and rose between consciousness and sleep for nearly an hour before dragging himself up and crossing the cold linoleum to urinate in his washbasin. He was laden with remorse. His life, he felt, had turned against him.[1]

Synopsis

Set in Stockton, California, in the late 1950s, this novel follows the lives of a number of has-been and wannabe boxers as they try to get or regain success in the ring. Focusing on the attempts of ex-boxer Billy Tully to advance the career of a new fighter, it documents life among the lowly in the tenements and bars on the bad side of town.

Critical Commentary

A moving and dramatic story of life on the fringes, *Fat City* provides insightful commentary on working-class life in the California of the 1950s—about those people who were not sharing in the prosperity of Eisenhower's America, but were actually sinking into despair. Some of them, however, are sustained at least temporarily by the hope of making it in the boxing ring. This is a novel about the fight game.

Fat City is defined by its strong descriptions of place. Gardner depicts the central valley of California and its flat agricultural landscape with precision, capturing the dust, the heat, and the oppressive effect of the land on the hopes and dreams of the dispossessed. The countryside contrasts with the abject poverty of urban Stockton—a city of concrete where even the shade trees have been cut down. The overall atmosphere is of oppressive sickness.

Caught in and tainted by this environment, Gardner's characters live aimless, pathetic lives. But there is constant action as the characters move around the city, scraping by on day-work jobs, spending their evenings in drunken stupors before stumbling back to their cheap hotel rooms—and dreaming of success in the ring.

Ultimately, what Gardner finally creates is a feeling of circularity, with everyone moving in the same patterns, both physically and emotionally, like fish confined in a tank. Even the dialogue reflects this with its feeling of endless repetition, as if the characters have already had all these conversations before.

The stories of Billy Tully and Ernie Minger run parallel, as old and young versions of the same dream. Another, larger dimension is introduced with the story of Arcadio Lucero, the Mexican boxer, whom the author uses to illustrate the universality of the themes he has been exploring. Poverty, striving, and failure are the common human condition, not something unique to a particular place or culture.

This classic novel about boxing features compelling fight sequences. However, to see it as a sports novel alone is to take too limited a view. Boxing functions as a plot device to propel greater themes and messages. Today, Gardner might have set the same story in an auto factory or a shipyard or a Wal-Mart and made an equally compelling book. It's a character-driven story and a pioneering book about lower-class life in California, in particular the lives of migrant workers, similar to Steinbeck's *The Grapes of Wrath*. It is a fascinating study of interest to anyone interested in boxing and, beyond that, an astute social commentary and depiction of California life.

Author Sketch

Gardner was born in 1934 in Stockton, California. He has written many articles and television screenplays, including the film *Tucker: The Man and his Dream* (1988). He received a National Book Award nomination for *Fat City* (1969). He lives in Marin County, California.[2]

Other Novels by the Author

None

Suggestions for Further Reading

Lindsay, Andrew. *Boxing in Black and White: A Statistical Study of Race in the Ring, 1949–1983*. Jefferson, NC: McFarland, 2004.

Mitchell, Don. *The Lie of the Land: Migrant Workers and the California Landscape*. Minneapolis: University of Minnesota Press, 1996.

Notes

1. Leonard Gardner, *Fat City* (New York: Vintage Contemporaries, 1986), p. 161.
2. *Contemporary Authors Online*, Gale, 2004.

Joseph Geha

Through and Through

Saint Paul: Graywolf Press, 1990

Originally published: 1990

Genre: Mainstream/Literary Fiction

Quote

> My father, Rasheed Yakoub, never got used to the snow and long winters of this country. In the middle of January or February he would walk home from work at the restaurant and grumble and stamp the snow from his shoes on the back porch. . . . Sitting next to the radio, he would grumble and devote long Arabic curses to the snow of this country, how it never stopped coming, how it stayed when it came, until my mother would tell him to hold his peace, or at least curse in English for the children's sake.[1]

Synopsis

In a series of eight interrelated vignettes, Geha follows the lives of a group of Lebanese and Syrian Christian immigrants in Toledo, Ohio, from the 1920s to the present. The story documents the experiences of characters ranging from the child Zizi to the elderly hit man Dip. Themes of displacement and the conflict between old and new permeate the interactions between the these characters as they remember their homelands while making lives in their new country.

Uhdrah's fiancée, newly arrived from Lebanon, appalls those around her when she, the greenhorn fresh from shepherding her father's goats, strokes the corpse of a mentally ill man, thinking to revive him. Issac's mother is still distrustful of Jews. Birds flying in the window are seen as a symbol of evil, and charms against the evil eye still are important. Through these poignant and descriptive images, Geha covers the full range of human experience from birth to marriage to raising a child to death.

Critical Commentary

How many average Americans can identify Naguib Mahfouz? Despite winning the Nobel Prize in Literature, he is, like the Icelandic Nobel laureate Halldór Kiljan Laxness, not terribly well known, even among literate Americans. Similarly, Americans have largely ignored the fact that there is an interesting body of literature about Middle Eastern life developing within their own country. *Through and Through* by Joseph Geha reminds us of this different culture in our midst.

It may be stretching it to call this book a novel, especially considering that it is subtitled "Toledo Stories." It could more accurately be considered a set of related vignettes about life in the Lebanese community. But in the sense that it does cover the story of a related group of people in one location over a period of decades, it can also be seen as an episodic novel.

73

What captivates readers here are the beautifully drawn characters—from the child Issac, to his unassimilated mother with her distrust of everything American and her insecurity about Jews, to an aging Toledo mobster on the lam for decades in Beirut, who returns to a country that he doesn't recognize and that has forgotten his crimes. There's also a wonderful sense of closeness among the characters. These are people with a sense of community.

The very unfamiliarity of these people with the country they live in directs a spotlight on American society. Looking at America as a strange land, they hold our practices and customs up to examination. Holding on to one's culture is a tender issue for many in America, where large numbers are so assimilated that ethnicity, ancestry, and tradition are often lost concepts..

A worthwhile quality in this book is its portrayal of a diverse Middle Eastern community. The main characters are Lebanese Christians. Although the Middle East is dominated by Islam, this book underlines the fact that it is also a region of multiple religions coexisting. In an era when understanding is desperately needed, and when many, especially the young, sometimes lack a clear sense of geography, this is valuable insight. (In 2002 a survey of American students found that on average they could identify only 3 of 11 Middle Eastern countries.) *Through and Through* is a useful reminder that, regardless of where people come from and despite their differences, in their human feelings they are very much like us. This is a short book that will be of interest not only to people interested in a good piece of fiction, but also to teachers and others who are developing programs on cultural pluralism and tolerance.[2]

Author Sketch

Geha was born November 5, 1944, in Zahleh, Lebanon, and educated at the University of Toledo (BA 1966, MA 1968). An academic, he has worked at Southwest Missouri State University (1968–71), Bowling Green State University (1971–76), and the University of Toledo (1976–77). He retired recently as a creative writing instructor at Iowa State University.[3]

Other Works by the Author

Holy Toledo. Story County Books, 1987.

Suggestions for Further Reading

Akash, Munir, and Khaled Mattawa, eds. *Post-Gibran Anthology of New Arab American Writing.* West Bethesda, MD, and Syracuse, NY: Kitab, distributed by Syracuse University Press, 1999.

Gillan, Maria M., and Jennifer Gillan. *Growing up Ethnic in America: Contemporary Fiction about Learning to Be American.* New York: Penguin Books, 1999.

Walker, Scott, ed. *The Graywolf Annual Seven: Stories from the American Mosaic.* Saint Paul, MN: Graywolf Press, 1990.

Notes

1. Joseph Geha, *Through and Through* (Saint Paul: Graywolf Press, 1990), p. 32.
2. http://www.nationalgeographic.com/geosurvey/download/RoperSurvey.pdf
3. *Contemporary Authors Online,* Gale, 2002; http://www.utoledo.edu/colleges/as/index.asp?id=348

Charlotte Perkins Gilman

Herland

New York: Pantheon Books, 1979

Originally published: 1915

Genre: Feminism/Utopian Fiction

Quote

> But to these women, in the unbroken sweep of this two-thousand-year-old feminine civiliza-
> tion, the word *woman* called up all that big background, so far as they had gone in social
> development; and the word man meant to them only *male*—the sex.[1]

Synopsis

A group of male explorers before World War I discovers an entirely female civilization living isolated on a plateau, where for more than 2,000 years women have been building a utopian
society entirely without men, even for reproduction. The three men are captured and learn
the language. Then they start having relationships with their captors and begin exploring this
civilization that appears to be perfectly balanced in almost all respects. After a great deal of
discussion and argument about what a society dominated by women actually means, the men
are sent back to the outside world with one of the women in tow so that she can find out about
the modern world and report back.

Critical Commentary

The idea of a utopia goes back in literature to classical times, starting with Plato's
Republic, carrying on through Thomas More's *Utopia,* and continuing to H. G. Wells in
the 1890s, Aldous Huxley in the 1940s, and countless others since then. Gilman's *Herland*
combines the utopian tradition with the popular adventure genre, popularized by H. Rider
Haggard's novels and Sir Arthur Conan Doyle's *The Lost World* (1911), to create a striking proto-feminist intellectual discussion of gender relationships that is both well-written
and often extremely funny. This is a book sure to appeal to people who like fantasy novels as
well as those interested in more serious discussions about the relationship between men and
women.

Herland is notable for Gilman's wonderful skill at effective (and for the men in the novel,
often devastating) description. She creates a vivid world that seems utterly believable, despite
some of the more fantastic elements that she introduces. One is asexual reproduction, a plot
device that by the post-Victorian standards of 1915 was shocking and probably accounts in
some part for the book's unpopularity. With an eye for human foibles and a keen ear for language, Gilman constructs an ideal society that enables her to criticize elements of her own
society, including sexual oppression, economic injustice, and war.

Despite its rather didactic intentions, the story never loses its sense of humor. Gilman is especially effective in creating female characters who, ignorant of men, ask simple yet insightful questions. It's literally a whole country of people asking "War? Poverty? What are those?"—and when these are explained, replying, "Oh come now, You can't be serious." Gilman makes good use of satire, of both men and women, to hold a light up to the flaws of both.

Herland might have a hard time getting published today, which is what makes it interesting. Given the ease of travel and communications in the early twenty-first century, it's difficult to realize how different the world of almost a century ago was. In 1915 an American in Europe (or in Herland) would have appeared as a rather exotic creature. People could still disappear off the map. Theodore Roosevelt, for example, became lost and missing for weeks on an expedition in the Amazon—after he had been president—a feat hard to imagine for a contemporary public figure. But in Gilman's time, the idea of a stranger in a strange land still worked.

It was also easier in 1915 to believe that somewhere there might be a lost island or unknown land. People had a sense of wonder and optimism that has, perhaps, lessened in our modern world of instant access. Today, every place on Earth is mapped and just a mouse click away. Gilman's book, more than anything it says about feminist ideals, reminds us that we have lost a few things in our march toward progress. All in all, *Herland* is a wonderful novel for those interested in feminism or, perhaps, for a class dealing with utopian fiction or the idea of progress.

Author Sketch

Born in Hartford, Connecticut, on July 3, 1860, Gilman was self-educated, with the exception of two years at the Rhode Island School of Design (1878–80). She worked as a designer of greeting cards before her marriage to Charles Walter Stetson in 1884. In 1888 Gilman separated from Stetson (they later divorced) and moved to California, where she began her writing career in the 1890s, focusing on the subjects of women and social roles. Gilman married her cousin George Gilman, a New York lawyer, in 1900 and lived in New York City and later Connecticut. She became famous for her lectures on women's issues, ethics, labor, and social concerns. She also created her own feminist magazine *Forerunner* from 1909 to 1916. In association with the noted American social reformer Jane Addams, she cofounded the Women's Peace Party in 1915. After her husband died in 1934, she returned to California to live near her daughter. Gilman died on August 17, 1935, in Pasadena, California.[2]

Other Works by the Author

In This Our World. Boston: Small, Maynard, 1898.
Concerning Children. 2nd ed. Boston: Maynard, 1901.
Human Work. New York: McClure, Philips, 1904.
The Forerunner [magazine]. 1909–1916.
The Man-Made World; or, Our Androcentric Culture. New York: Charlton, 1911.
Moving the Mountain. New York: Charlton, 1911.
Suffrage Songs and Verses. New York: Charlton, 1911.
Women and Economics: A Study of the Economic Relation between Men and Women as a Factor in Social Evolution. 9th ed. London: G. P. Putman, 1920.

The Man-Made World; Or, Our Androcentric Culture. Series in American Studies. New York: Johnson Reprint, 1971.

The Home; Its Work and Influence. Urbana: University of Illinois Press, 1972.

The Yellow Wallpaper. New York: Feminist Press, 1973.

The Living of Charlotte Perkins Gilman: An Autobiography. Reprint ed. Salem, NH: Ayer, 1987.

Women and Economics: A Study of the Economic Relation between Men and Women as a Factor in Social Evolution. Berkeley: University of California Press, 1998.

His Religion and Hers: A Study of the Faith of Our Fathers and the Work of Our Mothers. Classics in Gender Studies. Walnut Creek, CA: AltaMira Press, 2003.

Stetson, Charles Walter, Mary Armfield Hill, and Charlotte Perkins Gilman. *Endure: The Diaries of Charles Walter Stetson.* Philadelphia: Temple University Press, 1985.

Suggestions for Further Reading

Allen, Polly W. *Building Domestic Liberty: Charlotte Perkins Gilman's Architectural Feminism.* Amherst: University of Massachusetts Press, 1988.

Berkin, Carol Ruth. *Private Woman, Public Woman: The Contradictions of Charlotte Perkins Gilman.* New York: G. K. Hall, 1992.

Knight, Denise D. *Charlotte Perkins Gilman: A Study of the Short Fiction.* New York: Twayne, 1997.

———, ed. *"The Yellow Wall Paper" and Selected Stories of Charlotte Perkins Gilman.* Newark: University of Delaware Press, 1994.

Lane, Ann J. *The Charlotte Perkins Gilman Reader.* New York: Pantheon, 1980.

———. *To Herland and Beyond: The Life and Work of Charlotte Perkins Gilman.* Charlottesville: University Press of Virginia, 1997.

Notes

1. Charlotte Perkins Gilman,, *Herland* (New York: Pantheon Books, 1979), p. 137.
2. http://www.library.csi.cuny.edu/dept/history/lavender/386/cgilman.html

Ellen Anderson Gholson Glasgow

Virginia

New York: Penguin Books, 1989

Originally published: 1913

Genre: Mainstream/Literary Fiction/Domestic Romance

Quote

> With arms interlaced, they stood gazing down into the street, where the shadow of the old lamplighter glided like a ghost under the row of pale flickering lights. From a honeysuckle-trellis on the other side of the porch, a penetrating sweetness came in breaths, now rising, now dying away.[1]

Synopsis

Virginia Pendleton is a young girl growing up in small Dinwiddie, Virginia, in the 1880s, brought up by her minister father and her mother to be a wife and mother herself. In a moment of romantic impulse, she abandons her staid bourgeois upbringing and makes an inappropriate marriage with the artistic Oliver Treadwell. Their relationship, despite the birth of several children, goes quickly on the skids as Treadwell becomes a successful playwright who spends most of his time in New York, leaving Virginia to fend for herself back in Dinwiddie. After her parents, her main source of emotional support, both die, Virginia is left alone to deal with her children, who also eventually leave her to go to college. Eventually, the philandering Treadwell leaves Virginia for an actress. After falling into a state of depression and virtual collapse, she is relieved when her son Harry returns home to take care of her—which is, at best, only a temporary solution.

Critical Commentary

In *Virginia*, Ellen Glasgow has written a compelling and interesting novel of small-town Southern life that, through its focus on the life experience of one woman, Virginia Pendleton, reveals the ambiguities that the people of that era felt about women and their role in society. It also provides a timeless psychological portrait of a woman trapped in a loveless marriage in a small Southern town. Glasgow has created what might be considered an anti-love story— where a romantic relationship goes horribly wrong.

Structured in a three-part arc—"The Dream," "The Reality," and "The Adjustment"— the novel traces Virginia's life as she tries to adapt her strict Victorian values, given to her in childhood, to a world that increasingly deems them irrelevant. As a result, she becomes more and more unable to cope with the circumstances resulting from her marriage to Oliver Treadwell, whose own ambitions leave her increasingly deserted, both physically and emotionally.

This novel provides a vivid and heart-wrenching story about the circumstances of women in the postbellum American South. With an interesting and compelling storyline, well-developed characters, and thoughtful psychological insights, Glasgow produced a classic work of American fiction. Although she worked in what could be considered a traditional kind of romantic style, she avoided clichés and stereotypes, with the result that the novel doesn't seem dated or out of fashion decades after its publication. The concerns of Virginia, which fundamentally boil down to the question of how one lives a good life, are the stuff of classic and enduring fiction.

For modern readers this is a revealing look at the traditions and morals of a past century, when social conventions and alternatives for women were much more limited and prescribed. The typical response of a modern woman in Virginia's situation—to get a job, to move to another city, or to simply drag her errant husband through the courts (or the marriage therapist's office)—was simply not an option. Women, especially given the state of education (or rather women's lack of education), rarely had options outside the home and marriage. *Virginia* reveals to what degree people of that era, rather than living in small, cozy, caring communities full of supportive family and neighbors, were often on their own in dealing with personal problems. It is a thought-provoking work for anyone interested in women's studies or Southern history.

Author Sketch

Born April 22, 1873, in Richmond, Virginia, Ellen Glasgow was largely home-educated. In the 1890s, she began a writing career, which over the next 40 years gained her a certain amount of fame and popularity. Heavily influenced by the modernist traditions in literature, she produced a series of novels, mostly dealing with life in postbellum Virginia, to popular and critical acclaim. From the early 1930s onward, she received a series of honorary degrees from various institutions, including Duke University (1938), in recognition of her writing talent. She died on November 21, 1945.[2]

Other Works by the Author

The Voice of the People. New York: Burt, 1900.
The Freeman, and Other Poems. New York: Doubleday, Page, 1902.
The Deliverance. New York: Doubleday, 1904.
The Ancient Law. New York: Doubleday, Page, 1908.
The Romance of a Plain Man. New York: Macmillan, 1909.
The Miller of Old Church. Garden City, NY: Doubleday, Page, 1911.
Life and Gabriella: The Story of a Woman's Courage. Garden City, NY: Doubleday, Page, 1916.
The Builders. Garden City, NY: Doubleday, Page, 1919.
The Shadowy Third: And Other Stories. Garden City, NY: Doubleday, Page, 1923.
Barren Ground. London: John Murray, 1925.
The Romantic Comedians. Garden City, NY: Doubleday, Page, 1926.
They Stooped to Folly, A Comedy of Morals. New York: The Literary Guild, 1929.
The Sheltered Life. Garden City, NY: Doubleday, Doran, 1932.
Vein of Iron. New York: Harcourt, Brace, 1935.
In This Our Life. New York: Harcourt, 1941.

Suggestions for Further Reading

Glasgow, Ellen Anderson Gholson, and Pamela R. Matthews. *Perfect Companionship: Ellen Glasgow's Selected Correspondence with Women.* Charlottesville: University of Virginia Press, 2005.

Goodman, Susan. *Ellen Glasgow: A Biography.* Baltimore, MD: Johns Hopkins University Press, 1998.

Raper, Julius Rowan. *From the Sunken Garden: The Fiction of Ellen Glasgow, 1916–1945.* Southern Literary Studies. Baton Rouge: Louisiana State University Press, 1980.

Saunders, Catherine E. *Writing the Margins: Edith Wharton, Ellen Glasgow, and the Literary Tradition of the Ruined Woman.* Cambridge, MA: Dept. of English and American Literature and Language, distributed by Harvard University Press, 1987.

Scura, Dorothy McInnis. *Ellen Glasgow: The Contemporary Reviews.* New York: Cambridge University Press, 1992.

Wagner-Martin, Linda. *Ellen Glasgow, Beyond Convention.* Austin: University of Texas, 1982.

Notes

1. Ellen Glasgow. *Virginia* (New York: Penguin Books, 1989), p. 23.
2. *Contemporary Authors Online,* Gale, 2003; *Dictionary of Literary Biography,* Vol. 12: *American Realists and Naturalists,* ed. Donald Pizer and Earl N. Harbert (Detroit: Gale, 1982), pp. 213–226.

John Hawkes

The Lime Twig

New York: New Directions, 1961

Originally published: 1961

Genre: Mainstream/Literary Fiction

Quote

He was running in final stride, the greatest spread of legs, redness coming across the eyes, the pace so fast that it ceases to be motion, but at its peak becomes the long downhill deathless gliding of a dream until the arms are out, the head thrown back, and the runner is falling as he was falling and waving his arm at Rock Castle's onrushing silver shape, at Rock Castle who was about to run him down and fall.[1]

Synopsis

Not only is the experience of reading *The Lime Twig* dreamlike; the novel is actually *about* dreaming. Hawkes considers what might happen if a person's most intimate repressed desires came true—if the boundary between fantasy and reality collapsed. The dreamers in this novel, which is set in post-war England, are William Hencher, the first-person narrator who is soon killed, and a married couple, Michael and Margaret Banks. Hencher becomes "the seedbed," according to Hawkes, of the pathetic dreams and lives of the Banks.

Through his contacts with a local gang, Hencher helps Michael achieve his dream of obtaining a racehorse. By being the front for the stolen horse, Michael unwittingly becomes involved with the ruthless gang that is responsible not only for Hencher's death but also for the later kidnapping and fatal beating of Michael's wife. For Michael the horse is the embodiment of power, sexual potency, beauty, and danger—"knowing that his own worst dream, and best, was of a horse which was itself the flesh of all violent dreams." Knowing and yet innocent, Michael pursues his dream, realizes the fulfillment of sexual pleasures, and is ultimately destroyed when he plunges in front of the galloping horse to end the race and dash the gang's chance of wealth.

Critical Commentary

John Hawkes uses *The Lime Twig* to reinvent and question the conventional stereotypes of the literary mystery genre, taking the story of a criminal heist and turning it into a stunning psychological drama. This novel creates a wonderfully dark vision of ordinary people slipping into a world of excess, madness, and death. This is a novel that should appeal to readers who enjoy psychological thrillers filled with twists and turns.

The central themes are those of erasure and sacrifice. Two primary characters, Michael Banks and his wife, become involved in a plot to steal a racehorse. Michael slips from his ordinary life into criminality, which represents for him a new life of glamour. But when his wife is pulled in, it quickly becomes a fantasy-nightmare that leaves both of them dead. The criminals in this case literally erase the Banks, cleaning out their apartment to the bare walls. Imagery and symbolism fill the novel, from the title reflecting the lime twig, which is used to snare birds, to such names as Sybilline, which comes straight from Greek mythology and the Sybil of Cuma—the seer. One knows even at the beginning that as in a Greek tragedy, Michael Banks's character is his fate.

Hawkes uses three voices—Hencher's, Larry's, and that of newspaper columnist Sidney Slyter—to tell the story. Slyter never actually appears except through his column as a somewhat detached observer who suspects that something is going on, but is unclear on the details. As a result, the reader sees the story from a series of differing perspectives—from Slyter to Hencher to Larry—each with a different level of knowledge and, it is implied, a different level of moral guilt and responsibility. The actions of the story are further dramatized in contrast to the book's mundane setting, a racetrack in the English countryside

Not for the fainthearted, this violent story is filled from the beginning with images of war and the destruction of World War II London, from which it quickly moves into the smaller war waged by criminals against society. There are continual, vivid descriptions of violence and, even more disturbingly, the suggestion of evil and perversions—sexual and other—culminating in the senseless murder of an innocent child and Banks's self-sacrifice. The latter can be seen as an attempt at redemption; Banks's going willingly, like C. S. Lewis's Aslan, to the slaughter again relates very directly to classical mythology and a theme of sacrifice.

In this dramatic piece of experimental fiction, Hawkes has taken conventional story elements and rearranged them as a visual artist might create a collage, to create a novel that, though it appears in the guise of a murder mystery, is really a dramatic tale of murder and betrayal almost as intense as a classic Greek play. It is a book recommended, not only for mystery buffs, but also for those interested in literary writing generally.

Author Sketch

Born August 17, 1925, in Stamford, Connecticut, Hawkes graduated from Harvard University (BA 1949). From the late 1940s, he was a prolific and critically acclaimed (if not widely popular) novelist, as well as a literature professor or writer in residence at a number of institutions, including MIT (1959), University of Virginia (1965), and Stanford (1966–67). He also received several awards for his writing, including a Guggenheim Fellowship (1962–63), the Prix du Meilleur Livre Etranger (1973), and the Prix Medicis Etranger (1986) for best foreign novel translated into French, for *Adventures in the Alaskan Skin Trade*. He died of a stroke on May 15, 1998, in Providence, Rhode Island.[2]

Other Works by the Author

The Cannibal. Norfolk, CT: New Directions, 1949.
Second Skin. New York: New Directions, 1964.
The Innocent Party; Four Short Plays. New York: New Directions, 1966.
The Beetle Leg. London: Chatto & Windus, 1967.
Lunar Landscapes; Stories & Short Novels, 1949–1963. New York: New Directions, 1969.
The Blood Oranges. New York: New Directions, 1971.

Notes on Writing a Novel. Providence, RI: Brown University, 1973.

Travesty. New York: New Directions, 1976.

The Passion Artist. New York: Harper & Row, 1979.

Virginie, Her Two Lives. New York: Harper & Row, 1982.

Humors of Blood and Skin: A John Hawkes Reader: Autobiographical Notes. New York: New Directions, 1984.

Adventures in the Alaskan Skin Trade. New York: Simon & Schuster, 1985.

Whistlejacket: A Novel. New York: Weidenfeld & Nicolson, 1988.

The Owl; and, the Goose on the Grave: Two Short Novels. Los Angeles: Sun & Moon Press, 1994.

Sweet William: A Memoir of Old Horse. New York: Penguin Books, 1994.

The Frog. New York: Viking, 1996.

An Irish Eye. New York: Viking, 1997.

Regulus and Maximus. Providence: Paradigm Press, 1999.

Hawkes, John, Robert Coover, and Patrick McGrath. *The Lime Twig; Second Skin; Travesty.* Penguin Twentieth-Century Classics. New York: Penguin Books, 1996.

Hawkes, John, Anthony C. Santore, and Michael N. Pocalyko. *A John Hawkes Symposium: Design and Debris. Insights 1: Working Papers in Contemporary Criticism.* New York: New Directions, 1977.

Suggestions for Further Reading

Harrisson, Tom. *Living through the Blitz.* London: Collins, 1976.

Smiley, Jane. *A Year at the Races: Reflections on Horses, Humans, Love, Money and Luck.* New York: Knopf, 2004.

Notes

1. John Hawkes, *The Lime Twig* (New York: New Directions, 1961), p. 171.

2. "John Hawkes," in *Dictionary of Literary Biography,* Vol. 227: *American Novelists Since World War II, Sixth Series,* ed. James R. Giles and Wanda H. Giles (Detroit: Gale, 2000), pp. 168–183.

Ernest Hebert

The Dogs of March

New York: Penguin Books, 1979

Originally published: 1979

Genre: Mainstream/Literary Fiction

Quote

> He paused by an overturned wheelbarrow to survey his land. Birches, a score of junk cars, a swing on the limb of a giant maple, a bathtub in the garden, a gray barn, a house with fading asphalt shingles, a washing machine riddled with bullet holes—to Howard these things were all equal in beauty. He saw no ugliness on his property.[1]

Synopsis

Howard Elman lives a poverty-stricken existence in rural New Hampshire. With the loss of his job and the influx of rich newcomers who want to buy his property, his marginal but relatively happy life is turned upside down. Although he tries to fight progress—even going so far as to burn down his house—he eventually makes some compromises that offer both him and his children the chance for a better life.

Critical Commentary

In *The Dogs of March*, Ernest Hebert gives readers a delightful and engaging novel about change in the New England countryside—about the conflict between a traditional way of life and the influx of new people with different values and culture. Funny and tragic, the story evocatively depicts the problems facing people everywhere when they are confronted by progress and change.

Modernity is the essential theme of this novel—or the clash between modernity and tradition. Howard Elman really wants very little from life, but suddenly finds himself confronted with crisis in various forms—lack of employment, family problems, and most of all, new neighbors wanting his small farm. Within a traditional narrative structure, Hebert's language to describe both the people and the landscape of New England is dead on. This is not the slick and shiny New England of postcards and such holiday movies as *White Christmas*, but the grimy, dirty New Hampshire of abandoned factories and rural poverty—and more precisely of the back roads in northern New Hampshire lined with 50-year-old trailers on blocks next to the hulks of rusted-out '46 Cadillacs.

The conflict between Elman and his neighbors, in particular Mrs. Cutter, epitomizes the differences between a traditional subsistence culture, symbolized by Elman's attachment to his farm, and the emerging society of New Hampshire. That society is dominated by educated white-collar professionals, largely from Taxachusetts directly to the south, who are abetted by an impersonal yet paternalistic government. In the end, Elman makes a compromise that, although it doesn't leave him untouched, allows him a small moral victory. It's obvious that his life will be changed forever, but there is still hope that because of his sacrifice, his children will have better lives.

Today we see the struggle of Howard Elman being reenacted on a daily basis throughout New England and indeed the nation, as people are outsourced or replaced or they suddenly find that the world has moved on beyond their comprehension. Howard's story, told with touching truthfulness and authenticity, will resonate with many contemporary readers. Howard Elman is a kind of Everyman, trying to make his way in a world not of his making.

Author Sketch

Born May 4, 1945, in Keene, New Hampshire, Hebert worked a variety of jobs, including as a telephone installer and gas station manager, before graduating from Keene State College (1969). He worked on the *Keene Sentinel* newspaper in the 1970s and then moved into academia. He is currently on the faculty of Dartmouth College where he teaches English and creative writing.[2]

Other Works by the Author

A Little More than Kin. New York: Viking, 1982.
Whisper My Name. New York: Viking, 1984.
The Passion of Estelle Jordan. New York: Viking, 1987.
Live Free or Die. New York: Viking, 1990.
Mad Boys: A Novel. Hanover, NH: University Press of New England, 1993.
The Old American: A Novel, Hardscrabble Book. Hanover, NH: University Press of New England, 2000.
Spoonwood, Hardscrabble Books. Hanover, NH: Dartmouth College Press, 2005.

Suggestions for Further Reading

Feintuch, Burt, David H. Watters, and University of New Hampshire Center for the Humanities. *The Encyclopedia of New England: The Culture and History of an American Region.* New Haven: Yale University Press, 2005.
Heffernan, Nancy Coffey, and Ann Page Stecker. *New Hampshire: Crosscurrents in Its Development.* 3rd ed. Hanover, NH: University Press of New England, 2004.
Purchase, Eric. *Out of Nowhere: Disaster and Tourism in the White Mountains.* Baltimore, MD: The Johns Hopkins University Press, 1999.

Notes

1. Hebert, Ernest. *The Dogs of March* (New York: Penguin Books, 1979), pp. 1–2.
2. http://www.dartmouth.edu/~english/faculty/hebert.html

Marion Hedges

Iron City

Beloit: Beloit College Press, 1994

Originally published: 1919

Genre: Mainstream/Literary Fiction

Quote

> As John Cosmus looked back upon that second winter at Crandon Hill College it seemed
> one long stretch of exasperation. Upon one side he saw America's pitiable need of a great
> unifying passion, on the other, the immobility of the college, its servile worship of the past,
> its short-circuiting of great ideas. He did not escape despair, or that withering sense of
> failure, which comes to all men who see principles rather than things, masses rather than
> individuals.[1]

Synopsis

John Cosmus takes a position as an instructor of sociology at Crandon Hill College. With his
energy and idealism, he firmly believes that the purpose of education is to create positive change
in society. But he quickly runs up against the stodgy conservatism of the college and the town. The
town eventually becomes overcome by labor disputes and political issues related to the outbreak of
World War I. Despite his best efforts to raise the community's consciousness of such progressive
issues as labor rights, Cosmus is unsuccessful; eventually, he is fired from his job and driven away.

Critical Commentary

The early twentieth century was marked by social tensions, including those based on sex,
race, and the growing number of immigrant workers in American industry. This influx of immigrants significantly changed the ethnic makeup of many urban areas and smaller towns.
The literature of the period reflected the changes brought on by this. One of the period's books,
Marion Hedge's *Iron City*, caused an enormous controversy at the time of its publication,
largely because of its thinly veiled and documentary-like descriptions of Beloit, Wisconsin, and
Beloit College—and all of their problems. *Iron City* is a fascinating read for anyone interested
in social history.

Iron City tells the story of a labor management conflict in a Midwestern mill town, but it
is also an indictment of the complacency and boorishness of the local community and the
academic community. The local college, rather than being a place of inquiry and change, is
depicted as a tool for preserving the status quo. John Cosmus, the new, idealistic college instructor, runs up against the harsh realities of this insular Midwestern town.

The characters in this novel represent types—the idealistic teacher, the feminist, the factory
owners, the board of trustees—and are meant to serve as expressions of particular social and

political ideologies, rather than in-depth individuals. Hedges tells the story in a simple narrative and lets the banality of the situation speak for itself, condemning the town in the process. The symbolism in the novel (e.g., closing off the college street to prevent workers from soiling the campus) is obvious. More subtly, however, Hedges creates a dark psychological climate of increasing menace and violence, tempered only at the conclusion by the hope of love for Cosmus and Sarah.

In biting social commentary, Hedges anticipates the flowering of 1920s American modernism in literature and art, taken to its conclusion in the works of such writers as Sinclair Lewis and such artists as Edward Hopper, with his glorious portraits of an abundant yet empty American landscape. The stark, almost documentary, feel of the novel adds to its influence. In *Iron City*, Hedges creates a capsule picture of the tensions of the era, with its conflict between the existing society and an emerging technical civilization—a situation that makes this novel remain relevant in our own troubled age.

Author Sketch

Hedges, born in Winamac, Indiana, on September 14, 1888, graduated from DePauw University in 1910. He served at his alma mater as instructor of English composition He then became professor of English at Iowa Wesleyan College (1912) and at Beloit College (1913–1920). From 1920 to 1924, he was a reporter for the *Minneapolis Star*. In 1924 he went to Washington, D.C., where he was research director of the International Brotherhood of Electrical Workers. During the 25 years he held this position, he was also editor of the *Electrical Workers Journal* and became an internationally recognized expert on labor issues before retiring in 1954. He died in 1959 in Chevy Chase, Maryland.[2]

Other Works by the Author

Dan Minturn. New York: Vanguard Press, 1927.

Suggestions for Further Reading

Lambert, Josiah Bartlett. *"If the Workers Took a Notion": The Right to Strike and American Political Development.* Ithaca, NY: ILR Press/Cornell University Press, 2005.

Moreno, Paul D. *Black Americans and Organized Labor: A New History.* Baton Rouge: Louisiana State University Press, 2006.

Segal, Howard P. *Recasting the Machine Age: Henry Ford's Village Industries.* Amherst: University of Massachusetts Press, 2005.

Strohmeyer, John. *Crisis in Bethlehem: Big Steel's Struggle to Survive.* Bethesda, MD: Adler & Adler, 1986.

Notes

1. Marion Hedges, *Iron City* (Beloit: Beloit College Press, 1994), pp. 102–103.

2. *New York Times*, January 9, 1959, p. 25; http://www.depauw.edu/library/archives/ijhof/inductees/hedges.htm

William Herrick

Hermanos!

Sag Harbor, NY: Second Hand Press, 1983

Originally published: 1969

Genre: Adventure Fiction/War Stories

Quote

> Ballard shook his head to clear the frogs from his eyes, and stepped, shaking, from the car. He stood on a precipice. Below were red-tiled roofs hidden among golden mimosa, fresh green cypress standing a guard of honor. Beyond he saw the Mediterranean, yellow crimson from the dawning sun.[1]

Synopsis

Jacob Starr is a young Jewish Communist from New York. He goes to Europe to fight in the Spanish Civil War. Although he is initially assigned to rear guard duties, he is eventually thrown into combat, where he becomes a heroic figure—which wasn't the intention of his Communist leaders who were hoping he would simply be killed. Starr is then assigned to become an assassin for the party, a role he rebels against, and eventually, after helping some people he was assigned to kill to escape instead, he is executed by the Party for breach of discipline.

Critical Commentary

The Spanish Civil War is an event largely lost to Americans today. Even the participation of Americans in that conflict is given only a small mention in most history books. In *Hermanos!* William Herrick offers readers a brilliant and piercing portrait of the people, Americans as well as those other nationalities, who joined in an unlikely coalition in late 1930s Spain to combat fascism and of what turned out to be a dress rehearsal for World War II. Far from being simply a period piece, this story is germane to modern readers because it reveals the role that politics and belief can play in inspiring men to armed conflict—an especially relevant and important statement in our present age of ideology-based terror—as well as being an exciting and action-packed adventure story full of intrigue and romance.

Through his central character, Jake Starr, Herrick develops the story, following an ideological arc. Starr starts as a fervent believer in the party, to the point of accepting the necessity of a political assassination. But he becomes seasoned by war, which opens his eyes to reality, and he dies as something of a heretic. Herrick has accurately and movingly depicted the ideological development of a young man from callow youth to maturity. Starr faces the same problems of reconciling the reality of the world with his values and ideology that we as individuals face today.

This is also a wonderfully realized novel of men at war, based on Herrick's own war experiences (he served in the Spanish Civil War). Herrick's accurate character studies include the

88

good-natured professional adventurer Joe Garms, who could have done something better in life but was ruined by war, which became all he knew or wanted to know; and the ideological zealot Vlanoc, dedicated to the cause of a faceless and impersonal world revolution. In contrast, the novel's subplot focuses on the love story between Jake Starr and Sarah Ruskin.

Echoing other novels about this period, most notably Hemingway's *The Sun Also Rises* and George Orwell's *Homage to Catalonia,* with which this novel can be favorably compared, Herrick details the events of the Spanish Civil War, creating vivid word portraits of the violence and misery of a war in which ultimately there were no winners. In particular, Herrick's realistic descriptions of the sufferings of the Spanish villagers, whose only crime was to be living in the wrong place at the wrong time, should resonate with modern readers who have witnessed the suffering of modern innocents, from the Balkans and Darfur to Lebanon and Iraq.

Ultimately, readers will come away from this story with a greater sense of universality. Although the story is set in 1930s Spain, its characters could be fighting in a war anywhere and anytime. Herrick transcends his subject, creating not only a fiction dealing with a particular time and place, but also a novel that deals with permanent and important themes: human truth and one's personal obligation to fight against injustice. This is recommended for those interested in history or simply a gripping and intriguing story.

Author Sketch

Born January 10, 1915, in Trenton, New Jersey, Herrick was a veteran of the Spanish Civil War, in which he fought as a member of the Abraham Lincoln Battalion against Franco. From 1943 to 1969 he worked as a court reporter. After 1969 he increasingly turned to fiction, writing a number of novels and a memoir. He died on January 31, 2004, in Old Chatham, New York.[2]

Other Works by the Author

Strayhorn. New York: McGraw-Hill, 1968.
The Last to Die. New York: Simon & Schuster, 1971.
Shadows and Wolves: A Novel. New York: New Directions, 1980.
Love and Terror: A Novel. New York: New Directions, 1981.
Kill Memory: A Novel. New York: New Directions, 1983.
That's Life: A Fiction. New York: New Directions, 1985.
Bradovich: A Novel. New York: New Directions, 1990.
Jumping the Line: The Adventures and Misadventures of an American Radical. Madison: University of Wisconsin Press, 1998.

Suggestions for Further Reading

Bermack, Richard. *The Front Lines of Social Change: Veterans of the Abraham Lincoln Brigade.* Berkeley, CA: Heyday Books, 2005.
Ealham, Chris, and Michael Richards. *The Splintering of Spain: Cultural History and the Spanish Civil War, 1936–1939.* Cambridge, UK, and New York: Cambridge University Press, 2005.
Keene, Judith. *Fighting for Franco: International Volunteers in Nationalist Spain during the Spanish Civil War, 1936–1939.* London and New York: Leicester University Press, 2001.

Orwell, George, P. H. Davison, and George Orwell. *Orwell in Spain: The Full Text of Homage to Catalonia, with Associated Articles, Reviews and Letters from the Complete Works of George Orwell*. London: Penguin, 2001.

Seidman, Michael. *Republic of Egos: A Social History of the Spanish Civil War*. Madison, WI: University of Wisconsin Press, 2002.

Notes

1. William Herrick, *Hermanos!* (Sag Harbor, NY: Second Hand Press, 1983), p. 292.

2. *New York Times*, February 9, 2004, p. A25; http://www.albany.edu/writers-inst/herrick.html; http://www.albany.edu/writers-inst/tuherrik.html

Chester Himes

Lonely Crusade

New York: Knopf, 1947

Originally published: 1947

Genre: Crime Fiction/Suspense

Quote

> He had never told her how much he was afraid of going into the white world in quest of
> what he felt was rightfully his. Not always afraid of anything that he could name, define, put
> his finger on—seldom that. Afraid, for the most part, of his own fear, of this emotion that
> came unbidden to him and that he had no power to dispel.[1]

Synopsis

Lee Gordon, a college-educated African American in 1940s Los Angeles, can't get a
good job. Having lost several positions because of racism, he is finally offered a position as a
labor organizer for an aircraft factory. Despite his initial good feelings, he becomes increasingly dispirited as he finds the union overrun and controlled by ardent Communists. At the
same time, Lee also experiences marital problems with his wife, Ruth; their relationship is
punctuated by episodes of drunkenness and adultery. Ultimately, events spiral out of control,
and Gordon becomes involved in a crime that, in an odd way, allows for a reconciliation with
his wife.

Critical Commentary

Lonely Crusade takes on significant issues of racism and alienation in modern America. Although its concern with communism and labor unions may seem somewhat dated to modern
readers, this remains an intriguing story that combines politics with romance in a film-noir
atmosphere.

Dominated by dialogue, the novel includes extensive passages on Communist politics of the
late 1930s and early 1940s. The minor characters are rather stereotypical. (For example, Himes's
depiction of most Communists as Jewish may seem simplistic if not offensive to today's readers). But Himes uses the characters effectively in developing his plot, and in his main characters, Lee and Ruth Gordon, Himes hits his stride—because this novel really is a love story.

Himes has centered his plot on the story of Lee Gordon's work as an African American labor
organizer. By tracing the events in Gordon's life, showing his development as a human being in
the face of institutional racism and, in particular, his love affair with his wife, Himes develops a
universal human character. The couple's enduring relationship in the face of obstacles is reminiscent of some nineteenth-century European novels, such as Zola's *The Earth*—with careful
attention to detail and the emotional growth of the characters.

Himes's description of life in wartime Los Angeles makes this one of the better novels about industrial life to come out of the period. He writes about a Los Angeles that no longer exists—before the advent of freeways. Murder introduces a noir element to the story, increasing its dramatic tension.

The political issues that populate this novel, such as the concern regarding Communist infiltration of labor unions, may be unfamiliar to contemporary audiences—who may be driven to the Internet for definitions of such terms as Popular Front—and will likely make this enjoyable for history buffs. It is as a heartfelt story of the corroding effects of racism where *Lonely Crusade* most maintains its value. This is a sharp, edgy novel that remains an interesting read—and it is especially recommended for classes that want to have a discussion about the history of race in America.

Author Sketch

Himes, the son of a teacher in Mississippi, was born on July 29, 1909, in Missouri. He attended Ohio State University until he was dismissed. Subsequently, he drifted into a life of petty crime and was sentenced in 1936 to 25 years in the Ohio State Penitentiary for armed robbery. After his parole in 1944, he worked at many jobs while developing his career as a writer. Himes published several novels to mixed reception and then moved to Europe in the mid-1950s, where he was much better received, especially in France, his primary adopted country. From 1959 on, Himes received increasing attention, especially in Europe, for his series of crime novels, one of the most noted being *Cotton Comes to Harlem* (1965), which was later made into a movie (1970). He died on November 12, 1984, in Moraira, Spain.[2]

Other Works by the Author

If He Hollers Let Him Go. Garden City, NY: Doubleday, Doran, 1945.
Cast the First Stone, A Novel. New York: Coward-McCann, 1952.
The Third Generation. Cleveland: World Pub., 1954.
The Primitive. New York: New American Library, 1955.
The Third Generation. New York: New American Library, 1956.
The Crazy Kill. New York: Avon, 1959.
All Shot Up. New York: Avon, 1960.
The Big Gold Dream. New York: Avon, 1960.
Pinktoes. Paris: Olympia Press, 1961.
Cotton Comes to Harlem. New York: Putnam, 1965.
A Rage in Harlem. New York: Avon, 1965.
The Heat's On. New York: G. P. Putnam's Sons, 1966.
The Autobiography of Chester Himes. 2 vols. Garden City, NY: Doubleday, 1972.
Black on Black; Baby Sister and Selected Writings. Garden City, NY: Doubleday, 1973.
Come Back Charleston Blue. Harmondsworth, UK: Penguin Books, 1974.
A Case of Rape. New York: Targ Editions, 1980.
Blind Man with a Pistol. London and New York: Allison & Busby, 1986.
The Third Generation: A Novel. New York: Thunder's Mouth Press, 1989.
The Collected Stories of Chester Himes. New York: Thunder's Mouth Press, 1990.
The End of a Primitive. New York: Norton, 1997.

Yesterday Will Make You Cry. New York: Norton, 1998.

Himes, Chester B., and Hélène Devaux-Minié. *Plan B.* Paris: Lieu Commun, 1983.

Thompson, Willa, and Chester B. Himes. *Garden without Flowers.* Boston: Beacon Press, 1957.

Suggestions for Further Reading

Bailey, Frankie Y. *Out of the Woodpile: Black Characters in Crime and Detective Fiction.* Westport, CT: Greenwood, 1991.

Copjec, Joan, ed. *Shades of Noir: A Reader.* New York: Verso, 1993.

Freese, Peter. *The Ethnic Detective: Chester Himes, Harry Kemelman, Tony Hillerman.* Essen: Die Blaue Eule, 1992.

Lundquist, James. *Chester Himes.* New York: Ungar, 1976.

Skinner, Robert E. *2 Guns from Harlem: The Detective Fiction of Chester Himes.* Bowling Green, OH: Bowling Green State University Popular Press, 1989.

Woods, Paula. *Spooks, Spies, and Private Eyes: Black Mystery, Crime, and Suspense Fiction.* New York: Doubleday, 1995.

Notes

1. Chester Himes, *Lonely Crusade* (New York: Knopf, 1947), p. 6.
2. http://www.math.buffalo.edu/~sww/HIMES/himes-chester_BIO.html

Alice Tisdale Hobart

Oil for the Lamps of China

Indianapolis: Bobbs-Merrill, 1933

Originally published: 1933

Genre: Historical Fiction/Mainstream/Literary Fiction

Quote

> Down the worn stairs of the hong they carried the coffin, not half a man's load. For a mo-
> ment they halted in the hall. Above them on the wall hung the picture of the great skyscraper
> of the Oil Company. Then they moved on to the white man's cemetery, a tiny unsheltered
> spot among the ricefields.[1]

Synopsis

Stephen Chase is sent to work in China by a large American oil company. While on leave in Japan, he finds that the woman he planned to marry has rejected him, so he quickly finds another woman, Hester, and marries her—largely because if he doesn't return to China with a wife, he will lose status with his boss. Stephen, with his new wife, is assigned to a remote region of China, where Hester suffers a miscarriage—partially because Stephen was attending to company business, an oil tank fire, and wasn't around to help the doctor. Despite this setback, the couple stays together and is transferred to southern China. There they deal with disease, famine, and a Communist insurrection. In the end the company recognizes Stephen's sacrifices—as well as his innovation in inventing a cheap oil lamp—and gives him a promotion.

Critical Commentary

The three main characters in this story are the protagonist, the company that employs him, and China itself. The interaction of these three makes for a highly readable story that, though written in a standard narrative mode leading to a certain predictability of plot, provides interesting insights into the growth of modernity in a traditional society and the costs this has— both on those becoming modernized and the modernizers.

The strength of this book lies in the realization that it is actually about the conflict between differing perceptions of time. The Chinese live mostly in the past, and Stephen Chase lives mostly in the future (he hopes to eventually be posted back to the United States or, barring that, somewhere in China that is "civilized"). And then there is the company that lives in its own impersonal present, not really caring about anything but maintaining markets and profits. It is the conflict among these three that gives the book its interest.

In the interstices between these three live the other characters, including Stephen's wife, Hester, who is forced to live a poor-quality life lacking love and marked by the death of her child. Hester's husband largely ignores her as he tries to get on with the company; with Kin, the servant who is intent on squeezing Westerners for every extra bit of cash he can; and with the endless parade of company men who drift from place to place, never really questioning anything. These minor characters pay the price for the decisions of the major players, all the while having no real input themselves.

The novel is laudable for its vivid descriptions of China and foreign business practices of that time. This is not a piece of socialist realism that sacrifices plot for a mania for accuracy, but the story rings true. The author, being the wife of an American oil executive in China during the same era, certainly had the chance for firsthand observation, and this shows.

With echoes of Pearl Buck, whose famous novel of China, *The Good Earth,* came out in 1931, this book shows that the fascination of Americans with China is not a new thing—a fact worth remembering and one that is relevant to contemporary readers. It also is a cautionary tale for those who think that loving their corporations is a good strategy. Despite the somewhat happy ending of this story, the underlying message is that businesses have the bad habit of not loving people back. The book will be of interest not only to those interested in Chinese culture, but also to anyone working (or planning) to work in business. It might be of particular interest to business ethics and business history classes as well as those in Chinese studies.

Author Sketch

Born in Lockport, New York, on January 28, 1882, Hobart attended Northwestern University and the University of Chicago before her marriage to American oil executive Earle Tisdale in 1914. She then lived with her husband in China until 1927. After their return to the United States, she began her writing career. She died in Oakland, California, on March 14, 1967.[2]

Other Works by the Author

Hobart, Alice Tisdale Nourse. *Pioneering Where the World Is Old (Leaves from a Manchurian Note-Book).* New York: Holt, 1917.
By the City of the Long Sand; A Tale of New China. New York: Macmillan, 1926.
Pidgin Cargo. New York and London: Century, 1929.
River Supreme. Indianapolis: Bobbs-Merrill, 1934.
Yang and Yin: A Novel of an American Doctor in China. Indianapolis and New York: Bobbs-Merrill, 1936.
Their Own Country. Indianapolis and New York: Bobbs-Merrill, 1940.
The Cup and the Sword. Indianapolis and New York: Bobbs-Merrill, 1942.
The Peacock Sheds His Tail. Indianapolis: Bobbs-Merrill, 1945.
The Cleft Rock. Indianapolis: Bobbs-Merrill, 1948.
Venture into Darkness. New York: Longmans, 1955.
Hobart, Alice Tisdale, and Florence Wheelock Ayscough. *Within the Walls of Nanking.* London: J. Cape, 1928.

Suggestions for Further Reading

Cohen, Paul A. *History in Three Keys: The Boxers as Event, Experience, and Myth.* New York: Columbia University Press, 1997.
Lu, Hanchao. *Street Criers: A Cultural History of Chinese Beggars.* Stanford, CA: Stanford University Press, 2005.

Palace, Wendy. *The British Empire and Tibet 1900–1922.* RoutledgeCurzon Studies in the Modern History of Asia. London and New York: Routledge, 2005.

Spence, Jonathan D. *The Search for Modern China.* 2nd ed. New York: Norton, 1999.

Notes

1. Alice Tisdale Hobart, *Oil for the Lamps of China* (Indianapolis: Bobbs-Merrill, 1933), p. 286.

2. *New York Times,* April 10, 1974, p. 44; *New York Times,* March 15, 1967, p. 47; *New York Times,* November 11, 1951, p. BR11.

Paul Hoover

Saigon, Illinois

New York: Vintage Contemporaries, 1988

Originally published: 1988

Genre: Mainstream/Literary Fiction

Quote

> The draft board, Local 13 in Malta, was famous already. There had been an article about it in *Life*, describing a young man being dragged away from his wife's hospital room while she was giving birth to their first child. He was sent off to Vietnam, and a month later he was killed. The Malta *Prairie-Sun* put the news of his death on page eight, next to ads for cars.[1]

Synopsis

In 1968 Jim Holder, a 20-something slacker who basically just wants to have a good time and escape from his repressive rural upbringing, becomes a conscientious objector during Vietnam, less from a sense of morality than a desire not to get himself killed, and as his alternative service, he is engaged as an orderly at an inner-city Chicago hospital. There he deals with a menagerie of patients and staff and has experiences that range from the deaths of patients to the petty politics of the hospital administration to his girlfriend's pregnancy and abortion. The hospital is a Kakfaesque bureaucracy where counting sheets counts more than the welfare of the patients. Off duty, Jim lives with a group of people in an apartment sublet from a revolutionary who is busy somewhere in South America. Everyone at the apartment is engaged in some form of protest against society, taking everything, including themselves, much too seriously. Eventually, Jim offends his hospital superior and loses his job, which triggers an odyssey through his past before he decides to run away to the West Coast.

Critical Commentary

What is one's duty in wartime? Fight? Flight? Passive resistance? In this comic novel, Paul Hoover raises these important issues. What is the obligation of the citizen? For the characters in this novel, the answer is some middle course of outward obedience to society but actual resistance, even if their resistance in most cases simply takes the form of apathy. These questions are just as relevant today as they were when Hoover's book was published.

Structured episodically—perhaps reflecting Hoover's experience as a poet—the story, like its protagonist, really goes nowhere. Very little actually happens. All of the characters in this book live in a kind of timeless space. We know it is the Vietnam era, but it could just as easily be World War II or the war in Iraq. Jim Holder works; experiences various forms of death and suffering, mostly as a detached observer; and has a mindless series of political/sexual/emotional adventures in his private life. Incapable of making any real difference, these individuals are in the grip of a merciless universe that neither knows of their existence nor cares. The reader may be left with a sense of alienation and meaninglessness, yet also asking important questions. In the current milieu, such questions must be raised.

This is a very well-written book about one person's response to the insanity of war. In addition, it is a wonderfully humorous novel, similar in tone in some respects to Heller's *Catch-22,* about how people try to deal with situations that they cannot control and that have no real solutions.

Author Sketch

Born April 30, 1946, Hoover received degrees from Manchester College (BA 1968) and the University of Illinois (MA 1973). He worked as a university press editor and as poet in residence at several universities, including Columbia College, the School of the Art Institute of Chicago, and San Francisco State University. He has received numerous honors, including a poetry fellowship from the National Endowment for the Arts, 1980; artists' fellowships from the Illinois Arts Council, 1983, 1984, and 1986; and the San Francisco Literary Laureates Award from the Friends of the San Francisco Public Library, 2000.[2]

Other Works by the Author

The Monocle Thugs. Chicago: OINK! Press, 1977.
Letter to Einstein Beginning Dear Albert: Poems. Chicago: Yellow Press, 1979.
Somebody Talks a Lot. Chicago: Yellow Press, 1982.
Idea. Great Barrington, MA: The Figures, 1987.
The Novel: A Poem. New York: New Directions, 1990.
Viridian: Poems. Athens: University of Georgia Press, 1997.
Totem and Shadow: New and Selected Poems. Jersey City, NJ: Talisman House, 1999.
Rehearsal in Black. Cambridge, UK: Salt, 2001.
Winter (Mirror). Chicago: Flood Editions, 2002.
Fables of Representation: Essays, Poets on Poetry. Ann Arbor: University of Michigan Press, 2004.
Poems in Spanish. Richmond, CA: Omnidawn, 2005.
Hoover, Paul, ed. *Postmodern American Poetry: A Norton Anthology.* New York: Norton, 1994.
Tunström, Göran, and Paul Hoover. *The Christmas Oratorio: A Novel.* Boston: Godine, 1995.

Suggested Readings

Brock, Peter, Nigel Young, and Peter Brock. *Pacifism in the Twentieth Century.* Syracuse, NY: Syracuse University Press, 1999.
Dickerson, James. *North to Canada; Men and Women against the Vietnam War.* Westport, CT: Praeger, 1999.
Short, William, Willa Seidenberg, and Addison Gallery of American Art. *A Matter of Conscience: GI Resistance During the Vietnam War.* Andover, MA: Addison Gallery of American Art Phillips Academy, 1992.
Tollefson, James W. *The Strength Not to Fight: An Oral History of Conscientious Objectors of the Vietnam War.* Boston: Little, Brown, 1993.

Notes

1. Paul Hoover, *Saigon, Illinois* (New York: Vintage Contemporaries, 1988), p. 2.
2. *Contemporary Authors Online,* Gale, 2002.

Maureen Howard

Bridgeport Bus

New York: Penguin Books, 1980

Originally published: 1965

Genre: Mainstream/Literary Fiction

Quote

> So I have to saturate this city, this neighborhood, this apartment with sorrow, love, hate, happiness. My!—girlish My!—and will this bring me eventually to the same bondage? Yes—but the time and the scene of action will be mine. The exits will be mine.[1]

Synopsis

Mary Agnes Keely is 30-something and lives at home in Bridgeport, Connecticut, under the thumb of her widowed Catholic mother, whom she supports with a job as a secretary in a zipper factory. Tiring of her life, she abandons her situation and moves to New York City—where she gets a job in advertising, rents an apartment, and has an affair with a man who gets her pregnant. This ultimately drives her to return home to Bridgeport where, back in the hands of her mother, she is confined to a Catholic home for wayward girls. Strangely enough, this doesn't bother her all that much. Keely's story is told concurrently with the stories of her cousin Sherry, née Mary Elizabeth Hurley, who fails in show business and commits suicide, and Lydia Savaard, a wealthy society woman who spends every weekend visiting her husband in an upscale mental institution.

Critical Commentary

Mary Agnes Keely is a talented woman trying to break away from her conventional upbringing to a better life. This story of a young person leaving the provinces for the metropolis is an old one going back at least as far as Dick Whittington and his cat, but Howard infuses this familiar tale with freshness and vigor in this early feminist novel.

Bridgeport Bus has little storyline in the conventional sense. Howard has not abandoned the conventional linear time-driven narrative, but has eschewed the extended development of a conventional plot. Mary Agnes is simply sent on a rocketing arc from the dingy streets to Bridgeport to New York and back again. Along the way we see her interactions with the other characters, especially her cousin Sherry, a failed show-business ingénue, and Lydia Savaard, an older woman who spends every weekend with her husband in the mental institution. Their stories contrast with Mary Agnes's growth into a fully realized human being, symbolized at the end of the novel by her pregnancy—she is literally full of life. Even though she is by this time confined in a Catholic home for wayward girls, she is no longer confined by her old life, at least not psychologically.

One might say Howard has created three different novels, in which the stories of Sherry and Lydia run concurrently with that of Mary Agnes. The responses to life by the first two, who seek approval from either the public or a particular individual, are ultimately failures. The contrast with Mary Agnes, who seeks inner liberation, is apparent and makes this novel more structurally complex than it at first appears.

Compelling descriptions of New York life—not the rich world of magazine covers, but the gritty working professional life of late 1950s and early 1960s New York—add color and depth to the novel. This was a time when the commercial world bumped up against the slightly sleazy demimonde of art—symbolized here by Mary Agnes's sometime commercial artist boyfriend, Stanley, and the slightly crazed set of artists and poets who find Mary Agnes good for an easy handout, when they aren't carving her kitchen linoleum into modern art. All this is contrasted with the stagnant life in Bridgeport of Mary Agnes's mother, increasingly imprisoned by old age, illness, and her own narrow worldview.

In depicting what can happen when people reject the desire to seek the approval of others in favor of fulfilling their own needs as human beings, Howard has written a feminist novel, but its lessons could be applied to men as well. It is a thoughtfully written novel with wide appeal.

Author Sketch

Born June 28, 1930, in Bridgeport, Connecticut, Howard received a BA from Smith College (1952) and later worked in advertising and publishing. Since 1967, she has been a teacher and lecturer at a number of universities, including the New School for Social Research, the University of California at Santa Barbara, Columbia University, Yale University, Amherst College, and Brooklyn College. She was awarded a Guggenheim Fellowship in 1967 and the National Book Critics Circle Award in 1980. She is currently a member of the English department at Yale.[2]

Other Works by the Author

Not a Word about Nightingales. New York: Atheneum, 1962.
Before My Time. Boston: Little, Brown, 1974.
Facts of Life. Boston: Little, Brown, 1978.
Grace Abounding. Boston: Little, Brown, 1982.
Expensive Habits: A Novel. New York: Summit Books, 1986.
Natural History: A Novel. New York: Norton, 1992.
A Lover's Almanac. New York: Viking, 1998.
Big as Life: Three Tales for Spring. New York: Viking, 2001.

Suggestions for Further Reading

Coulter, Moureen. "Bridgeport Revisited." *Belles Lettres* 9, no. 1 (Fall 1993): 15.
Flower, Dean. "Politics and the Novel." *Hudson Review* 46 (Summer 1993): 395–402.
Kearns, Caledonia. *Cabbage and Bones: An Anthology of Irish American Women's Fiction.* New York: Holt, 1997.
Leonard, John. "Up from Bridgeport." *New York Times Book Review,* July 1, 2001, p. E10.
Perrin, Noel. "The Lure of the Bright Lights." *Washington Post Book World,* May 27, 1984, p. 11.

Notes

1. Maureen Howard, *Bridgeport Bus* (New York: Penguin Books, 1980), p. 39.
2. *Washington Post Book World,* November 22, 1992, p. 6; *Contemporary Authors Online,* Gale, 2005.

William Dean Howells

The Rise of Silas Lapham

New York: New American Library, 1980

Originally published: 1885

Genre: Mainstream/Literary Fiction

Quote

> So long as the people that own the barns and fences don't object, I don't see what the public has got to do with it. And I never saw anything so very sacred about a big rock, along a river or in a pasture, that it wouldn't do to put mineral paint on it in three colors. I wish some of the people that talk about the landscape, and WRITE about it, had to bust one of them rocks OUT of the landscape with powder, or dig a hole to bury it in, as we used to have to do up on the farm; I guess they'd sing a little different tune about the profanation of scenery.[1]

Synopsis

Silas Lapham is a Vermont entrepreneur who, having made a fortune selling a special mineral paint, moves his family to Boston. Once in Boston, the family begins some awkward social climbing, encouraging their daughters to pursue the rich offspring of an old Boston family—whose parents are appalled by this prospect. In the process of coming to terms with this situation, Lapham suffers a variety of social and financial reverses that, ultimately, ruin him materially and force him and his family back to Vermont, sans wealth, but with his character intact.

Critical Commentary

In one of the first novels to focus on the life of an American businessman, William Dean Howells takes a seemingly commonplace person, the self-made paint magnate Silas Lapham, and creates a masterpiece of modern realism. Today, in the era of Internet nouveau riche, *The Rise of Silas Lapham* takes on new meaning.

The story is a fairly straightforward one. Initially, Silas Lapham is financially and socially successful. The novel traces his collapsing fortunes and the emergence of his true character, which eventually leads to his moral if not financial success. Howells, while rejecting many of the conventions of the traditional Victorian sentimental novel, still works somewhat in that paradigm. In fact, a major criticism of the novel is its lack of ugliness—the world of Boston seems a remarkably clean one, both physically and emotionally, and blissfully ignorant of the realities of the emerging urban immigrant culture.

In this unexpectedly comic novel, Howells traces the confrontation of old traditional culture with the emerging capitalist society. He never falls prey to excesses of naturalism, but depicts the status- and class-conscious world of nineteenth-century Boston with clarity and verve. The character of Lapham can be seen as representing the emerging business class; yet ultimately he is unwilling to stoop to the depths of his competitors, therefore losing his business but not his self-respect. Howells's portrayal of Lapham is positive, especially in comparison with later depictions of businessmen by writers such as Sinclair Lewis.

This book has been taught in college English classes over the years, and it continues to be taught. However, reading for personal edification and reading for class assignments are two different things. Most people who have read this novel have done so well before they come upon situations in their own lives that would make the book meaningful—financial problems, job difficulties, corporate intrigue. By the time they do encounter such experiences, when the book should and could be useful and valuable, memories of *Silas Lapham,* an enjoyable and enlightening read, have faded. Although written as mainstream, literary fiction, the book can also be enjoyed by contemporary readers as a historical novel.

Author Sketch

Howells, born in Martins Ferry, Ohio, on March 1, 1837, worked as a typesetter and later as a reporter for the *Ohio State Journal.* He was hired to write the campaign biography of Abraham Lincoln. *The Lives and Speeches of Abraham Lincoln and Hannibal Hamlin* was published in 1860. Lincoln appointed Howells as American counsel in Venice (1861–65), which resulted in a book—*Venetian Life* (1878). In 1865 he began publishing novels as well as pursuing a career as an editor with various magazines, including *Atlantic Monthly* and *Harper's.* Howells was a founding member of the NAACP in 1909. He died in New York City on May 11, 1920.[2]

Other Works by the Author

Venetian Life (Boston: Osgood, 1878).
A Fearful Responsibility, and Other Stories. Boston: Osgood, 1881.
An Imperative Duty. A Novel. New York: Harper & Brothers, 1892.
The World of Chance, a Novel. New York: Harper & Brothers, 1893.
Their Wedding Journey. Boston and New York: Houghton Mifflin, 1895.
The Great Modern American Stories, an Anthology. New York: Boni and Liveright, 1920.
Mrs. Farrell; a Novel. New York: Harper & Brothers, 1921.
Eighty Years and After. New York: American Academy of Arts and Letters, 1937.
Indian Summer: A Novel. New York: Fromm, 1985.
Novels, 1886–1888. New York: Library of America, 1989.
Howells, William Dean, and Ruth Bardon. *Selected Short Stories of William Dean Howells.* Athens, OH: Ohio University Press, 1997.

Suggestions for Further Reading

Cady, Edwin Harrison. *The Realist at War; the Mature Years, 1885–1920, of William Dean Howells.* Syracuse, NY: Syracuse University Press, 1958.
———. *The Road to Realism: The Early Years 1837–1885 of William Dean Howells.* Westport, CT: Greenwood Press, 1986.
Crowley, John William. *The Dean of American Letters: The Late Career of William Dean Howells.* Amherst: University of Massachusetts Press, 1999.

Goodman, Susan, and Carl Dawson. *William Dean Howells: A Writer's Life.* Berkeley: University of California Press, 2005.

Nettels, Elsa. *Language, Race, and Social Class in Howells's America.* Lexington: University Press of Kentucky, 1988.

Notes

1. Howells, William Dean, *The Rise of Silas Lapham* (New York: New American Library, 1980), p. 18.

2. "William Dean Howells," in *Dictionary of Literary Biography,* Vol. 189: *American Travel Writers, 1850–1915,* ed. Donald Ross and James J. Schramer (Detroit: Gale, 1998), pp. 172–192; http://www.spartacus.schoolnet.co.uk/USAhowellsWD.htm

Charles Richard Johnson

Oxherding Tale

New York: Grove Weidenfeld, 1982

Originally published: 1982

Genre: Historical Fiction

Quote

> The beauty of the night made me shout a cry that set sleeping dogs to barking and hummed for minutes afterwards in my ears. A fine rain fell. I sang out, now to trees that nodded respectfully in return, now to invisible blackbirds that called from the bushes.[1]

Synopsis

Andrew Hawkins, a mulatto slave in the 1850s American South, desiring freedom, starts on an odyssey of escape to the North. Along the way he encounters a fantastic set of characters who include Karl Marx, the Communist philosopher; Flo Hatfield, whose sexual appetites have put at least one slave in the ground; Reb, an all-knowing black slave; and Horace Bannon, Southcatcher, a fugitive slave hunter par excellence.

Critical Commentary

In Western literary tradition, the story of a young man on a journey is common. In *Oxherding Tale,* Charles Johnson captures a similar sense of adventure and motion within the context of the slave narrative tradition.

The story requires close attention by the reader, yet is rewarding because of its lively comic style and highly enjoyable characterizations. Johnson introduces elements that might be seen as completely silly, such as having Karl Marx make a visit to the plantation, and in less able hands, this might have fallen flat, but the scene is simply drop-dead funny—and it effectively advances the intellectual argument Johnson is making. Although the novel is filled with literary and scholarly allusions, these don't overwhelm the narrative. Johnson truly understands the need to be, first and foremost, a good storyteller. The result is an enjoyable read, even when weighty issues are tackled.

The theme of the story is the movement from sin to salvation, from Andrew's dubious origins, conceived in the bed of his father's master by his father and the master's wife, to his growing up and his education well beyond his station. Eventually, Andrew flees to freedom, impelled by his growing awareness of the dichotomy between the liberty of his mind and the enslavement of the body.

As Andrew makes his way to freedom, Johnson uses various narrative and stylistic conventions, while turning those conventions on their head for comic effect. Andrew meets up with characters and situations that range from the silly to the evil in a wonderfully comic meditation on the human condition as well as on the absurdity of American racial attitudes.

Undercutting fixed ideals of identity, *Oxherding Tale* shows how, in actuality, race is protean. Andrew, operating with several identities, recognizes that the perception of others creates reality. He uses this fact to his advantage in effecting his own liberation and in developing his own sense of identity. The result is a fascinating book that should be of interest to anyone interested in the issue of racial identity—as well as just those who want to read a rip-roaring piece of picaresque humor.

Author Sketch

Born in Evanston, Illinois, on April 23, 1948, Johnson graduated from Southern Illinois University in 1971. He continued study for graduate degrees in philosophy at SIU and later SUNY–Stony Brook, while developing his writing career. Since 1976, while working as a professor and editor, he has written a number of well-received novels. He received the National Book Award in 1990 for *Middle Passage* and a MacArthur Fellowship in 1998.[2]

Other Works by the Author

The Sorcerer's Apprentice, Contemporary American Fiction. New York: Penguin Books, 1987.
Being & Race: Black Writing since 1970. Bloomington: Indiana University Press, 1988.
Middle Passage. New York: Atheneum, 1990.
Dreamer: A Novel. New York: Scribner, 1998.
Soulcatcher and Other Stories. San Diego: Harcourt, 2001.
Turning the Wheel: Essays on Buddhism and Writing. New York: Scribner, 2003.

Suggestions for Further Reading

Faust, Drew Gilpin. *The Ideology of Slavery: Proslavery Thought in the Antebellum South, 1830–1860.* Baton Rouge: Louisiana State University Press, 1981.
Fox-Genovese, Elizabeth. *Within the Plantation Household: Black and White Women of the Old South, Gender & American Culture.* Chapel Hill: University of North Carolina Press, 1988.
Fox-Genovese, Elizabeth, and Eugene D. Genovese. *Fruits of Merchant Capital: Slavery and Bourgeois Property in the Rise and Expansion of Capitalism.* New York: Oxford University Press, 1983.
Genovese, Eugene D. *Roll, Jordan, Roll; The World the Slaves Made.* New York: Pantheon Books, 1974.

Notes

1. Charles Johnson, *Oxherding Tale* (New York: Grove Weidenfeld, 1982), p. 19.
2. "Charles Johnson," in *Dictionary of Literary Biography,* Vol. 278: *American Novelists Since World War II, Seventh Series,* ed. James R. Giles and Wanda H. Giles (Detroit: Gale, 2003), pp. 201–211.

Louis B. Jones

Ordinary Money

New York: Viking Penguin, 1990

Originally published: 1990

Genre: Mainstream/Literary Fiction

Quote

> And he had lived, ever since, a life of evasion of that perpetually unsolved equation. The
> sight of the classified advertising pages stung his vision. He kept wafting the big pages past.
> Or, if he looked, he let his eyes run to those large contemptible ads promising to "dynamic"
> or "ambitious" candidates an unrealistically huge income in the first month, which to con-
> template made him snugger in his torn bathrobe.[1]

Synopsis

Friends Randy and Wayne live on the edge of poverty in California, pursuing lousy jobs
and get-rich-quick schemes. They get involved with a mysterious, strangely named man, Bim
Auctor, who, it appears, is running a counterfeiting operation. Randy and Wayne decide to cut
themselves in on some of the money to improve their humdrum lives. This causes them endless trouble with the government. In the end, although some of the details of the scheme come
to light, the real motivations behind the plot remain a mystery. Randy and Wayne question
their lives and try to plan something different and better for the future.

Critical Commentary

What is money really? Is it something with a value pegged to an external resource, like gold
or bread? Or is it something that has value in and of itself? And, if you came into a large sum
of money, what would you do? Would it be possible to undo your mistakes? Or run away from
them? These are only a few of the important questions raised in *Ordinary Money*, a comic story
that takes a serious look at the underbelly of the American economy and asks questions about
what success really means.

Marin County, California, is home to some of the most successful people in America. It is also
the home of some of the biggest losers. Randy and Wayne, who have an almost Damon Runyon
quality to their personalities—of loveable losers always looking for their lucky break—fall into
the second category. Both search for success and then have it dumped in their laps. But is it real?
The ambiguity of the money's reality becomes a metaphor for the ambiguity of their lives.

None of the characters in this novel are living in a truly authentic and truthful manner—
either with the people in their lives or with themselves. Jones uses the various comic misadventures of his two main protagonists to illustrate this fact. With echoes of *Don Quixote*, Randy
and Wayne engage in a journey to find the reality behind their lives. Their benefactor, Bim

Auctor, never really appears in a substantial way in the novel and instead is depicted as a kind of Wizard of Oz character who, if they will simply follow the path he's laid out, will bring them what they want.

Here is life on the margins of the California dream. This is the Marin County of the strip-mall employee, not the California of the Silicon Valley millionaire. The lives of the characters are scruffy and dirty—one day ahead of the repo man and a bank foreclosure notice. The 1980s economic boom in California ignored people like this, leaving them trapped in a kind of middle-class ghetto, with aspirations toward the lifestyle of their richer neighbors, but not a clue (or the life skills) to get there. Jones captures it all in lush descriptive writing.

In the absence of any real beliefs or spiritual framework for their lives, the two main characters are easily led astray into get-rich-quick schemes. They have no way to define their lives other than in terms of material success, so when offered the opportunity to have a pile of money, of dubious provenance and even more dubious legitimacy, they fall for it.

Jones has written a story around the premise of the adage to be careful what you wish for. He writes with a fine sense of satire and, in places, whimsy, providing readers with a priceless and hilarious depiction of a government that, in the end, is so inept at determining whether money is real that it simply gives up trying to figure out the truth. Although this novel can be read with serious issues in mind, it never takes itself too seriously. The result is a small gem of a book that is highly enjoyable, eminently readable, and without pretension.

Author Sketch

Born in Chicago, Jones attended the University of Illinois. After graduation he became a full-time writer. He lives in northern California in the San Francisco Bay area.[2]

Other Works by the Author

Ordinary Money. New York: Viking, 1990.
Particles and Luck. New York: Pantheon Books, 1993.
California's Over. New York: Pantheon Books, 1997.

Suggestions for Further Reading

Degen, Robert A. *The American Monetary System: A Concise Survey of Its Evolution since 1896.* Lexington, MA: Lexington Books, 1987.

Goetzmann, William N., and K. Geert Rouwenhorst. *The Origins of Value: The Financial Innovations That Created Modern Capital Markets.* New York: Oxford University Press, 2005.

Locke, John, and P. H. Kelly. *Locke on Money.* Oxford and New York: Clarendon Press/Oxford University Press, 1991.

Smith, Adam, and Laurence Winant Dickey. *An Inquiry into the Nature and Causes of the Wealth of Nations: Selections.* Indianapolis: Hackett, 1993.

Notes

1. Louis B. Jones, *Ordinary Money* (New York: Viking Penguin, 1990), p. 6.
2. http://www.stmarys.ca.edu/academics/adult_graduate/programs_by_school/school_of_liberal_arts/programs/mfa/Mary/archive/Mary_spring2002/jones.html

Sylvester Judd

Margaret: A Tale of the Real and the Ideal, Blight and Bloom; Including Sketches of a Place Not before Described, Called Mons Christi

Boston: Jordan and Wiley, 1845

Originally published: 1845

Genre: Historical Fiction

Quote

> The child Margaret sits in the door of her house, on a low stool, with a small wheel, winding spools, in our vernacular, "quilling," for her mother who, in a room near by, is mounted in a loom, weaving and smoking, the fumes of her pipe mingling with the whiz of the shuttle, the jarring of the lathe, and the clattering of treadles. From a windle the thread in conducted to the quills, and buzz, buzz goes Margaret's wheel, while a grey squirrel, squatted on her shoulder, inspects the operation with a most profound gravity.[1]

Synopsis

Margaret is a child being raised by her rough and irreligious family in rural postrevolutionary New England. As a child she encounters the repressive Calvinism of her community, which doesn't attract her. Eventually, Margaret is removed from her harsh environment by her foster father, Pluck, who gives her a proper education and upbringing. After her brother is wrongly hanged for manslaughter, she flees to New York and Boston, where, after trials and tribulations, she is united with her husband Mr. Evelyn. Armed with both knowledge and wealth, the adult Margaret and her husband return to her home village and create a utopian community without prisons, capital punishment, or poverty and where everyone lives in harmony.

Critical Commentary

People think of the 1960s as the "radical" decade in American history with "flower power" and the rest, but in reality, the 1960s was matched by the 1840s as a period of social and philosophical experimentation. With the development of religious groups such as the Mormons and the Shakers, the communes of the Oneida Colony, and the antiauthoritarian writings of such people as Emerson, this decade was equally innovative. Sylvester Judd's *Margaret* is a novel that follows this tradition, and it is an outstanding example of Transcendentalist thought, as well as a well-written and compelling romantic novel.

In this novel Judd gives readers a spiritual biography. He takes Margaret, found in a state of nature and innocence, and follows her through her life as she matures and as she eventually works to develop an idealistic utopian colony. Judd's descriptions of life in postrevolutionary New England, with details of everyday life—clothing, food, and the rest—are dead on. With Judd's excellent eye for nature, this is also a delightful description of unspoiled outdoors New England.

More striking than the material details, however, is Judd's attention to inner life. In the characters of Margaret; her family, including three brothers, Nimrod, Hash, and Chilion; Obed Wright; his mother the Widow Wright; the local herbalist; and Bartholomew Elliman, "the Master," Judd creates a fully realized community of characters as interesting and colorful as any to be found in Dickens.

Despite its philosophical overtones, this is a well-developed and fast-moving novel that offers the reader a great deal of action and romance, including a long aside explaining the pasts of several of the characters. In this, along with plot elements that include a hanging, Judd seems to follow the traditional narrative impulses commonly found within traditional eighteenth-century Gothic novel such as *The Monk*. However, beyond this simple desire to provide an interesting readable story, Judd shows the influence of the developing modern American ideals of the period—the merging concerns with social welfare, the rights of women, and the development of a just society.

At times, because of the language and the ideas presented, the story slows, which may be off-putting to contemporary readers. Simply put, this is a novel written by an author and for a readership that had the time to read. However, patience is rewarded. This is, ultimately, a fascinating and well-crafted novel with an important message about human dignity and potential. It is an excellent example of a piece of radical writing that retains its relevance today, and it will especially appeal to history buffs interested in the social and religious concerns of the 1840s.

Author Sketch

Judd was born July 23, 1813, in Westhampton, Massachusetts. He was educated at Hopkins Academy and Yale, where he graduated with honors (1836). After a religious conversion to Unitarianism, he trained for the ministry, afterward accepting a position with the Unitarian Church of Augusta, Maine (1840). He worked as a minister while also publishing several novels and other works. He died January 26, 1853, in Augusta.[2]

Other Works by the Author

A Moral Review of the Revolutionary War, Or Some of the Evils of That Event Considered. A Discourse Delivered at the Unitarian Church, Augusta, Sabbath Evening, March 13th, 1842, with an Introductory Address, and Notes. Hallowell, ME: Glazier, Masters & Smith.

A Discourse Touching the Causes and Remedies of Intemperance Preached February 2, 1845. Augusta, ME: William T. Johnson.

Philo: An Evangeliad. Boston: Phillips, Sampson.

Richard Edney and the Governor's Family: A Rus-Urban Tale Simple and Popular, Yet Cultured and Nobel of Morals, Sentiment, and Life Practically Treated and Pleasantly Illustrated Containing, also Hints on Being Good and Doing Good. Boston: Phillips, Sampson, 1850.

True Dignity of Politics: A Sermon. Augusta, ME: William T. Johnson, 1850.

Suggestions for Further Reading

Brockway, P. J. *Sylvester Judd (1813–1853): Novelist of Transcendentalism.* Orono, ME: University Press, 1941.

Dedmond, F. B. *Sylvester Judd.* Boston: Twayne, 1980.

Delano, S. F. *Brook Farm: The Dark Side of Utopia.* Cambridge, MA: Belknap Press of Harvard University Press, 2004.

Malpas, J. E. *From Kant to Davidson: Philosophy and the Idea of the Transcendental.* London and New York: Routledge, 2003.

Versluis, A. *The Esoteric Origins of the American Renaissance.* New York: Oxford University Press, 2001.

Notes

1. Sylvester Judd, *Margaret* (Boston: Jordan and Wiley, 1845), p. 6.

2. F. B. Dedmond, *Sylvester Judd* (Boston: Twayne, 1980); http://etext.virginia.edu/eaf/authors/sj.htm

John Keeble

Yellowfish

New York: Harper & Row, 1987

Originally published: 1980

Genre: Mainstream/Literary Fiction

Quote

The fog, they say, its density and in winter its bitterness, is worst in Chinatown of all places in San Francisco. Its bitterness is traditional. The fog is used here, as a measure of divination as the moon's aureole is used elsewhere, or the snow level on a mountain, the radiance of a distant glacier, the depth of a creek, the anxiety of cattle in a pasture, the crick in one's knee joint.[1]

Synopsis

Wesley Erks, a criminal who would like to retire with his wife to his farm in Washington State, must undertake one last human smuggling operation in order to realize his dream. So he transports Ginarn Taam, an illegal Chinese immigrant who is being chased by both the U.S. government and the Chinese Triad, across the American-Canadian border. The story follows Erks as he moves his passenger down the West Coast from British Columbia to San Francisco's Chinatown—along the way dealing with betrayal, desperation, and murder.

Critical Commentary

American Wesley Erks is what we often call a "coyote"—one of those people willing to transport people across the border illegally for a fee. Although this phenomenon has been well documented from the Mexican perspective, to view the issue from the Canadian perspective is unusual.

Like the characters in Chaucer's *Canterbury Tales* and Steinbeck's *Grapes of Wrath*, these individuals have embarked on a kind of pilgrimage, each hoping to obtain some kind of redemption. Although the reader knows little about some of the characters' backgrounds or motivations for the journey, as in the case of the Chinese people featured in the book, the characters are nonetheless realistically portrayed.

This book raises an interesting moral dilemma. The reader is left questioning who the real criminals are: the illegal aliens, Erks, or the members of society who are unwilling or unable to perform menial tasks—working in fields, restaurants, or laundries—and so turn a blind eye to the existence and suffering of those who do this work. Or perhaps the criminal is the federal government, with its inconsistent and unevenly enforced immigration policies.

There is also the larger issue of Erks's own alienation. A generation or two ago, such people as Erks had a place in society. Members of the lower middle class or the working poor—even

111

the unskilled or the unlucky—could find employment in factories or on farms. This allowed a basic subsistence and the hope of something better coming along. Someone like Erks, technically and mechanically skilled, would have had a good life.

In our modern economy, many such jobs have been eliminated, replaced by technology or moved to the very places (such as China) that the illegal aliens in this novel are trying to escape. Erks, like the other characters in this novel, has been alienated from his own country. He is an internal refugee with neither the material nor the spiritual resources to hope for a better day.

Keeble's atmospheric invocation of the spirit of the Pacific Northwest is infused with keen skills of observation and a loving ear for the English language, which endows this journey of the Chinese aliens and their American guide with a sense of mystery. The almost hauntingly lyrical depiction of the Pacific Northwest provides a scenic backbeat that adds contrast and authenticity to the storyline. Evocative descriptions of both the land and its native people make this a wry and sophisticated commentary on the moral conditions of the characters and on the state of modern American society.

Author Sketch

Keeble, born November 24, 1944, in Winnipeg, Manitoba, Canada, has written four novels as well as shorter fiction and nonfiction in publications such as *Outside, Village Voice, American Short Fiction,* and *Best American Short Stories.* He has worked at Grinnell College (1962–1972) and from 1973 at Eastern Washington University, where he is now a professor emeritus of the MFA writing program. He has been distinguished visiting chair in creative writing at the University of Alabama several times.[2]

Other Works by the Author

Crab Canon. New York: Grossman, 1971.
Broken Ground. New York: Harper & Row, 1987.
Out of the Channel: The Exxon Valdez Oil Spill in Prince William Sound. New York: HarperCollins, 1991.
Nocturnal America. Lincoln: University of Nebraska Press, 2006.
Jeffery, Ransom, and John Keeble. *Mine.* New York: Grossman, 1974.

Suggestions for Further Reading

Chin, Ko-lin. *Smuggled Chinese: Clandestine Immigration to the United States.* Philadelphia: Temple University Press, 1999.
Lee, Erika. *At America's Gates: Chinese Immigration during the Exclusion Era, 1882–1943.* Chapel Hill: University of North Carolina Press, 2003.
McCoy, Robert R. *Chief Joseph, Yellow Wolf, and the Creation of Nez Perce History in the Pacific Northwest.* New York: Routledge, 2004.
O'Connell, Nicholas. *On Sacred Ground: The Spirit of Place in Pacific Northwest Literature.* Seattle: University of Washington Press, 2003.
Smith, Paul J. *Human Smuggling: Chinese Migrant Trafficking and the Challenge to America's Immigration Tradition.* Significant Issues Series. Washington, D.C.: Center for Strategic & International Studies, 1997.

Notes

1. John Keeble, *Yellowfish* (New York: Harper & Row, 1980), p. 1.
2. http://www.ewu.edu/getlit/2004/author19.html; *Contemporary Authors New Revision Series,* Vol. 14, p. 257.

John Keene

Annotations

New York: New Directions, 1995

Originally published: 1995

Genre: Mainstream/Literary Fiction

Quote

By the autumn of his childhood they had abandoned their prefab in the ghetto for a ranch house in a suburb whose property values and lack of crime could boast of national renown. No one, you understand, carped at the size of the required down payment, since it was assumed that they would eventually own their own property. Ignorance is incapable of concealing itself.[1]

Synopsis

Tracing the life of an African American man in St. Louis from his childhood in the early 1960s through adulthood, this story describes various stages—early life, school days, family gatherings, and the protagonist's eventual awakening, intellectually and sexually, into mature adulthood. All are placed against the ever-present backdrop of the city of St. Louis.

Critical Commentary

On the border between novel and epic poem, this novel causes the reader to question the usual definitions of the terms. Keene follows the general convention in novels of a roughly linear narrative, moving forward in time from the 1960s until his character's acceptance at Harvard. However, he also uses a wide range of literary techniques; writes in a variety of voices, ranging from the humorous to the serious; and borrows from a range of genres to create an insightful commentary of African American life.

The book is organized in 18 chapters, all of which, because of Keene's choice not to use paragraphs, end up reading like poetry. His use of language is outstanding, not only in his choice of words, but also in his phrasing, which is sensitive and elegant. Skillfully painting a realistic picture of American family life in an era of transitions, Keene captures the essence of growing up in the Midwest in the 1960s and 1970s.

Each chapter is bracketed with carefully chosen epigrams that function as poetic caesura, giving a pause to the rhythmic flow of the work—as well as being thoughtful meditations on what is to come. Interestingly, Keene also chooses to end the novel with a set of footnotes and a list of references.

At only 78 pages, one may hesitate about calling this a novel, but what it lacks in length it makes up for in emotional impact. Keene is writing in a semiautobiographical manner, a form that can, depending on the experience of the writer, turn either maudlin or bitter in quick order. He expertly avoids this pitfall by the force of his convictions, which come through on every page. Keene has given readers a wonderful ode to his childhood, as well as one of the most interesting and sensitive portraits of St. Louis as a city ever put to paper—a small gem of literary genius.

Author Sketch

Keene, born June 18, 1965 in St. Louis, Missouri, has a BA (Harvard) and an MFA (New York University). He currently teaches at Northwestern University where he specializes in fiction and cross-genre writing and African American and diasporic literature. He is a member of the Dark Room Writers Collective of Cambridge and Boston and is a Graduate Fellow of Cave Canem. In 2001 he was Northwestern's inaugural Simon Blattner Visiting Assistant Professor. Recognitions for his writing have included four Pushcart Prize nominations, several fellowships, the 2000 John Cheever Short Fiction Prize, and the Solo Press/SOLO Magazine Poetry Prize.[2]

Other Works by the Author

Seismosis (with Christopher Stackhouse). New York: The Center for Book Arts, 2003.

Suggestions for Further Reading

Collins, Earl A. *Folk Tales of Missouri*. Boston: Christopher Publishing House, 1935.
Franklin, John Hope. *From Slavery to Freedom*. New York: Vintage, 1969.

Notes

1. John Keene, *Annotations* (New York: New Directions, 1995), p. 51.
2. http://www.english.northwestern.edu/people/keene.html; http://authors.aalbc.com/john_keene.htm

Lynn Lauber

White Girls

New York: Vintage Contemporaries, 1991

Originally published: 1990

Genre: Mainstream/Literary Fiction

Quote

It was only we younger girls who admitted to the discontent that grew in us like the tumors our mothers whispered about—big as a pea, an apple, a grapefruit, we heard them say.[1]

Synopsis

Loretta Dardio is a young white woman growing up in the 1950s and 1960s in grimy Union, Ohio—a town that the future has passed by. As she matures, she reflects on her life with a growing awareness of the world around her, and she begins to question the status quo, especially that which has unjustly deemed blacks as second-class citizens. Loretta openly crosses across the color barrier and eventually decides to have a child with her black boyfriend, but things begin to unravel. Rather than having a happy ending, Loretta ends up in a home for unwed mothers.

Critical Commentary

In a deeply moving, honest, and sometimes humorous set of vignettes about life in small-town Ohio during the 1950s and 1960s, Lauber delivers compelling portraits of a young person growing into adulthood within a changing society.

Lauber's visualizations of life in a small town, lost on the edges between rural America and urbanization, accurately catch the sense of hopelessness—as well as the total lack of aesthetic value—in the community. Union, Ohio is always a vacant concrete schoolyard at 5 A.M. in August—empty, orderly, pregnant with the possibility of what might happen, but as yet barren.

A number of colorful characters, from the rebellious protagonist and narrator Loretta Dardio to the bag lady who lives in the ladies room of the local department store, inhabit this universe. Though obviously influenced by Sherwood Anderson's *Winesburg, Ohio,* Lauber makes her story original by placing the focus on the development of a young woman in a more modern setting.

Beneath the mundane events of this story lies a sensitivity to critical social issues, such as the relationship between children and parents, the small-mindedness of rural towns, and the influence of bigotry. There's a lifetime of curiosity between Loretta and the black inhabitants of the town, the latter gradually taking larger and larger roles within the story. Eventually, these people play a central role in Loretta's process of maturity and her decision to keep her black boyfriend's child rather than give it up or have an abortion.

Loretta's act of rebellion ends badly, underlining the ambiguity of her life and the lives of those around her. Yet implicit in the event is the hope and possibility of change toward a positive future.

Author Sketch

Born July 23, 1952, Dayton, Ohio, Lauber was educated at Ohio State. She worked in the publishing industry before becoming a full-time writer and teacher. Lauber lives in New York State.[2]

Other Works by the Author

21 Sugar Street. New York: Norton, 1993.
Listen to Me: Writing Life into Meaning. New York: Norton, 2004.

Suggestions for Further Reading

Baum, Bruce David. *The Rise and Fall of the Caucasian Race: A Political History of Racial Identity.* New York: New York University Press, 2006.
Carr, C. *Our Town: A Heartland Lynching, a Haunted Town, and the Hidden History of White America.* New York: Crown, 2006.
Davis, Thomas J. *Race Relations in America: A Reference Guide with Primary Documents.* Major Issues in American History. Westport, CT: Greenwood Press, 2006.
Schultz, Mark. *The Rural Face of White Supremacy: Beyond Jim Crow.* Urbana: University of Illinois Press, 2005.

Notes

1. Lynn Lauber, *White Girls* (New York: Vintage Contemporaries, 1991), p. 35.
2. "Lynn Lauber," in *Contemporary Authors Online*, Gale, 2002; http://www.lynnlauber.com/

Gus Lee

China Boy

New York: Dutton, 1991

Originally published: 1991

Genre: Mainstream/Literary Fiction/Immigrant Fiction

Quote

> There are times when I think that San Francisco was designed by the architects who laid out
> Disneyland. With the ease of a park visitor crossing from Fantasyland to Tomorrowland, a
> City tourist can leave the Tenderloin, traverse the business district, and enter North Beach
> or Chinatown. A tourist can stand on Broadway and Grant and see Sicilian, Chinese, Nea-
> politan, Bohemian and Basque neighborhoods.[1]

Synopsis

In the 1950s, Kai Ting Lee, son of a distinguished Chinese military officer, immigrates with his family to San Francisco. Living in poverty, with little knowledge of either the English language or American culture, Kai Ting, who quickly earns the street nickname of "China Boy," is subject to almost constant physical and verbal abuse from his peers in his poor neighborhood, where physical prowess in fighting is considering a prerequisite for survival. His problems are complicated by the death of his mother and his father's remarriage to an American woman who has no sympathy for his Chinese ways. In spite of this, Kai Ting perseveres and, with the help of a group of boxers at the local YMCA, learns enough about defending himself and about American culture to take care of himself and gain some self-respect as well as respect from his peers.

Critical Commentary

In *China Boy* Gus Lee gives readers a delightful and touching coming-of-age story of a Chinese boy in a tough San Francisco neighborhood during the 1950s. In the character of Kai Ting Lee, he creates one of the more memorable and interesting individuals in recent fiction, and, in the process, he presents a wonderful meditation on the issues of loss, growing up, and coming to terms with the realities of a new country.

This is a story filled with many colorful and memorable characters, centered around Kai Ting, the "China Boy" of the title, who, because of his lack of English language skills, small size, and general naïveté about how things work in America, becomes the target of every neighborhood bully. To add to his woes, Kai Ting is faced with the death of his beloved mother and his father's remarriage to an Anglo woman from Philadelphia, whose lack of knowledge (or interest) in things Chinese is only matched by her inept parenting skills. (On occasion, Lee uses the stepmother's lack of Chinese to humorous effect, so this is a novel not without its comic elements.)

The novel's cast of characters includes blacks, Hispanics, and whites, and Kai Ting interacts with them all—Big Willy Mack, the neighborhood tough; Kai's friend Toussaint La Rue, who does his best to help Kai get with the program; and Kai's Uncle Shim. In the end, Kai improves both his English skills and his physical skills, thus gaining some self-respect from his neighbors, but the story of how he does that is a classic one.

In his wonderfully descriptive and thoughtful story of growing up in poverty in San Francisco in the 1950s, Lee writes with verve and detail, creating a fast-moving story that holds the reader's interest and emotions. This is a book that should interest anyone who appreciates a story about an underdog fighting against great odds, as well as people interested in knowing more about the Chinese immigrant experience in America.

Author Sketch

Born August 8, 1946, in San Francisco, California, Gus Lee was educated at West Point and at the University of California, Davis, where he received his BA (1969) and JD (1976). He was recognized for his distinguished service in the U.S. Army and later became a practicing attorney in the State of California with the Sacramento District Attorney's Office; he also practiced with private firms. He is active with the state bar association and other civic groups, such as the Boys and Girls Club. Married, with three children, Lee has received numerous military and civic awards for his legal work as well as his community service. He currently resides in Colorado Springs, Colorado.[2]

Other Works by the Author

Honor and Duty. New York: Knopf, 1994.
Tiger's Tail: A Novel. New York: Knopf, 1996.
No Physical Evidence. New York: Fawcett Columbine, 1998.

Suggestions for Further Reading

Chung, Sue Fawn, and Priscilla Wears. *Chinese American Death Rituals: Respecting the Ancestors.* Lanham, MD: Alta Mira Press, 2005.

Kao, George. *Cathay by the Bay: Glimpses of San Francisco Chinatown in the Year 1950.* Hong Kong: Chinese University Press, 1988.

McCann, Ruthann Lump. *An Illustrated History of the Chinese in America.* San Francisco: Design Enterprises of San Francisco, 1979.

———. *Chinese American Portraits: Personal Histories 1828–1988.* San Francisco: Chronicle Books, 1988.

Shah, Mayan Bhupendra. "San Francisco's 'Chinatown': Race and the Cultural Politics of Public Health, 1854–1952." PhD dissertation, University of Chicago, 1995.

Yung, Judy. *Unbound Feet: A Social History of Chinese Women in San Francisco.* Berkeley: University of California Press, 1995.

Notes

1. Gus Lee, *China Boy* (New York: Dutton, 1991), p. 297.

2. *Dictionary of Literary Biography*, Vol. 312: *Asian American Writers*, ed. Deborah L. Madsen (Detroit: Gale, 2005), pp. 195–201.

Milton Lesser

Earthbound

Philadelphia: Winston, 1952

Originally published: 1952

Genre: Speculative Fiction/Science Fiction

Quote

> Each of the thousand thousand tiny motes in the asteroid belt caught the sun's light, un-
> shielded by any intervening atmosphere, and reflected it back at Pete. Each one shone like
> an individual jewel, and this close, Pete could detect their swirling, chaotic movement. Each
> looked like a gleaming jewel—but each could be a deadly missile of destruction.[1]

Synopsis

Cadet Peter Hodges is about to graduate from the Space Academy and realize his dream of being a space pilot when he is dismissed because of a previously overlooked heart condition. Getting a job at traffic control in a spaceport, Hodges falls in with a group of space pirates who blackmail him into helping them. Quickly arrested, Hodges is drugged, jailed, kidnapped from jail, and flown to Antarctica by the criminal gang, who need his skill in computing spaceship orbits. With the aid of an undercover agent, Hodges escapes, brings the gang to justice, and returns home, where he finds that one of his academy friends is stranded in the asteroid belt. Stymied by bureaucracy, he steals a spaceship and rescues his friend—a heroic act that gets him reinstated to the Space Academy.

Critical Commentary

Earthbound is a straight adventure story obviously designed for a young audience. Lesser's writing is almost journalistic, notable for its use of short declarative sentences. The language, particularly in conversations between characters, moves the plot along without a great deal of, if any, discussion or personal introspection on the part of the characters.

It might be said that Lesser's style echoes the early twentieth-century writer (or writers) "Victor Appleton" and his Tom Swift books, where the focus of the descriptions is on the technological wonders of the time—rocket ships, moon bases—the real stars of this novel. Lesser's characters are clearly defined in black and white terms (or good and evil). Even when the primary protagonist Hodges becomes involved in crime, it is clear that he is a victim of circumstance and will eventually return to the side of light.

An artifact of post–World War II American triumphalism, this engaging space opera can be read as a piece of nostalgia, showing the early 1950s romance with nuclear power and technology in general. However, a closer examination of the events and themes of the book reveals serious relevance for the modern reader.

For example, the role of the state is ever-present. Space is a highly regulated government enterprise, from the selection and training of astronauts to space flight itself. The functioning of an interplanetary society depends on a controlled economy, as illustrated by the control towers in which the protagonist finds himself working. Clearly capitalist, although state-regulated, it is an economy that works, as evidenced by the fact that space men are allowed, nay ordered, to retire young.

At the same time, this book celebrates the role of the individual. Despite advances in technology, the state is unable to control crime. Outlaws still exist despite the best efforts of the government. But one individual, Pete Hodges, travels easily, finds work, and eventually steals a spaceship with little interference from the authorities. And in the end, it is this freedom of action that allows him to save the day and meet his own ambition.

Earthbound is, first and foremost, entertainment. However, it is also an example of anti-totalitarian propaganda. It celebrates the power and ability of the individual as opposed to the enforced conformity of an authoritarian regime. Trapped in our own battles with technology and tyranny, today's readers will find in this book an important message about the immutability of human nature. It's also an exciting piece of escapist 1950s science fiction that will be entertaining for anyone who enjoys a classic adventure story ala Flash Gordon filled with rockets and ray guns.

Author Sketch

Milton Lesser is the birth name of the American mystery writer Stephen Marlowe. Born in 1928, Marlowe, who adopted his pen name in 1958, was educated at the College of William and Mary (1949). Marlowe has had a long, well-recognized writing career in a variety of genres, including, most notably, a series of mystery-crime books including the Chester Drum novels.[2]

Other Works by the Author

Earthbound. Philadelphia: Winston, 1952.
Looking Forward. (Editor). New York: Beechhurst Press, 1953.
The Star Seekers. Philadelphia: Winston, 1953.
The Golden Ape (Under pseudonym Adam Chase). New York: Bouregy, 1959.
Recruit for Andromeda. New York: Ace Books, 1959.
Find Eileen Hardin— Alive (Under pseudonym Andrew Frazer). New York: Avon, 1960.
The Fall of Marty Moon (Under pseudonym Andrew Frazer). New York: Avon, 1961.
Passport to Peril. New York: Ace Books, 1961.
Stadium beyond the Stars. New York: Holt, 1961.
Spacemen, Go Home. New York: Holt, 1962.
Lost Worlds and Men Who Found Them. Racine, WI: Whitman, 1962.
The Summit: A Novel. New York: Geis, 1970.
Colossus: A Novel about Goya and a World Gone Mad. New York: Macmillan, 1972.
The Man with No Shadow. Englewood Cliffs, NJ: Prentice-Hall, 1974.
The Cawthorn Journals: A Novel. Englewood Cliffs, NJ: Prentice-Hall, 1975. Also published as *Too Many Chiefs.* London: New English Library, 1977.
Translation: A Novel. Englewood Cliffs, NJ: Prentice-Hall, 1976.
The Valkyrie Encounter. New York: Putnam, 1978.

1956: A Novel. New York: Arbor House, 1981.

Deborah's Legacy. New York: Zebra, 1983.

The Lighthouse at the End of the World: A Tale of Edgar Allan Poe. New York: Dutton, 1995.

The Death and Life of Miguel de Cervantes: A Novel. London: Bloomsbury, 1991.

Suggestions for Further Reading

Aldiss, Brian W., with David Wingrove. *Trillion Year Spree: The History of Science Fiction.* New York: Atheneum, 1986.

Sullivan, C. W., III., ed. *Science Fiction for Young Readers.* Westport, CT: Greenwood Press, 1993.

Notes

1. Milton Lesser, *Earthbound* (Philadelphia: Winston, 1952), p. 187.

2. *Contemporary Authors Online,* Gale, 2006. Reproduced in *Biography Resource Center* (Farmington Hills, MI: Thomson Gale. 2006).

Deena Linett

The Translator's Wife

San Jose: Arts and Humanities Press, San Jose State University, 1986

Originally published: 1986

Genre: Mainstream/Literary Fiction

Quote

> She will go to the little telephone table under Beulah's wall-hanging and sit, staring at the parallelogram of sunlight on the grey carpet. She will know with perfect clarity that she has been getting ready for this moment for a long time and that it will have consequences she cannot imagine.[1]

Synopsis

Vida is a middle-aged woman in an unhappy marriage to a failed academic, and she is attempting to remake herself by entering graduate school. In the course of a trip to South America with her husband Mac, she engages in an affair with a Peruvian archaeologist. At the same time, the story moves backward in time and reviews Vida's life—her relationship with her family, her early love affairs—to see how she got to this stage of life.

Critical Commentary

What makes a life well lived? Material success? Happiness? Balance? In *The Translator's Wife* Deena Linett examines this classic philosophical question in an original and thoughtful novel. Through the story of Vida, a middle-aged American woman who is attempting to create a new life for herself through a love affair and her graduate studies, Linett takes a traditional and well-worked theme and develops it with originality and grace.

Linett takes some traditional story conventions and turns them on their heads. For example, Vida enters an affair with a Peruvian archaeologist, Carlos Urquiaga, who is markedly different from her husband, Mac, surely one of the more unappealing professor characters in recent fiction, who, largely because of his whining and unpleasant character, was deservedly turned out from his university post. This familiar theme is made fresh through Linett's creative and daring approach to abandon the linear flow of time, having the novel flow backward and forward in time. This allows the reader to examine the origins of Vida's actions in an interesting and dramatic fashion. In addition, Linett's talent for dialogue and eye for description make her literary technique, which could be confusing, work in an effective and dramatic matter.

By looking back weeks, months, and in some cases years, the reader sees the influences that caused Vida to make the choices that have made her present life one of discontent. One sees her life with her family, including her sister Beulah and her mother—both of whom, in their own ways, imposed their own expectations on Vida. At the same time, the reader witnesses the development of Vida's romantic affairs, both with Mac in the past and with Carlos in the near past and present—the latter of which relationships seems to have the possibility of happiness, yet is also constrained by a set of previous choices.

In quantum physics, one principle is that in any given moment, multiple possibilities exist. It is only when the actual observation of events is made that these multiple opportunities, or waves of possible futures, collapse into a fixed and immutable present. In *The Translator's Wife* Linett expresses this idea in a compelling and innovative novel.

Author Sketch

Born in Boston, Massachusetts, around August 39, 1938, Deena Linett was raised on the Gulf Coast of Florida. She attended the University of Florida (1956–58), Boston University (BA 1960), and Rutgers (EdD 1982). She taught English at Somerset County College, New Jersey (1977–79), at Rutgers (1980–1982), and at Stockton State College (1982–83). She is currently a professor at Montclair State College, in the department of English, where she began in 1983. She has been the recipient of various fellowships, including fellowships to the Hawthornden Castle International Retreat for Writers in Scotland (1996, 2002) and a residency fellowship to the Baltic Centre for Writers and Translators, Sweden, in Summer 2004. Divorced, she has three children.[2]

Other Works by the Author

On Common Ground. Albany: State University of New York Press, 1983.
Rare Earths: Poems. Rochester, NY: BOA Editions, 2001.

Suggestions for Further Reading

Ford, K. W. *The Quantum World: Quantum Physics for Everyone.* Cambridge, MA: Harvard University Press, 2004.
Reinhard, J. *The Ice Maiden: Inca Mummies, Mountain Gods, and Sacred Sites in the Andes.* Washington, D.C.: National Geographic Society, 2005.
Robinson, L. S. *Modern Women Writers.* New York: Continuum, 1996.
Schwartz, G. M., J. J. Nichols, et al. *After Collapse: The Regeneration of Complex Societies.* Tucson: University of Arizona Press, 2006.

Notes

1. Deena Linett, *The Translator's Wife* (San Jose, CA: Arts and Humanities Press, San Jose State University, 1986), p. 1.
2. *Contemporary Authors Online*, Gale, 2002; http://boaeditions.org/authors/linett.html

Ross Lockridge Jr.

Raintree County

Boston: Houghton Mifflin, 1948

Originally published: 1948

Genre: Historical/Mainstream/Literary Fiction

Quote

> A small boy had wandered out into the morning of America and down far ways seeking the Lone Star Republic and the Oregon Trail. A small boy had dreamed forever westward, and the dream had drawn a visible mark across the earth. But the boy had never gone that way. He had only dreamed it.[1]

Synopsis

This novel follows the events of July 4, 1892, in Raintree County, Indiana. Beginning with his awakening at dawn, the story tracks Mr. John Wickliff Shawnessy through his day and through his interactions with a wide range of characters, including Senator Garwood Jones, Professor Jerusalem Webster Stiles, and General Jacob Johnson, straight through the last explosion of fireworks and the departure of Professor Stiles at midnight. Interspersed among these encounters are flashbacks to numerous county events of the past half century—wars, droughts, and strikes—and how they have shaped existence, of both individuals and the community.

Critical Commentary

The epic scope and sprawling exuberance of *Raintree County* take it beyond regional novel status into being a great American saga. Through his use of modernist writing techniques, Lockridge created an innovative and compelling work that covers a single day, July 4, 1892, interweaving the history of its characters against the backdrop of American history and especially the Civil War. The protagonist, the teacher John Wickliff Shawnessy, is drawn in layers of metaphor—the legendary and symbolic American who embodies the deepest fears and hopes of the culture.

But the central symbol of the novel is the raintree, representing the tree of life and also the tree of knowledge that gives wisdom to the individual. Through a series of flashbacks, Lockridge highlights crucial events in Shawnessy's life, setting his great expectations and marriage difficulties against the history of a growing country. Shawnessy's mission in life is illuminated by poetic prose, full of vision, beauty, and Midwestern light.

Various American archetypes play against the protagonist. Garwood (later Senator) Jones, a cynical, unscrupulous materialist, sells democracy short but ultimately has a heart of gold. Cassius Carney, the "poet of finance," dies of ulcers and success. The "Perfesser," a homespun Voltaire, knows something about everything and respects nothing. And there are Shawnessy's first great love, Nell Gaither, and his wife, Susannah Drake, a slaveholding Southerner whose obsession with issues of race and identity drives her mad.

In the groping and anxiety-ridden 1940s, when the United States was grappling with how to wage a victorious peace, it would have been surprising if someone had not written a book like *Raintree County*. But rather than simply offer nostalgia, Lockridge created a fascinating psychological portrait of a nation (and its citizens) trying to cope with change and trying to integrate their new experiences into their existing mythology and ethics. Lockridge was, quite possibly, the finest writer Indiana ever produced—and deserves to be better acknowledged as such.

Author Sketch

Born April 25, 1914, in Bloomington, Indiana, Ross (Franklin) Lockridge Jr. was a brilliant student at Indiana University and Harvard. He was an instructor in English at Indiana University (1936–39) and assistant professor of English at Simmons College (1941–46). He died just two months after the publication of *Raintree County*, on March 6, 1948.[2]

Other Works by the Author

None

Suggestions for Further Reading

Anderson, David D., ed. *Myth, Memory, and the American Earth: The Durability of Raintree County.* A Midwestern Heritage Book. East Lansing: Midwestern Press, Center for the Study of Midwestern Literature and Culture, Michigan State University, 1998.

Leggett, John. *Ross and Tom; Two American Tragedies.* New York: Simon & Schuster, 1974.

Lockridge, Laurence S. *Shade of the Raintree: The Life and Death of Ross Lockridge, Jr., Author of Raintree County.* New York: Viking, 1994.

Notes

1. Ross Lockridge Jr., *Raintree County* (Boston: Houghton Mifflin, 1948), p. 21.

2. *Dictionary of Literary Biography Yearbook, 1980* (Detroit: Gale, 1981), pp. 246–251; "Ross Lockridge, Jr.," in *Dictionary of Literary Biography*, Vol. 143: *American Novelists since World War II, Third Series,* ed. James R. Giles and Wanda H. Giles (Detroit: Gale, 1994), pp. 111–117.

Grace Lumpkin

To Make My Bread

Urbana and Chicago: University of Illinois Press, 1995

Originally published: 1932

Genre: Historical Fiction

Quote

> She went out of the door into the barren front yard where the ground met her feet. She missed the soft ground of the mountains that was rich with growth. There was plenty of mud on the roads here, as in the streets of the village. But on the mountains the black soil sank under her feet, and in it grew small flowers and plants she liked to pick in the spring.[1]

Synopsis

The McClures, a poor Appalachian family, live a subsistence-level lifestyle, filled with community, nature, and religion, until they are forced by poverty to abandon their mountain home to move to town and work as poorly paid and exploited mill workers. In the course of this journey into modern society, they meet pain, more poverty, and oppression, which results in family members becoming increasingly radicalized. Eventually, one sister is killed during a mill strike, causing her brother to become a Communist and carry on the struggle.

Critical Commentary

By the early twentieth century, the American South was, for practical purposes, an economic colony of the North. Reconstruction had subrogated the local economy and culture to the needs of an expanding Northern industrial society. The people of Appalachia were one of the groups most affected—first, by the exploitation of their land by extractive industries (such as coal mining) and second, by the exploitation of their labor in the new developing Southern industries such as textile manufacturing. In *To Make My Bread*, Lumpkin dramatically documents these changes through the lives of several generations of the McClure family.

Through her vivid descriptions and accurate portrayals of traditional Southern folkways, Lumpkin provides insight into the life of mountain farmers, contrasting this lifestyle with the new challenges presented by the emerging market economy, such as having to purchase food rather than being self-sufficient or living in a money economy rather than one based largely on barter. In addition, once they move to town, they have to deal with a variety of new technologies, such as electricity, as well as a diversity of ideologies—such as women in the workforce—which are often at odds with their fundamentalist religious and social views. Carefully avoiding romanticism, Lumpkin carefully depicts the joys and hardships of mountain life. Her characterization of Grandpop, who represents the traditional lifestyle, is highly emotive, and she introduces elements such as the Lost Cause myth without falling into typical stereotypes about poor Southern whites.

As the story moves along its arc through the second McClure generation, the reader clearly sees the compromises and hardships facing new factory workers. Lumpkin uses religion as a plot element linking the various generations, with religious arguments made by local preachers to the mill workers, urging them to accept hardship in this world for a reward in the next, echoing those arguments made to slaves in the same region generations before. The character of Brother Basil, who appears only occasionally, is moving , especially when he is depicted as trying to fit into a modern society that will never truly accept him, and by his absence from the narrative, he becomes a particularly interesting and appealing, although ultimately sad, figure.

At the story's conclusion, the third McClure generation, Bonnie and John, develop a practical response for confronting paternalism and exploitation. They reject religion in favor of an emerging political consciousness. Their acceptance of African Americans is in marked contrast to the racism of earlier generations. The murder and violence of the story are not presented in a gratuitous manner and are effectively counterpointed by the understated ending and the author's poignant use of the symbol of John's red armband.

This is a significant book for its sensitive treatment of a number of marginalized social groups (women, Appalachians, poor whites, union workers). Nonetheless, because of her politics, Lumpkin ended up in obscurity. Her Communist past and her writing, with its celebration of marginalized peoples, bothered the political right and eventually made her a victim of Cold War hysteria over Communism. And her later testimony against Communists in the 1950s did not go over with the political left. However, readers who take the time to find this novel will find it a powerful piece of writing with an important message about the need for social justice—and what people will do to achieve it.

Author Sketch

Lumpkin was born into an upper-class Milledgeville, Georgia, family around 1892; her family moved to South Carolina in 1900. After college, she began working for various publications, which led her to become involved with left-wing causes and eventually the Communist Party. She began her writing career in the 1930s, with polemical novels promoting the Communist cause. But in the 1950s, she broke with the party, and in 1953 she testified as a friendly witness before the Subcommittee on Government Operations, providing many specifics about her Communist affiliations. After this break with the party, Lumpkin became increasingly religious and spent much of her later life attacking Communism. She died in 1980.[2]

Other Works by the Author

Some Take a Lover. New York: Macaulay, 1933.
A Sign for Cain. New York: Lee Furman, 1935.
Full Circle: A Novel. Boston: Western Islands, 1962.
The Wedding. Carbondale: Southern Illinois University Press, 1976.
Bein, Albert, and Grace Lumpkin. *Let Freedom Ring: A Play in Three Acts.* New York: S. French, 1936.

Suggestions for Further Reading

Fink, Gary M., and Merl Elwyn Reed. *Race, Class, and Community in Southern Labor History.* Tuscaloosa: University of Alabama Press, 1994.

Hine, Lewis Wickes, and John R. Kemp. *Lewis Hine: Photographs of Child Labor in the New South.* Jackson: University Press of Mississippi, 1986.

Newby, I. A. *Plain Folk in the New South: Social Change and Cultural Persistence, 1880–1915.* Baton Rouge: Louisiana State University Press, 1989.

Simon, Bryant. *A Fabric of Defeat: The Politics of South Carolina Millhands, 1910–1948.* Chapel Hill: University of North Carolina Press, 1998.

Notes

1. Grace Lumpkin, *To Make My Bread* (Urbana and Chicago: University of Illinois Press, 1995), p. 295.

2. http://www.georgiaencyclopedia.com/nge/Article.jsp?id=h-2473

Michael Malone

Dingley Falls

Naperville, IL: Sourcebooks, 2002

Originally published: 1980

Genre: Mainstream/Literary/Speculative Fiction

Quote

Dingleyans had watched the riotous sixties on television and were happy to have missed them. They were proud that in 1976, as all around Great Societies puffed themselves up and blew themselves away, here in Dingley Falls the true America had been safely preserved, like an artifact in a time capsule.[1]

Synopsis

Dingley Falls is a picture-perfect Connecticut town. Under the peaceful façade, however, the town is filled with a wide range of strange behaviors and alliances. Something odd is going on—with strange lights appearing in the forest, threatening hate letters being stuffed in mailboxes, and perfectly healthy people dropping dead. As it turns out it, all of these events are related to a secret germ-warfare lab on the edge of town.

Critical Commentary

Conspiracy theory—American literature and history are filled with it. In *Dingley Falls,* Michael Malone spins conspiracy theory in a new direction by combining elements from John Frankenheimer's movie *Seven Days in May* with the traditional small-town story represented in such titles as Sherwood Anderson's *Winesburg, Ohio.* In short, he gives us a humorous tragedy with elements of science fiction.

In the setting of Dingley Falls, Malone offers readers a fully realized Connecticut town, complete with history and map. Within this beautifully described geography he places well-developed characters who cover the entire socioeconomic, political, and religious spectrum. From the fading aristocracy of the village's industrial past to a Vietnamese immigrant to a local political crank and Nazi—all live together in imperfect harmony. Engaging dialogue and the in-depth development of the characters' backgrounds create an emotional range that sustains reader interest.

Subplots within the story involve infidelity, business problems, and mysterious deaths—all existing in the context of the larger plot, which revolves around a secret government germ-warfare lab on the edge of town that is secretly infecting the population. This combination of plotlines makes for a great piece of black comedy—a meeting place somewhere between *Peyton Place* and *The Andromeda Strain.* Concluding the novel with an insane general in a scoutmaster's uniform dropping a bomb out of a Cessna? As the credit card commercials say, it's "priceless."

Malone makes some serious points about government secrecy, the insularity of small-town life and its attendant hypocrisies, and the inner pain of people forced by life to sacrifice their dreams. But the tone is satiric, and the story is written with both flair and subtlety. There is also a certain irony in placing the novel in 1976—the bicentennial year when a number of colonial descendants were certainly neither free nor able to pursue happiness.

Novels portraying a town or country threatened by some sinister force but saved at the last moment are something of a staple of American popular fiction. One only has to consider the popularity of Clive Cussler and his peerless hero Dirk Pitt—or the box-office success of Vin Diesel's movie *xXx*. But novels focusing on technology and the single uber-hero lack the elements of political satire and humor that one finds in Malone's novel. The result is a well-written and complex commentary on American life that should appeal to the sophisticated reader as well the person just looking for an interesting book for a long vacation.

Author Sketch

Born in November 1942 in North Carolina, Malone was educated at the University of North Carolina and Harvard. He worked as a professor at various colleges, including Yale and Swarthmore, and from 1991 to 1996 was head writer for the television soap opera *One Life to Live*, where his scripts were highly praised by viewers.[2]

Other Works by the Author

Painting the Roses Red. New York: Random House, 1975.
The Delectable Mountains: A Novel. New York: Random House, 1976.
Psychetypes: A New Way of Exploring Personality. New York: Dutton, 1977.
Heroes of Eros: Male Sexuality in the Movies. New York: Dutton, 1979.
Handling Sin: A Novel. Boston: Little, Brown, 1986.
Foolscap: A Novel. Boston: Little, Brown, 1991.
First Lady: A Novel. Naperville, IL: Sourcebooks, 2002.
Red Clay, Blue Cadillac: Stories of Twelve Southern Women. Naperville, IL: Sourcebooks Landmark, 2002.

Suggestions for Further Reading

Cole, Leonard A. *Clouds of Secrecy: The Army's Germ-Warfare Tests over Populated Areas.* Totowa, NJ: Rowman & Littlefield, 1988.

Harris, Robert, and Jeremy Paxman. *A Higher Form of Killing: The Secret Story of Gas and Germ Warfare.* London: Chatto & Windus, 1982.

Michaelsen, Christopher. *The Use of Depleted Uranium Ammunition in Operation Iraqi Freedom: A War Crime?* Canberra: Strategic and Defence Studies Centre, Australian National University, 2005.

Regis, Edward. *The Biology of Doom: The History of America's Secret Germ Warfare Project.* New York: Holt, 1999.

Notes

1. Michael Malone, *Dingley Falls* (Naperville, IL: Sourcebooks, 2002), p. 5.
2. *Contemporary Authors Online,* Gale, 2003.

Dexter Masters

The Accident

New York: Knopf, 1955

Originally published: 1955

Genre: Mainstream/Literary Fiction

Quote

> Sunday's air was the softest of air and the day was a day of sunny glory. Spring was in full flood that day, across the mesas, up and down the canyon walls, in the calls of birds and the mists of flowers in the sheltered fields; the sky was a limitless glow of light and the snow made a dainty fringe on Truchas.[1]

Synopsis

The Accident revolves around the events during a week in 1946 in Los Alamos, New Mexico, following scientist Louis Saxl's exposure to a fatal dose of radiation, which he receives during an experiment that goes wrong. The reactions of various people—David Thiel, a scientist; Dr. Pederson, the physician treating Saxl; and others, including Saxl himself—are documented as Saxl slowly dies. At the same time, the individual story of Saxl is contrasted with the larger story of the development of the atomic bomb and the construction of Los Alamos from nothing.

Critical Commentary

The voice of *The Accident* is sophisticated. The author uses a dramatic nuclear accident to form a nuanced and thoughtful portrayal of the slow death of a single human being—counterbalanced by the fuss and fury of a government entity in full panic and damage-control mode. This emotional yet thoughtful novel openly criticizes the excesses committed in the name of developing the nuclear state.

The contrast of a scientist's gradual death against this backdrop creates an emotional and disturbing view of the human condition. Clinical descriptions of the death process contrast with the natural setting in which the characters find themselves. Despite the development of Los Alamos, the story is still dominated by the grandeur of this setting. It is this juxtaposition of the natural world (and the characters' interactions with it) and the cold, scientific, man-made environment that gives this book its dramatic quality and sense of reality.

The Accident effectively illustrates the fact that when one adopts a technology, one also inevitably adopts the ideology underlying it. The scientists in this novel have been smart enough to build an atomic weapon that works. Yet from the first pages, it's clear that they have little understanding of the effects of their creation, in either a physical or a moral sense. The reader knows from the beginning that the injured man is doomed. The doctors treating him have little more to go on than some basic observations of the effect of radiation on rats. In reality, the patient becomes little more than an experiment to them—a carefully measured case study in how someone dies.

In a larger philosophical sense, it's also clear that the scientists involved in this project—in both the medical effort and the overshadowing bomb development—are morally confused. Their training as scientists has engendered in them the desire to find truth, but their efforts are blunted by their acceptance of the military strictures of compartmentalization and secrecy imposed on them by the government as a condition of their participation. More seriously, they have also accepted the moral blinders that prevent them from looking objectively and rationally at the long-term effects of their work. In the effort to defeat the fascist menace, they have accepted some of the worst philosophical aspects of those regimes to further their own ends, and even though the war is over, they remain trapped in their Faustian bargain.

For today's readers, this book is significant because it portrays the end of individual science and the beginning of the corporate, governmental science establishment that dominates today. The questions the book raises about atomic weapons are equally relevant when applied to modern scientific problems such as the human genome project or the development of new drugs. Science is no longer an effort of individual discovery, but a group effort in which both the objectives of research and the outcomes are controlled by nonscientific entities—either the government in the name of secrecy and defense or a corporation in the name of profit.

Today, we know much more about the history of the nuclear industry (and its abuses) than we did in 1955, when this book was written. In retrospect, Masters seems almost prescient in his ability to correctly outline the consequences of the development of nuclear power. Anyone who reads this book and is willing to apply its moral lessons to aspects of contemporary society, such as the close relationship between university medical researchers and the international pharmaceutical companies that finance their research, will come away deeply troubled and concerned about the future. It's quite clear from this book that no one, then or now, walks away with clean hands.

Author Sketch

Born June 15, 1908, in Springfield, Illinois, Masters was one of the early critics of the atomic bomb. A nephew of the famed American poet Edgar Lee Masters, he worked as a writer in the 1930s at several prestigious publications, including *Time* and *Fortune*. During World War II, he was employed at the Radiation Lab at MIT on the development of radar. After the war, he became an outspoken advocate against atomic weapons, writing a Peabody Award–winning radio series about nuclear weapons in 1947. Between 1958 and 1963, Master directed the Consumers Union, where he had worked since 1936. He died on January 5, 1989, in Springfield, Illinois.[2]

Other Works by the Author

The Cloud Chamber. Boston: Little, Brown, 1971.

Masters, Dexter, and Katharine Way, eds. *One World or None.* Essay Index Reprint Series. Freeport, NY: Books for Libraries Press, 1972.

Suggestions for Further Reading

Conant, Jennet. *109 East Palace: Robert Oppenheimer and the Secret City of Los Alamos.* New York: Simon & Schuster, 2005.

Hacker, Barton C. *The Dragon's Tail: Radiation Safety in the Manhattan Project, 1942–1946.* Berkeley: University of California Press, 1987.

Lawren, William. *The General and the Bomb: A Biography of General Leslie R. Groves, Director of the Manhattan Project.* New York: Dodd, Mead, 1988.

McMillan, Priscilla Johnson. *The Ruin of J. Robert Oppenheimer, and the Birth of the Modern Arms Race.* New York: Viking, 2005.

Sparks, Ralph C. *Twilight Time: A Soldier's Role in the Manhattan Project at Los Alamos.* Los Alamos, NM: Los Alamos Historical Society, 2000.

Wilson, Jane, and Charlotte Serber. *Standing by and Making Do: Women of Wartime Los Alamos.* Los Alamos, NM: Los Alamos Historical Society, 1988.

Notes

1. Dexter Masters, *The Accident* (New York: Knopf, 1955), p. 400.
2. *Contemporary Authors Online,* Gale, 2000; *New York Times,* January 6, 1989, p. D15.

William Maxwell

They Came Like Swallows

Boston: Nonpareil Books, 1988

Originally published: 1937

Genre: Mainstream/Literary Fiction

Quote

> They would not have been that way, he felt, if he had not been doing what she wanted him
> to do. For it was Elizabeth who had determined the shape that his life should take, from
> the very first moment he saw her. And she had altered that shape daily by the sound of her
> voice, and by her hair, and by her eyes which were so large and dark. And by her wisdom
> and her love.[1]

Synopsis

Told from the three perspectives of different family members—young Bunny; Robert, the
older child; and their father—this is the story of the Morisons, who live in a small town in Illinois in 1918, and how the family is impacted and changed by the influenza epidemic that kills
the mother, Elizabeth. The book shows how, over time, their lives are influenced by the spread
of the epidemic—in small ways such as school closings and not being allowed to play outside
to greater and greater changes, culminating in Elizabeth's death from the flu.

Critical Commentary

In this insightful and emotionally charged psychological portrait, created with simplicity
and care, Maxwell uses the death of a mother and its effects on the family to reveal profound
truths about the human experience.

The story of a mother's death during the great influenza of 1918, in addition to being told
from three different perspectives, also moves through different perspectives of time, from the
experience of the youngest child through that of the father, James. The story is deepened by
these layers, and readers come away with a sense of parallel development—like watching intersecting ripples in a pond.

The theme of limitation runs through the novel. Despite their apparent outward freedom,
each of the characters is restricted in some way. The middle son, Robert, for example, has lost a
leg; this doesn't apparently limit his physical mobility, but even when engaged in outside activities like climbing on a rooftop, he is obviously limited in his emotional perspective. Everyone
in this novel, whether restricted physically to a room, house, or yard or emotionally restrained
in a marriage, echoes that limitation within the larger context of family and social relations.
In the end, one of the characters ends up within the confines of a coffin, Maxwell's metaphor
taking concrete shape.

However, the overall tone of this novel is one of love and tranquility: the peaceful, structured, well-running household—like Robert's lead soldiers fixed in their box—contrasted with the ominous threat of the outside world. That threat is symbolized by disease, that is, the ever-present Spanish influenza, which increasingly and more virulently intrudes until the entire family structure has been destroyed. Society, too, crowds in and threatens the family. For example, the crowded train where the mother catches the disease that kills her contrasts with the empty interurban car running on parallel tracks and symbolizing the erosion of well-ordered family life.

Although not intended as a historical novel, *They Came Like Swallows* works as one. It presents a dramatic picture of the Midwest under siege by the Spanish flu, with all the fear and concern that the disease evoked. Despite the prevalence of diseases in our society and the effect they have had over time, there are few novels that deal with the consequences of epidemics. Where, for example, is the great novel about polio or tuberculosis—each of which killed tens of thousands?

It can be argued that this is (probably without the author's intention) something of a Christian allegory. The mother's story and the story told by the three other characters parallel the four gospels, which also tell the same story from various perspectives, while showing the power of a death to shake people from complacency into realizing that change is possible and there is hope of redemption—if they do not forget. Possibilities of religious allegory aside, this is an important piece of modernist writing that can be usefully read by students of literature as well as other individuals interested in a compelling and elegantly written story.

Author Sketch

Maxwell was born on August 16, 1908, in Lincoln, Illinois. Educated at the University of Illinois (BA 1930) and Harvard University (MA 1931), he later taught English at the University of Illinois. In 1936 he became an editor for the *New Yorker* magazine, working with noted authors including John Updike and J. D. Salinger. Maxwell also wrote a number of novels; his first, *Bright Center of Heaven*, was published in 1934. In 1945 Maxwell married Emily Gilman Noyes. They had two daughters, Katharine and Emily. His 1980 novel, *So Long, See You Tomorrow*, won the American Book Award. Maxwell died July 31, 2000, in New York City.[2]

Other Works by the Author

Bright Center of Heaven. New York: Harper & Brothers, 1934.
The Château. New York: Knopf, 1961.
The Folded Leaf. New York: Vintage Books, 1959.
All the Days and Nights: The Collected Stories of William Maxwell. New York: Knopf, 1995.

Suggestions for Further Reading

Barry, John M. *The Great Influenza: The Epic Story of the Deadliest Plague in History.* New York: Viking, 2004.
Burkhardt, Barbara. *William Maxwell: A Literary Life.* Urbana: University of Illinois Press, 2005.
Crosby, Alfred W. *America's Forgotten Pandemic: The Influenza of 1918.* New York: Cambridge University Press, 1989.

Duncan, Kirsty. *Hunting the 1918 Flu: One Scientist's Search for a Killer Virus.* Toronto and Buffalo: University of Toronto Press, 2003.

Notes

1. William Maxwell, *They Came Like Swallows* (Boston: Nonpareil Books, 1988), p. 173.
2. http://archives.cnn.com/2000/books/news/08/01/obit.maxwell.ap/;   http://www.britannica.com/eb/article-9104553

Robert McAlmon

Village

Albuquerque: University of New Mexico Press, 1990

Originally published: 1924

Genre: Mainstream/Literary Fiction

Quote

> With the coming of morning it was discovered that Deacon Pothatch's hayrack had been
> run into the town creek; and there it remained for some months, long after the creek had
> frozen over and was being used for a skating pond. Not until then did the Deacon remove
> it with malice aforethought, skaters believed, since two people skated right into the hole
> made in the ice, and up to their necks in freezing water.[1]

Synopsis

Tracing the developments in a small North Dakota town over a period of 15 years, McAlmon
gives readers a glimpse into the lives of villagers, both poor and rich. Most of the events he
documents are tragedies, ranging from the death of a child to alcoholism to suicide, although
occasional humorous vignettes, like the farmer's ruining winter ice skating as revenge for an
earlier prank, are also included.

Critical Commentary

Great writing is not always cheerful. Well-recognized novels, Dickens's *Bleak House* for example, are as often celebrated for their unsparing and truthful depictions of the harshness of
life as they are for their descriptions of joy. Robert McAlmon's *Village* is written in this same
vein. It is its very bleakness and negativity that give it its fascination and interest to the reader,
much in the same way that the paintings of Goya, depicting blood and carnage, give those
works their power.

McAlmon takes the story of small-town rural life, a well-used literary genre that often is
filled with sugary sentimentality, and turns it on its head. *Village*, a story of evil and loneliness,
rather than celebrating a nostalgic sense of community, honestly confronts the harsh realities
and failures of people living without hope. This book of extremes will resonate well with any
reader interested in psychological fiction. Although not strictly in the horror genre, the book
is sure to appeal to people who like their fiction dark—really dark.

In interrelated vignettes that occur over a period of 15 years, McAlmon tells the stories
of a cast of characters who must be among the most unhappy people in twentieth-century
literature. The town of Wentworth is peopled by losers of all types—failures in love, in business, and in life generally. McAlmon leads readers into a world of cynicism and hatred, filled
with various forms of scandal—sexual and other—that blight the lives of the characters. The

defining attribute of this small-town society is its hypocrisy, usually beneath the surface, but sometimes coming into the open through seemingly random acts of violence. Wentworth is the anti–Walnut Grove.

The format of the novel, which contains no plot in the conventional sense, lends itself well to this style, allowing the author to move from person to person and through time in an almost cinematic style. With writing distinguished by its spareness and simplicity, McAlmon displays the isolation and stagnation of life on the American plains. His descriptions of the North Dakota landscape add to this, with the barrenness of nature paralleling the characters' moral emptiness. One wouldn't think that a book this bleak would be interesting, but its very negativity becomes intriguing. One is continually drawn into the story, fascinated by the events of the novel. McAlmon shows how, as a writer, one can effectively use negativity, in the same way a painter uses blank space, to create a work of engaging interest.

In the book's brutal honesty, McAlmon spares no person and no institution. He even expresses a highly negative view of progress, showing how modernity and improvement have actually served to make things worse for the citizens of Wentworth. The daily train, rather than being a connection to the outside world, is where the local girls go to pick up traveling salesmen for quick assignations. The outside world and its cities, especially Chicago, are seen as places that instead of bringing in culture and energy, simply drain Wentworth of its young people. The theme of leaving, of abandonment, plays constantly throughout the novel. Thus, this is a novel that might also be engaging for those who have some interest in the history of urbanization as it shows the effects that migration to cities has on the life of a small town.

Almost violent in its intensity, at times the novel exhibits a somewhat documentary quality, seemingly a precursor to Truman Capote's *In Cold Blood*. A chilling picture of life in a nihilistic American heartland, this is definitely not a book for everyone, but it should appeal to some readers—perhaps fans of the *Blair Witch Project*—who don't mind a dose of evil in their leisure reading.

Author Sketch

McAlmon was born in Clifton, Kansas, in 1896, the youngest of 10 children of an itinerant Midwestern minister. He enrolled in the University of Minnesota (1916) and later the University of Southern California, without graduating. In 1919, after military service, he began a literary career, moving to New York in 1920. In 1921 he married the English poet Annie Winifred Ellerman and shortly thereafter moved to Paris, where he established friendships with such luminary writers as James Joyce. McAlmon, with the financial support of his wife's family, established a small publishing house, Contact, that published his own work as well as that of other writers.

In 1926 McAlmon divorced Ellerman, returning to the United States in 1940. He worked briefly for his family business in Arizona, but developed tuberculosis, which eventually killed him on February 2, 1956, in Hot Springs, California. Although McAlmon received little recognition for his own works—their homosexual themes made them effectively banned in the United States—he helped to promote the work of many other writers of the 1920s, including James Joyce and Ezra Pound.[2]

Other Works by the Author

Explorations. London: Egoist Press, 1921.

A Hasty Bunch. Paris: Contact Editions, 1922; Carbondale and Edwardsville: Southern Illinois University Press, 1977.

A Companion Volume. Paris: Contact Editions, 1923.

Post-Adolescence. Paris: Contact Editions, 1923.

Distinguished Air Grim Fairy Tales. Paris: Three Mountains Press, 1925; enlarged as *There Was a Rustle of Black Silk Stockings.* New York: Belmont, 1963.

The Portrait of a Generation, including the Revolving Mirror. Paris: Contact Editions, 1926.

North America Continent of Conjecture. Paris: Contact Editions, 1929.

Indefinite Huntress and Other Stories. Paris: Crosby Continental Editions, 1932.

Not Alone Lost. Norfolk, CT: New Directions, 1937.

Being Geniuses Together: An Autobiography. London: Secker & Warburg, 1938; republished as *Being Geniuses Together 1920–1930,* revised with additional material by Kay Boyle. Garden City: Doubleday, 1968; London: Joseph, 1970.

Suggestions for Further Reading

Carpenter, Humphrey. *Geniuses Together: American Writers in Paris in the 1920s.* Boston: Houghton Mifflin, 1987.

Fitch, Noel Riley. *Sylvia Beach and the Lost Generation: A History of Literary Paris in the Twenties and Thirties.* New York: Norton, 1983.

Knoll, Robert. *McAlmon and the Lost Generation: A Self Portrait.* Lincoln: University of Nebraska Press, 1962.

Smoller, Sanford J. *Adrift among Geniuses: Robert McAlmon, Writer and Publisher of the Twenties.* University Park: Pennsylvania State University Press,1975.

Taylor, Kimberly. "Passion and Pathos: The Rhetoric of Self-Preservation in the Writings of Robert McAlmon 1920–1938." MA thesis, Graduate School at the College of Charleston and The Citadel, 2002.

Notes

1. Robert McAlmon, *Village* (Albuquerque: University of New Mexico Press, 1990), p. 162.

2. Gabriele Griffin, *Who's Who in Lesbian and Gay and Writing* (London: Routledge, 2002); *Contemporary Authors Online,* Gale, 2006, reproduced in *Biography Resource Center* (Farmington Hills, MI: Thomson Gale, 2006), http://galenet.galegroup.com.ezproxy.uvm.edu/servlet/BioRC; *New York Times,* March 11, 1921, p. 11.

Mary McCarthy

The Groves of Academe

San Diego: Harcourt Brace Jovanovich, 1992

Originally published: 1951

Genre: Mainstream/Literary Fiction

Quote

> This finding convinced the trustees, who included the heads of two progressive schools, that the founder was ahead of his time, a stimulating man in the tradition of Pasteur and the early vivisectionists, whom history would give his due. He left the college the legacy of a strong scientific bent and a reputation for enthusiasm and crankishness that reflected itself in budgetary difficulties and in the prevalence of an "undesirable" type of student.[1]

Synopsis

Henry Mulcahy is a professor of English at a small progressive college in the 1950s. The college decides not to renew his teaching contract, and this leads to a controversy in the college community, especially among his faculty colleagues, who feel he is being unfairly persecuted for leftist political views. This controversy winds its way through faculty meetings, academic discussions, and a hilarious depiction of a literary conference. Eventually, it is revealed that, rather than being a Communist, Mulcahy is an apolitical opportunist who is using the college's own progressive views and guilt to blackmail it into keeping him.

Critical Commentary

Mary McCarthy uses *The Groves of Academe* to make fun of Senator Joseph McCarthy. This 1951 novel is a funny send-up of both the politics of anti-Communism and the internal politics of a private college. Those college politics are still around, which saves this book from being just Cold War nostalgia and in fact makes it a timeless classic.

The book tells the story of a badly run witch hunt. Mary McCarthy uses the setting of a small private college as a symbolic representation of the larger drama going on in the society at the time—much in the same way Arthur Miller used his play *The Crucible* during the same period. The story allows the author to develop the character of Henry Mulcahy, who rather than being a victim, is revealed by the end of the novel to be a fairly awful and unethical person who is using smear tactics, reminiscent of McCarthyism, to further his own career.

Mary McCarthy has created a vivid picture of the infighting and gamesmanship that surround a college personnel decision. She takes a fairly routine issue of reappointment and turns it into high drama. Her characterizations of various faculty members as well as descriptions of the college itself are not only funny but also a satiric tour de force of the abuses and compromises involved in higher education.

But it's doubtful that her fictional college would have given her an honorary degree.

Author Sketch

Born June 21, 1912, in Seattle, Washington, McCarthy was orphaned at six and raised by relatives. She graduated from Vassar College in 1933. McCarthy went on to become a successful writer and editor for such journals as *Partisan Review, Nation,* and *New Republic,* as well as having a career as a novelist. Her 1963 partly autobiographical novel about life at Vassar, *The Group,* gained her a wide readership. McCarthy won the National Medal for Literature and the MacDowell Medal in 1984. She died of cancer October 25, 1989, in New York City.[2]

Other Works by the Author

The Company She Keeps. New York: Simon & Schuster, 1942.

The Oasis. New York: Random House, 1949.

Cast a Cold Eye. New York: Harcourt, 1950.

The Groves of Academe. New York: Harcourt, Brace, 1952.

Venice Observed. Paris and New York: G. & R. Bernier, 1956.

Memories of a Catholic Girlhood. New York: Harcourt Brace Jovanovich, 1957.

The Stones of Florence. New York: Harcourt, 1959.

Vietnam. New York: Harcourt, 1967.

Winter Visitors. New York: Harcourt Brace Jovanovich, 1970.

Medina. New York: Harcourt Brace Jovanovich, 1972.

The Seventeenth Degree. New York: Harcourt Brace Jovanovich, 1974.

Ideas and the Novel. London: Weidenfeld and Nicolson, 1981.

Suggestions for Further Reading

McCormick, Charles H. *This Nest of Vipers: McCarthyism and Higher Education in the Mundel Affair, 1951–52.* Urbana: University of Illinois Press, 1989.

Redish, Martin H. *The Logic of Persecution: Free Expression and the McCarthy Era.* Stanford, CA: Stanford University Press, 2005.

Notes

1. Mary McCarthy, *The Groves of Academe* (San Diego: Harcourt Brace Jovanovich, 1992), p. 63.

2. *Dictionary of Literary Biography,* Vol. 2: *American Novelists since World War II, First Series,* ed. Jeffrey Helterman and Richard Layman (Detroit: Gale, 1978), pp. 310–317.

Jay McInerney

Story of My Life

New York: Atlantic Monthly Press, 1988

Originally published: 1988

Genre: Mainstream/Literary Fiction

Quote

I think Dean's doorman kind of likes me, he winks at me and lets me go right up. Guy's from one of those Communist countries that sounds like a disease, what's it called, where they used to have vampires and Dean's always loaning him money because he's completely in debt to these Korean gamblers who are going to kill him. Welcome to the free world, Igor.[1]

Synopsis

In 1980s New York, Alison Poole, an aspiring young actress, spends her time trying to get acting jobs, partying, and dealing with parental indifference, as well as with friends who have a variety of imbalances—social, chemical, and financial. Her life of excess ends when Alison crashes and burns, winding up in a Minnesota rehab facility.

Critical Commentary

In retrospect the 1980s are often seen as the decade of excess, with drugs, sex, and junk bonds dominating the culture. This novel is a small monument to another excess of that decade—a literary excess, which was marked by young writers publishing work that, in an earlier era, would never have made it out of their desk drawers. This coming-of-age story set among the spires of 1980s Manhattan stars the young people who lived there with too much time and money, but little or no common sense, and it is a wry tribute to a decade of decadence.

The only way to describe this story's pace is frantic. This is a work of nonstop interior monologue narrated by the heroine, Alison, who slightly resembles Holly GoLightly of *Breakfast at Tiffany's,* but who is apparently possessed by Satan and on the mother of all caffeine, jags. McInerney follows her and other superficial people in search of drugs, parties, sex, and money—not necessarily in that order. With no real moral purpose or agenda, he describes the way things are with just enough plot to move things along as the characters wander about Manhattan to clubs and apartments on their various quests.

The author has taken all of the worst excesses of the decade and thrown them onto a small group of people. Most of these kids are the neglected children of affluent families—but nothing really tells us anything more than their superficial reactions to events, including such crises as losing an apartment, running out of cocaine, and discovering that the roommate has stolen the rent money to buy designer clothes. The reader is pulled along by these events just to see what happens to these people.

Elements of plot and character aside, this is a funny novel, delivered crisply and intelligently. The scenarios, if not completely realistic, are cleverly drawn. Although it could hardly be called nostalgic, this book is likely to stir memories in older generations, while piquing the curiosity of the young.

Author Sketch

McInerney, born January 13, 1955, in Hartford, Connecticut, is a graduate of Williams College (BA 1976) and also attended Syracuse University. He worked as a newspaper reporter as well as in the publishing industry. He has written fiction for magazines such as *Esquire* and *Atlantic* and is the author of a number of novels. He lived in Tennessee before returning to Manhattan where he presently resides.[2]

Other Works by the Author

Bright Lights, Big City: A Novel. New York: Vintage Contemporaries, 1984.
Ransom: A Novel. New York: Vintage Books, 1985.
Brightness Falls: A Novel. New York: Knopf, 1992.
Cowboys, Indians and Commuters: The Penguin Book of New American Voices. New York: Viking, 1994.
The Last of the Savages: A Novel. New York: Knopf, 1996.
Model Behavior: A Novel and 7 Stories. New York: Knopf, 1998.
Bacchus & Me: Adventures in the Wine Cellar. New York: Lyons Press, 2000.
Marqusee, Mike, and Jay McInerney. *New York, an Illustrated Anthology.* Topsfield, MA: Salem House, 1988.

Suggestions for Further Reading

Greiner, Donald J. *Women without Men: Female Bonding and the American Novel of the 1980s.* Columbia: University of South Carolina Press, 1993.
London, Herbert Ira. *The Broken Apple: New York City in the 1980s.* New Brunswick, NJ: Transaction, 1989.
Nachbar, John G., and Kevin Lausé. *Popular Culture: An Introductory Text.* Bowling Green, OH: Bowling Green State University Popular Press, 1992.
Troy, Gil. *Morning in America: How Ronald Reagan Invented the 1980s.* Princeton, NJ: Princeton University Press, 2005.

Notes

1. Jay McInerney, *Story of My Life: A Novel* (New York: Atlantic Monthly Press, 1988), p. 126.
2. http://www.lovereading.co.uk/book/0747541574/isbn; http://oneweb.utc.edu/~tnwriter/authors/mcinerney.jay.html; "Jay McInerney," in *Contemporary Authors New Revision Series,* Vol. 116, ed. Scot Peacock (Detroit: Gale, 2003), pp. 221–225.

Truman John Nelson

The Sin of the Prophet

Boston: Little, Brown, 1952

Originally published: 1952

Genre: Historical Fiction

Quote

Not this in easy symbolism. The wave was a black wave on a white beach at night. The red bricks of the old revolutionary buildings in Boston where it mostly happened had faded into dusty pink and were dwarfed and shrunken by new cubes of granite setting forth the temples of law, money and religion.[1]

Critical Commentary

Thoughtful readers of history realize that revolutions are never neatly finished. They end, but they leave a multitude of loose ends for subsequent generations to sort out. The American Revolution is no exception to this general principle—its constitutional settlement was a compromise that left the issue of slavery festering like a boil, which eventually had to be lanced by the swords of the Civil War. *The Sin of the Prophet* performs a great service to readers by reminding us of this fact.

In this detailed historical novel, Nelson accurately depicts the hunt for a fugitive slave in antebellum Boston. His lush descriptions of the backdrop, the characters, and the events are wrought by a remarkable attention to period detail and an excellent ear for nineteenth-century language. The fast-paced story quickly draws the reader in, by the varying motivations of the characters, which are explained in depth. Today we say we are threatened by terrorism. This novel reminds us that terror is not unique to the twenty-first century. Nelson illustrates the inevitability of human conflict—especially the moral conflict that actions of the state create in the body politic.

Author Sketch

Born February 18, 1911, in Lynn, Massachusetts, Nelson was a professional writer and actor—working, among other places, with the noted Mercury Theatre—as well as a noted conservationist and civil libertarian. He died July 11, 1987.[2]

Other Works by the Author

The Sin of the Prophet. Boston: Little, Brown, 1952.
The Passion by the Brook: A Novel About Brook Farm. Garden City, NY: Doubleday, 1953.
The Surveyor. Garden City, NY: Doubleday, 1960.

The Long Hot Summer. Berlin: Seven Seas Books, 1967.

The Torture of Mothers. Boston: Beacon Press, 1968.

The Old Man; John Brown at Harper's Ferry. New York: Holt, 1973.

Nelson, Truman John, and William John Schafer. *The Truman Nelson Reader.* Amherst: University of Massachusetts Press, 1989.

Suggestions for Further Reading

Bordewich, Fergus M. *Bound for Canaan: The Underground Railroad and the War for the Soul of America.* New York: Amistad, 2005.

Coffin, Levi, William Still, George Hendrick, and Willene Hendrick. *Fleeing for Freedom: Stories of the Underground Railroad.* Chicago: Ivan R. Dee, 2004.

Grover, Kathryn. *The Fugitive's Gibraltar: Escaping Slaves and Abolitionism in New Bedford, Massachusetts.* Amherst: University of Massachusetts Press, 2001.

Hamilton, Virginia. *Anthony Burns: The Defeat and Triumph of a Fugitive Slave.* New York: Knopf, 1988.

Notes

1. Truman Nelson, *The Sin of the Prophet* (Boston: Little, Brown, 1952), p. 1.

2. *Contemporary Authors Online,* Gale, 2003.

Jay Neugeboren

Big Man

Boston: Mariner/Houghton Mifflin, 2000

Originally published: 1966

Genre: Mainstream/Literary Fiction

Quote

> Then he cackles the way he does. Oh yeah. I'm back in the bigtime. Me and Louie's Leap-
> ers, we burning up the league, win seventeen games in a row. These last few months,
> between games and Willa and those sessions with Rosen, you want to keep up with me,
> you got to run, man.[1]

Synopsis

Mack Davis, a young African American man, once had great promise. But after he got caught up in a basketball betting scandal at the university, he was expelled. Now he works at a marginal job in a car wash, a situation that has made him bitter and disillusioned. Years later, when he is offered an opportunity to play for a local semi-pro team, he is initially reluctant, but he decides to participate and thus finds moral redemption and more hope for his future.

Critical Commentary

Sports fiction is rarely written with literary grace. It's all too easy for authors to fall into clichés about sportsmanship or to substitute play-by-play description for the deeper work of novelists—examining serious questions of the nature of human existence. In *Big Man*, Jay Neugeboren deftly avoids the usual pitfalls of sports fiction and creates one of the best novels about basketball, and indeed about sports, in the last half-century.

Mack Davis, a basketball star felled by a gambling scandal, illustrates the ability of the human spirit to overcome obstacles. Neugeboren follows the consequences of that action, leading ultimately to Davis's having some hope of a future. He examines the psychology of the athlete with empathy and acuity, focusing not so much on basketball as a subject as on basketball as a process—a process of redemption.

Although based on real events (a 1950s New York betting scandal), the story avoids being either overly documentary or preachy. Neugeboren lets the people and events speak for themselves, developing a dramatic narrative that takes what could be a sad story and makes it into one of nobility and serious reflection on human character. He writes with empathy, a good ear for dialogue, and a sense of realism.

In a society obsessed with sports and gambling, it's surprising that there are so few novels dealing with both. For that reason, Neugeboren's novel should be required reading in every college locker room in the country.

Author Sketch

Neugeboren was born on May 30, 1938, in Brooklyn and educated at Columbia University (BA 1959) and Indiana University (MA 1963). After graduation he worked as a teacher in New York City before becoming a full-time writer. He has been at the University of Massachusetts since 1971 as a professor of English and has also taught at Columbia, Stanford, and Freiburg. Neugeboren has received numerous awards and citations, including a Guggenheim Fellowship (1978) and the Ken Book Award from the National Alliance for the Mentally Ill (2000), for *Transforming Madness: New Lives for People Living with Mental Illness*. He has also appeared in *Prize Stories: The O. Henry Awards*.[2]

Other Works by the Author

Corky's Brother. New York: Farrar Straus & Giroux, 1969.

Sam's Legacy; a Novel. New York: Holt Rinehart & Winston, 1974.

Before My Life Began: A Novel. New York: Simon & Schuster, 1985.

Imagining Robert: My Brother, Madness, and Survival: A Memoir. New York: Holt, 1998.

News from the New American Diaspora and Other Tales of Exile. Literary Modernism Series. Austin: University of Texas Press, 2005.

Foley, Martha, and Jay Neugeboren. *The Story of Story Magazine: A Memoir*. New York: Norton, 1980.

Suggestions for Further Reading

Blackwell, James. *On, Brave Old Army Team: The Cheating Scandal That Rocked the Nation: West Point, 1951*. Novato, CA: Presidio, 1996.

Grundman, Adolph H. *The Golden Age of Amateur Basketball: The AAU Tournament, 1921–1968*. Lincoln: University of Nebraska Press, 2004.

Isaacs, Neil David. *All the Moves: A History of College Basketball*. Rev. and updated ed. New York: Harper & Row, 1984.

Kirby, James. *Fumble: Bear Bryant, Wally Butts, and the Great College Football Scandal*. San Diego: Harcourt Brace Jovanovich, 1986.

Notes

1. Jay Neugeboren, *Big Man* (Boston: Mariner/ Houghton Mifflin, 2000), p. 117.

2. *Dictionary of Literary Biography*, Vol. 28: *Twentieth-Century American-Jewish Fiction Writers*, ed. Daniel Walden (Detroit: Gale, 1984), pp. 181–188.

Fae Myenne Ng

Bone

New York: HarperPerennial, 1993

Originally published: 1993

Genre: Mainstream/ Literary Fiction

Quote

> I believe in holding still. I believe that the secrets we hold in our hearts are our anchors, that even the unspoken between us is a measure of our every promise to the living and the dead. And all our promises, like all our hopes, move us through life with the power of an ocean liner pushing through the sea.[1]

Synopsis

This story revolves around a family of Chinese immigrants with three daughters, Leila, Ona, and Nina. As the book opens, Ona has committed suicide by jumping from the thirteenth story of an apartment building. The varying reactions of the family to this event include shame, guilt, and concern that somehow they were responsible through their own inaction or inattention. Each also fears that their family is somehow fated to unhappiness in a foreign land. Although the reason behind Ona's act is never explained, the result is a voyage of self-discovery for all concerned.

Critical Commentary

On the surface, *Bone* can be read as a coming-of-age tale of a young Chinese woman. Characters are central to the story, especially Leila, the protagonist, and Ng provides vivid details about her and her often-upsetting interactions with her mother and other family members. Domestic sensibilities play out in interior spaces, both emotionally and in the isolated private spaces of homes—and in the larger private space that is Chinatown. The fact that a vast part of a large American city is, in essence, an interior space is ironic, and Ng develops this irony with wit and authority.

Ng also portrays with intensity these first-generation Americans attempting to find their own identity in the context of their parents' lack of assimilation. Her characters are drawn with compassion and hopefulness, so what could have been a succession of stereotypes instead is a group of fully realized individuals with their own idiosyncrasies. These characters may not be initially likeable, but each grows in stature as the novel progresses.

Intertwining past and present, Ng takes the incomprehensible act of suicide and subjects it to an analysis that underscores the difficulty of understanding someone's motives in committing what is said to be the most selfish of human acts. In what could have been a dark tragedy, Ng has instead given us an enlightening and very human story.

Author Sketch

Ng (pronounced "Ing") was born in 1957 and is a first-generation American, educated at the Columbia University School of Arts, where she received an MA in 1984. Since 1989 she has lived in Brooklyn. Ng has received several awards and grants, including the Pushcart Prize, a National Endowment for the Arts award, a Lila Wallace–Reader's Digest Literary Fellowship, and a Fellowship in Literature from the American Academy of Arts and Letters.[2]

Other Works by the Author

In Her Mother's House: The Politics of Asian American Mother–Daughter Writing. Lanham. MD: AltaMira Press, 1999.

Suggestions for Further Reading

Cheung, King-Kok. *Articulate Silences: Hisaye Yamamoto, Maxine Hong Kingston, Joy Kogawa.* Ithaca, NY: Cornell University Press, 1993.

Christ, Carol P. *Diving Deep and Surfacing: Women Writers on Spiritual Quest.* Boston: Beacon, 1980.

Kafka, Phillipa. *(Un)Doing the Missionary Position: Gender Asymmetry in Contemporary Asian American Women's Writing.* Westport, CT: Greenwood Press, 1997.

Lim, Shirley Geok-Lin. "Feminist and Ethnic Literary Theories in Asian American Literature." *Feminist Studies* 19, no. 3 (Fall 1993): 571–595.

Whelehan, Imelda. *Modern Feminist Thought: From the Second Wave to "Post-Feminism."* New York: New York University Press, 1995.

Notes

1. Fae Myenne Ng, *Bone* (New York: HarperPerennial, 1993), p. 193.

2. http://voices.cla.umn.edu/vg/Bios/entries/ng_fae_myenne.html; *Contemporary Authors Online,* Gale, 2006; *New York Times,* January 29, 1993, p. C26.

Frank Norris

McTeague: A Story of San Francisco

New York: Norton, 1997

Originally published: 1902

Genre: Mainstream/Literary Fiction

Quote

> Below the fine fabric of all that was good in him ran the foul stream of hereditary evil, like a
> sewer. The vices and sins of his father and of his father's father, to the third and fourth and
> five hundredth generation, tainted him. The evil of an entire race flowed in his veins, Why
> should it be? He did not desire it, Was he to blame?[1]

Synopsis

McTeague is a dentist of questionable background operating a small practice in San Francisco. He has friends, a reasonable number of patients satisfied with his work, and generally,
good prospects in the world. He seems to prosper, both in his practice and in his marriage to
the attractive Trina, who brings a reasonable dowry to the marriage. As time goes on, however,
the marriage and the practice collapse, victim to McTeague's increasing alcoholism and lack
of attention to his marriage, which reveal the horrible character flaws that he has been hiding.
Ultimately, his increasing desperation leads him to murder and to his pursuit by a relentless
adversary across California and into the high Sierras, where events come to a thrilling and
surprising conclusion.

Critical Commentary

In *McTeague* Frank Norris has created a wonderfully realistic novel about life in the lower
depths of early twentieth-century San Francisco. His descriptions of life in the city are fully
in the tradition of naturalism, echoing the realism that one finds in other novelists of the period—such as Zola. However, beyond these period descriptions, Norris has written a wonderful character study sure to appeal to modern readers.

This is a book set in a low social milieu: from the central character of McTeague, a shady
dentist, to junk-collecting Maria Macapa to McTeague's wife Trina—all are urban poor trying
to keep up appearances. Norris has created a set of interesting and involving characters with
compelling backstories—from McTeague and his past as a shady dentist to the various characters that inhabit his particular quarter of San Francisco. Fundamentally, what Norris has done
is recreate, in tone and spirit, a realistic novel similar in style to the realistic novels of Zola and
other French novelists of the period, but distinctive in its American voice.

From this story of urban life, the narrative quickly devolves into a murder mystery—where,
although the murderer is not long in doubt, the adventures encountered in his escape move the

story from the urban slums of San Francisco to the high deserts of southern California. This juxtaposition of modern urban life with a struggle against nature makes this a compelling and interesting read. It is all in all a fascinating novel for those interested in California history or stories of urban life by one of the great practitioners of the realistic style.

Author Sketch

Born in Chicago on March 5, 1870, Norris moved to California at an early age because his father was a businessman with interests in the state. He was well educated, including art study at Atelier Julian in Paris (1887) before entering the University of California–Berkeley (1890). After leaving Berkeley, traveling abroad, and attending Harvard (1894), Norris began a career as a journalist and writer—including the publication of *McTeague* and other works that gained him some note for his realistic style, including *The Octopus* and *The Pit,* both part of an uncompleted trilogy about California. Norris died of appendicitis October 25, 1902.[2]

Other Works by the Author

Yvernelle, a Legend of Feudal France. Philadelphia: J. B. Lippincott, 1892.

Moran of the Lady Letty; A Story of Adventure Off the California Coast. New York: Doubleday & McClure, 1898.

Blix. New York: Doubleday & McClure, 1899.

Mcteague, a Story of San Francisco. New York: Doubleday & McClure, 1899.

The Octopus; A Story of California. New York,: Doubleday, Page, 1901.

The Pit; A Story of Chicago. New York,: Doubleday, Page, 1903.

The Joyous Miracle. London: Harper and Brothers, 1906.

The Third Circle. New York: J. Lane Company, 1909.

Shanghaied; A Story of Adventure Off the California Coast. London: T. Nelson & Sons, 1910.

The Surrender of Santiago; An Account of the Historic Surrender of Santiago to General Shafter, July 17, 1898. San Francisco: Paul Elder, 1917.

A Man's Woman; and, Yvernelle, a Legend of Feudal France. Introduction by Christopher Morley. Garden City, NY: Doubleday, Doran, 1928.

Vandover and the Brute. Introduction by H. L. Mencken. Garden City, NY: Doubleday, Doran, 1928.

Six Essays on the Responsibilities of the Novelist. New York: Alicat Bookshop Press, 1949.

The Letters of Frank Norris. Edited by Franklin Dickerson Walker. San Francisco: The Book Club of California, 1956.

Frank Norris Collected Letters. Edited and compiled by Jesse S. Crisler. San Francisco: Book Club of California, 1986.

Novels and Essays. New York: Library of America, 1986.

Glasgow, Ellen Anderson Gholson, and Frank Norris. *The Voice of the People.* New York: Doubleday, Page, 1900.

Suggestions for Further Reading

Graham, Don. *The Fiction of Frank Norris: The Aesthetic Context.* Columbia: University of Missouri Press, 1978.

Hankins, Barry. *God's Rascal: J. Frank Norris & the Beginnings of Southern Fundamentalism.* Lexington: University Press of Kentucky, 1996.

Hochman, Barbara. *The Art of Frank Norris, Storyteller.* Columbia: University of Missouri Press, 1988.

Jessup, Alexander, ed. *Representative American Short Stories.* Boston: Allyn and Bacon, 1923.

McElrath, Joseph R. *Frank Norris: A Descriptive Bibliography.* Pittsburgh: University of Pittsburgh Press, 1992.

McElrath, Joseph R., and Jesse S. Crisler. *Frank Norris: A Life.* Urbana: University of Illinois Press, 2006.

Pizer, Donald. *The Novels of Frank Norris.* Bloomington: Indiana University Press, 1966.

Schneider, Robert W. *Five Novelists of the Progressive Era.* New York: Columbia University Press, 1965.

Notes

1. Frank Norris, *McTeague: A Story of San Francisco* (New York: Norton, 1997), p. 22.

2. *Dictionary of Literary Biography,* Vol. 71: *American Literary Critics and Scholars, 1880–1900,* ed. John W. Rathburn and Monica M. Grecu (Detroit: Gale, 1988), pp. 168–179.

Myra Page

Moscow Yankee

Urbana: University of Illinois Press, 1995

Originally published: 1935

Genre: Mainstream/Literary Fiction

Quote

Snow, like charity, may cover a multitude of unpleasant facts. And so the brigade found—
rather, the supply depot. As the brigadiers crossed the plant yard toward the wide exit,
Natasha lifted her head, threw back her shoulders and breathed in the exciting air. First
hints of crocuses under the snow. Spring![1]

Synopsis

During the Great Depression, the dearth of work in Detroit sends Andy and two friends to
Moscow to work in a Moscow automobile plant. Whereas his colleagues (and the other Americans working in Moscow) simply see this as a temporary job—and spend most of their time
complaining about the situation—Andy gradually comes to like the new attitudes and philosophy of the workers he meets. He comes to see Russia as a place where the average worker can
make a difference without being oppressed by the capitalist bosses. In his conversion, he is also
encouraged, professionally and romantically, by his colleague Natasha, who is a "new soviet
woman" determined to build socialism. Eventually, Andy marries Natasha and decides to stay
in Russia permanently.

Critical Commentary

Moscow Yankee, an engaging realistic novel of the 1930s, reveals the hopes and dreams of a
people during a time when many believed that Communism could work and was a viable alternative to capitalism. Andy, unlike most characters in American literature about immigrants,
leaves America—for Russia, in this case. In his story, the reader finds a compelling study of the
awakening of political consciousness as well as an endearing romance.

The novel addresses the materialism of 1930s America. In his old life, the emphasis seems
to be on buying more and better—a philosophy that is rapidly making Andy miserable—as he
considers going to night school to please his girlfriend Elsie and become a man on the make.
Instead, he takes a left turn from Detroit, both physically and politically, to take a job in a Russian truck factory.

Andy discovers a different philosophy at work in Russia—one that in some respects is no
better than he had in Detroit. He finds that Communism, despite its glorious promises, still
involves its share of bureaucracy and difficulty in getting things done. Despite this, he meets
a group of people who are truly dedicated to a new vision of humankind. His fellow workers,

except for the occasional slacker and malcontent, are truly committed to their communist ideals, and this gradually wears off on Andy.

At the same time, Andy finds a new love in his pursuit of Natasha and also a different conception of the role of women. Of course, like Americans, Russians are not without their contradictions, but women are, in theory (and usually in practice), operating as the equals of men. Natasha exemplifies this equality; she is training to become an engineer. No one is contesting women's right to work on the assembly line or in other occupations that, in America, would be traditionally assigned to men. Yet in the character of the prostitute Zena, Page points out the contradictions within the new Soviet society. In a country that fully practiced equality, as the Soviets were proclaiming that they did, prostitution would have disappeared along with all other kinds of exploitation of one person by another. Yet it still existed. However, when Zena is persecuted by her fellow workers for her illegal activities, she is defended by Natasha, who sees in Zena's failing not so much a personal moral failure, but a failure on the part of the group. Zena's coworkers have been exploiting her rather than bringing her along the socialist path—that, along with her weaknesses for Western luxury goods, has been her undoing.

These 1930s Russians, despite the fact that they were working in the context of an ideology that has seemingly failed, were trying to work out the same important questions that we are: how to ensure equality between men and women and how to develop a society that celebrated diversity and equality where everyone had enough, but where a few people didn't have so much that they could dominate others. Readers interested in history, including women's history and the forgotten history of hundreds of American workers who went to Soviet Russia in the 1930s—and those just interested in a satisfying love story set in an interesting milieu—will find this a thought-provoking and interesting read.

Author Sketch

Myra Page was born Dorothy Page Gary in Newport News, Virginia, in 1897. A graduate of Westhampton College, she became active in the union-organizing movement in the 1920s and earned a PhD in sociology from the University of Minnesota (1928). From the 1930s onward, she was a journalist and writer, often working for Communist-sponsored newspapers such as the *Daily Worker,* for whom she was a correspondent in the Soviet Union in the 1930s. She wrote a number of novels and works of juvenile fiction and taught as well. She died in 1993.[2]

Other Works by the Author

Gathering Storm: A Story of the Black Belt. New York: International Publishers, 1932.
Daughter of the Hills: A Woman's Part in the Coal Miners' Struggle. New York: Feminist Press at the City University of New York, 1986.
Page, M., and A. Pogovsky. *Soviet Main Street.* Moscow and Leningrad: Cooperative Publishing Society of Foreign Workers in the USSR, 1933.

Suggestions for Further Reading

Fitzpatrick, S. *Everyday Stalinism: Ordinary Life in Extraordinary Times: Soviet Russia in the 1930s.* New York: Oxford University Press, 1999.

Kiaer, C., and E. Naiman. *Everyday Life in Early Soviet Russia: Taking the Revolution Inside.* Bloomington: Indiana University Press, 2006.

Pons, S., A. Romano, et al. *Russia in the Age of Wars, 1914–1945.* Milano: Feltrinelli, 2000.

Youngblood, D. J. *Russian War Films: On the Cinema Front, 1914–2005.* Lawrence: University Press of Kansas, 2007.

Notes

1. Myra Page, *Moscow Yankee* (Urbana: University of Illinois Press, 1995), p. 214.

2. http://www.lib.unc.edu/mss/inv/htm/05143.html;   http://www.press.uillinois.edu/f95/page.html; *Contemporary Authors Online,* Gale, 2006.

Américo Paredes

George Washington Gómez

Houston: Arte Público Press, 1990

Originally published: 1990. Written and unpublished, 1936–1940

Genre: Mainstream Literary Fiction/Latino American/Hispanic Literature

Quote

There were years when spring came early to the Golden Delta of the Rio Grande, and this was one of those years. The morning sun, shining from a clear-blue sky, gave a warm pleasant tang to the cool breeze that still smelled of winter. Already was the sour-orange tree by the fence putting out its delicate shoots that soon would become white perfume.[1]

Synopsis

This is the life story of George Washington Gómez, known as Gualinto, from his birth to Mexican immigrants in the Texas border town Jonesville-on-the Grande in 1915 through his education and eventual assimilation into the American mainstream. The novel starts with Gualinto's rather idyllic childhood—contrasted with the stories of his mother, father, and uncle, who must deal with the harsh realities of prejudice and economic survival—set against a world of bandits, machine politics, and smuggling. As Gualinto grows older, the story begins to focus on him and especially on his experiences in the school system, which cause him to have an almost dual personality: American at school, Mexican at home. Through the events of his life—his education, his experiences with prejudice, the economic hardships of the Depression, and eventually, his Americanization as represented by his taking of a government security job—the reader witnesses the conflict of dual cultural identities.

Critical Commentary

George Washington Gómez is a fascinating and insightful novel about a young man's coming-of-age on the Texas-Mexico border during the 1920s and 1930s. Vividly and colorfully written, this is the story of immigrant life, beginning with the challenges that George's parents faced in Texas, including poor education, racism, and ever-present economic hardship.

The work as a whole is wonderfully balanced. There's both tragedy and joy as one sees the whole spectrum of life experiences. For example, George bears the burden of his name with both pride and embarrassment. Paredes has captured joy and pathos in equal measure. Paredes also vividly illustrates the benefits of the Texas educational system, recognizing the value of bilingual education, and the drawbacks, including bigoted and ignorant teachers. This may be one of the best fictional descriptions ever published of what it was like to be a Latino student in the 1920s and 1930s that has ever been published.

The central character, George, ties the narrative together and lends coherence to the work. George is also the lynchpin on which one or two surprising plot twists revolve. Aside from George, the characters of his parents, Feliciano and Maria, dominate the story. Through the experience of Feliciano—in particular, his dealings with the local political machine that helps him and his family—the reader gets a sense of how things actually worked in the border regions. This was a time and area where elections were decided less on the basis of a free vote than according to the manipulations of the local politicians.

Supporting characters, such as George's schoolmates Miguel and El Colorado, flesh out the story of the Latino experience. They are contrasted with the local whites, who are portrayed as largely sympathetic, mostly because they are in the same economic boat as their Hispanic neighbors. However, there is a small group of local racists who, more or less under the color of law, go about fighting an irregular series of battles with local Hispanics who, for whatever reason, are living on the wrong side of the law.

The immigrant community is depicted as a real place. The characters are not abstract statistics, but flesh and blood people with both strengths and faults. One can't read this elegantly written book without having a real sense of empathy and compassion for the characters. This is a masterful example of what can happen when a talented writer moves beyond traditional definitions of literary form to create something that looks directly into the human spirit. The story should appeal to a wide range of readers, including those interested in Texas history, the history of education, immigration, and the experiences of Latinos in America. It should be required reading for anyone who wants to express an informed opinion about the life of Latinos in the border regions of Texas.

Author Sketch

Born in Brownsville, Texas, on September 3, 1915, Paredes was educated in the Brownsville Public School and at Brownsville Junior College, while also working at the local newspaper, the *Brownsville Herald*, as a writer and proofreader. After his military service in World War II, he earned a PhD from the University of Texas at Austin (1956) where, after a short teaching stint in El Paso, he returned and spent his career as a scholar of folklore and ethnomusicology, focusing on the area of the Southern borderlands. He was an activist in the struggle for the recognition of Mexican American studies in the university and academia generally, and he also published numerous well-received books and articles. He died on May 5, 1999.[2]

Other Works by the Author

"With His Pistol in His Hand," A Border Ballad and Its Hero. Austin: University of Texas Press, 1958.
Folktales of Mexico. Chicago: University of Chicago Press, 1970.
A Texas-Mexican Cancionero: Folksongs of the Lower Border. Urbana: University of Illinois Press, 1976.
Between Two Worlds. Houston: Arte Público Press, 1991.
Folklore and Culture on the Texas-Mexican Border. Austin: Center for Mexican American Studies, University of Texas, 1993.
Uncle Remus con Chile. Houston: Arte Público Press, 1993.
The Hammon and the Beans and Other Stories. Houston: Arte Público Press, 1994.
The Shadow. Houston: Arte Público Press, 1998.

Paredes, Américo, and Richard Bauman. *Toward New Perspectives in Folklore.* Publications of the American Folklore Society. Bibliographical and Special Series, vol. 23. Austin: University of Texas Press, 1972.

Paredes, Américo, Edward James Olmos, and Moctesuma Esparza Productions. *The Ballad of Gregorio Cortez.* Video recording. Los Angeles: Embassy Home Entertainment, 1984.

Paredes, Américo, and Raymund Paredes. *Mexican-American Authors.* Boston: Houghton Mifflin, 1976.

Paredes, Américo, and George Isidore Sánchez. *Humanidad: Essays in Honor of George I. Sánchez.* Los Angeles: Chicano Studies Center, University of California, 1977.

Paredes, Américo, and Ellen Jane Stekert. *The Urban Experience and Folk Tradition.* Publications of the American Folklore Society. Bibliographical and Special Series, vol. 22. Austin: University of Texas Press, 1971.

Suggestions for Further Reading

Almon, Bert. *This Stubborn Self: Texas Autobiographies.* Fort Worth, TX: TCU Press, 2002.

Bloom, Harold. *Hispanic-American Writers* Modern Critical Views. Philadelphia: Chelsea House Publishers, 1998.

Gonzales-Berry, Erlinda, and Charles W. Tatum. *Recovering the U.S. Hispanic Literary Heritage,* Vol. 2. Houston: Arte Público Press, 1996.

Kanellos, Nicolás, and Luis Dávila. *A Texas-Mexican Anthology.* Houston: Revista Chicano-Riqueño, 1980.

Ontiveros Miller, Linda Gloria. "The Other Side/El Otro Lado: The Chaos of Transition for Chicanas." MA thesis, University of Texas at El Paso, 2000.

Valdâes, Marâia Elena de. *The Shattered Mirror: Representations of Women in Mexican Literature.* The Texas Pan American Series. Austin: University of Texas Press, 1998.

Notes

1. Paredes, Américo. *George Washington Gómez* (Houston: Arte Público Press, 1990), p. 52.
2. http://www.lib.utexas.edu/benson/paredes/biography.html

Joseph Stanley Pennell

The History of Rome Hanks and Kindred Matters

Sag Harbor, NY: Second Chance Press, 1982

Originally published: 1944

Genre: Historical/Mainstream/Literary Fiction

Quote

All the way back to the gun there were pillagers, some shamefast and furtive, others bra-
zen. In blue, a Union boy with the beginning fuzz of a military beard looked up from a dead
man's pockets as Rome and I came up to him. It's Brother, he said. I'm a-goin' to take his
watch to Ma. We was in the same regiment. The dead man was dressed in gray, but he
may have been a Union man.[1]

Synopsis

In this panoramic Civil War novel, a young man, Robert Lee Harrington, remembering stories told to him by his grandfather and father, tries to imagine what the Civil War was like and
how it affected his ancestors. Moving backward and forward in time, as he visits people who
share their recollections, Harrington provides a vivid story of the war and his grandfather's experiences and associations with a variety of narrators—including the Rev. Dr. Wagnal, Robert's
Uncle Pinckney—each with their own unique version of events. Robert Harrington ends up
learning just as much about himself as he does about the past of his family.

Critical Commentary

In a nation characterized by mobility and change, it is the rare individual who can trace his
or her ancestry more than one or two generations with any accuracy. In *The History of Rome
Hanks and Kindred Matters,* Joseph Pennell offers an enthralling ode to personal ancestry, taking his primary character, Robert Lee Harrington, on a journey that acquaints him with his
family heritage, his country, and himself.

This is a novel of great scope, filled with detailed and insightful character portraits—from
the Rev. Thomas Wagnal, a doctor of divinity and former regimental surgeon; to Thomas Beckham, in the multicolored uniform of Drake's Zouaves; to Harrington's Great-Uncle Pink. These
are no mint-julep-soaked Southern colonels, still fighting for the cause from their verandahs.
Joseph Pennell goes beyond easy stereotypes to create authentic figures who although not entirely likeable, are always intriguing.

Pennell's command of period detail is striking; and for thoughtful readers this novel illumi-
nates some dark corners of American history, such as the fact that in the Civil War the medical

treatment soldiers received was often as deadly as combat itself—for example, having a leg amputated without benefit of anesthetic. The tragedy of a nation ill-prepared for war is shown in the descriptions of untrained recruits going off to battle with their Belgian muskets, which they replace at the first opportunity with more modern weapons stripped from the bodies of the Confederate dead. These pictures are counterpoised with the darkly humorous situations that Harrington stumbles into during his journey and the strange involvements in which he and the other characters find themselves.

Pennell takes liberties with the novel form, sometimes including sonnets, sometimes experimenting with capitalization and punctuation (e.g., he abandons quotation marks); but these elements don't detract from the readability of the book. This is a fascinating piece of fiction by an accomplished writer.

Author Sketch

Born in Junction City, Kansas, in 1908, Pennell was educated at the University of Kansas and at Oxford. In addition to writing novels, he worked as a newspaper reporter and teacher. He died in 1961.[2]

Other Works by the Author

The History of Nora Beckham, a Museum of Home Life. New York: Scribner's, 1948.
Darksome House: The Collected Poems of Joseph Stanley Pennell. Coffeyville, KS: Zauberberg Press, 1959.

Suggestions for Further Reading

Ambrosius, Lloyd E. *A Crisis of Republicanism: American Politics in the Civil War Era.* Lincoln: University of Nebraska Press, 1990.
Berlin, Ira. *Free at Last: A Documentary History of Slavery, Freedom, and the Civil War.* New York: The New Press, 1992.
Smith, John David. *Black Soldiers in Blue: African American Troops in the Civil War Era.* Chapel Hill: University of North Carolina Press, 2002.
Watford, Christopher M. *The Civil War in North Carolina: Soldiers' and Civilians' Letters and Diaries, 1861–1865.* Jefferson, NC: McFarland, 2003.

Notes

1. Joseph Pennell, *The History of Rome Hanks and Kindred Matters* (Sag Harbor, NY: Second Chance Press, 1982), p. 31.
2. http://libweb.uoregon.edu/speccoll/guides/lit.html

Anne Lane Petry

The Street

Boston: Houghton Mifflin, 1946

Originally published: 1946

Genre: Mainstream/Literary Fiction

Quote

Her finger moved over the glass, around and around. The circles showed up plainly on the dusty surface. The woman's statement was correct, she thought. What possible good has it done to teach people like me to write?[1]

Synopsis

Lutie Johnson, an intelligent and strong black woman, does her best to be a good single mother to her son—despite the racism and poverty that face her in 1940s America. Streetwise Lutie even sidesteps a tricky situation and turns the tables on a con man who planned to exploit her. Despite her intelligence, she can't avoid being dragged into the justice system, where she is forced to make some unjust and life-changing sacrifices in order to survive.

Critical Commentary

In *The Street,* Ann Petry creates two characters, Lutie Johnson and her son Bub, who stand for everyone oppressed by racism. This novel poignantly and credibly addresses the larger problems of society within the context of an individual's hard work and good intentions.

Lutie Johnson's existence is a nightmare with no real hope. Her pain stems from the fact that, unlike many of the people around her, she is aware of her situation and not lulled by the artificial painkillers the others are using to avoid the truth. This is an American apartheid where everyone is a victim, and Petry questions the essential elements of the paradigm that posits America as a meritocracy, despite evidence to the contrary. Lutie tries to conform and succeed but is constantly thwarted, until her murder of would-be rapist Boots, when she is dragged back into the very mire she has sought so earnestly to escape.

The Street is credible, in part because of Petry's accurate and well-drawn descriptions of Lutie's environment—the dingy apartments and dangerous neighborhoods that contrast dramatically with the wealthy white environments where she sometimes works. There's no doubt who the have and have-nots are. This is a valuable novel in the realistic and naturalistic tradition of Henry James that accurately depicts the struggles of the individual against the forces of a largely uncaring society—giving the modern reader a message about the corrosive effects of racism and poverty on the human spirit, a message that is still relevant and important today.

Author Sketch

Born October 12, 1908, in Old Saybrook, Connecticut, Petry was educated at the University of Connecticut (PhG 1931). She worked as a pharmacist and a journalist in addition to being a professional writer. She died April 28, 1997.[2]

Other Works by the Author

Country Place. Boston: Houghton Mifflin Company, 1947; Cambridge: The Riverside Press, 1947.
Harriet Tubman, Conductor on the Underground Railroad. New York: Crowell, 1955.
The Narrows. New York: New American Library, 1955.
The Common Ground. New York: Crowell, 1964.
Tituba of Salem Village. New York: Crowell, 1964.
Miss Muriel and Other Stories. Boston: Houghton Mifflin, 1971.
Petry, Ann Lane, and Olof Högstadius. *Gatan.* Stockholm: Ljus, 1947.
Petry, Ann Lane, and Susanne Suba. *The Drugstore Cat.* New York: Crowell, 1949.

Suggestions for Further Reading

Breines, Winifred. *The Trouble between Us: An Uneasy History of White and Black Women in the Feminist Movement.* New York: Oxford University Press, 2006.
Davis, David Brion. *Inhuman Bondage: The Rise and Fall of Slavery in the New World.* New York: Oxford University Press, 2006.
Jonas, Gilbert. *Freedom's Sword: The NAACP and the Struggle against Racism in America, 1909–1969.* New York: Routledge, 2005.
West, Michael Rudolph. *The Education of Booker T. Washington: American Democracy and the Idea of Race Relations.* New York: Columbia University Press, 2006.

Notes

1. Ann Lane Petry, *The Street* (Boston: Houghton Mifflin, 1946), p. 436.
2. *Contemporary Authors Online,* Gale, 2003; http://www.pocanticohills.org/womenenc/petry.htm

Elizabeth Stuart Phelps

Doctor Zay

New York: The Feminist Press at The City University of New York, 1987

Originally published: 1882

Genre: Mainstream/Literary/Feminist Fiction

Quote

> He remembered into how many sick-rooms she must bring her bloom and bounteousness, and for the first time in his fortunate life he understood how corrosive is the need of the sick for the well. He remembered he was but one of—how many? dependent and complaining creatures, draining upon the life of a strong and busy woman.[1]

Synopsis

Waldo Yorke, a young man from Boston, takes a business trip to the wilds of Maine in the late nineteenth century, where he has a serious accident. Upon regaining consciousness, he finds that he is under the care of a female physician, Dr. Zaidee Atalanta Lloyd—Dr. Zay. Dr. Zay, a homeopathic doctor trained in Europe, has chosen to practice in rural Maine, largely focusing on women and children. At first, Yorke is reluctant to be treated by a female doctor, but as his extended recovery progresses, he finds himself falling in love with Dr, Zay, who is then faced with a choice between matrimony and her practice. After a long romance and a great deal of reflection, Dr. Zay decides to marry Waldo Yorke.

Critical Commentary

The late nineteenth century represented a transitional period in America from an agricultural to an industrial society. Along with these changes came changes in conception of both what constituted a profession and the role of women. In *Doctor Zay* Elizabeth Stuart Phelps gives readers a traditional and heartwarming romance novel—albeit with an interesting role reversal—along with an insightful portrait of the emergence of women into the medical profession.

The structure of the novel is simple, and the narrative follows the arc of a love story. Over the course of the story, as Waldo Yorke and Dr. Zay become increasingly involved with each other, the reader finds a detailed and fascinating description of the practice of medicine in the nineteenth century—an era with none of the modern medicines and devices we take for granted.

At the same time, it is a character study of two individuals who, unlike the characters in a traditional romance, play opposite roles in the love match, which is particularly interesting because of the time period when this book was written. This creates a compelling dynamic between the two main characters.

This novel also gives us a picturesque and detailed portrait of life in a rural New England community. The reader sees the isolation and problems of these remote communities that lack not only what we might consider luxuries, but also even the basic amenities and communication with the outside world. These people truly rely on their own resources. The contributions of Dr. Zay to this underserved community cannot be understated—especially for the women and children who, even more than the men, suffer from lack of medical care. Phelps has created a psychological portrait of an entire community where their inner problems are revealed in the interactions and observations of the two educated outsiders—Yorke and Zay—who have dropped, either by choice or happenstance, into their community.

Doctor Zay raises important questions about gender, class relations, and the dynamic between one's personal life and the demands of professional obligation. In contemporary society, where women have seemingly achieved more than their nineteenth-century counterparts, these issues still ring true and raise thought-provoking questions for modern audiences. An essential read for anyone interested in the history of women in the professions, this work should also appeal to readers who are interested in the history of medicine or to those readers simply seeking a thoughtful love story.

Author Sketch

Born in Boston, Massachusetts, August 31 1844, Phelps was privately educated at the Abbot Academy and Mrs. Edwards' School for Young Ladies. From the 1860s onward, she wrote a series of popular novels and fiction for magazines that were well received by the public. Her book *The Gates Ajar* sold over 100,000 copies—a fantastic number for the time period. She continued to write until shortly before her death in Newton Center, Massachusetts, on January 28, 1911.[2]

Other Works by the Author

Mercy Gliddon's Work. The Sunday-School Series of Juvenile Religious Works. Boston: Henry Hoyt, 1865.

Tiny. Boston: Massachusetts Second Universalist Society, 1866.

The Gates Ajar. Boston: Fields, Osgood, 1869.

Hedged In. Boston: Fields, Osgood, 1870.

The Silent Partner. Boston: Osgood, 1871.

Poetic Studies. Boston: Osgood, 1875.

Gypsy's Sowing and Reaping. New York: Dodd, Mead, 1876.

The Story of Avis. Boston: Osgood, 1877.

The Boys of Brimstone Court. Boston: D. Lothrop, 1879.

Sealed Orders. Boston: Houghton, Osgood, 1879. Microform.

Beyond the Gates. Boston and New York: Houghton, 1883.

Songs of the Silent World: And Other Poems. Boston and New York: Houghton, Mifflin, 1884.

An Old Maid's Paradise. Boston and New York: Houghton, Mifflin, 1885.

Burglars in Paradise. Boston and New York: Houghton, Mifflin, 1886.

The Madonna of the Tubs. Boston and New York: Houghton, Mifflin, 1886.

The Gates Between. Boston and New York: Houghton, Mifflin, 1887.

Jack the Fisherman. Boston and New York: Houghton, Mifflin, 1887.

The Madonna of the Tubs. Boston and New York: Houghton, Mifflin, 1887.

Old Maids, and Burglars in Paradise. Boston and New York: Houghton, Mifflin, 1887.

The Master of the Magicians. Boston: Houghton, Mifflin, 1890. Microform.

Fourteen to One. Boston and New York: Houghton, Mifflin, 1891.

Austin Phelps; A Memoir. New York: Scribner's, 1892.

Donald Marcy. Boston and New York: Houghton, Mifflin, 1893.

The Supply at Saint Agatha's. Boston and New York: Houghton, Mifflin, 1896.

Suggestions for Further Reading

Bennett, Mary Angela. "Elizabeth Stuart Phelps." PhD Thesis, University of Pennsylvania, 1938–1939.

Kelly, Lori Duin. *The Life and Works of Elizabeth Stuart Phelps, Victorian Feminist Writer.* Troy, NY: Whitston, 1983.

Kessler, Carol Farley. *Elizabeth Stuart Phelps.* Boston: Twayne, 1982.

Privett, Ronna Coffey. *A Comprehensive Study of American Writer Elizabeth Stuart Phelps, 1844–1911: Art for Truth's Sake.* Lewiston, NY: Edwin Mellen Press, 2003.

Notes

1. Elizabeth Phelps, *Dr. Zay* (New York: The Feminist Press at The City University of New York, 1987), p. 66.

2. *Dictionary of Literary Biography,* Vol. 221: *American Women Prose Writers, 1870–1920,* ed. Sharon M. Harris (Detroit: Gale, 2000), pp. 294–304; http://www.readseries.com/auth-oz/phelps-daught.html

Connie Porter

All-Bright Court

New York: HarperPerennial, 1992

Originally published: 1991

Genre: Mainstream/Literary Fiction

Quote

> "Boys like you be coming in here all the time. But let me tell you something, The way you be working, you liable not to make enough money to cross the street."
> "Sir?" Samuel said. He was annoyed.
> "Boy, keep your mind on your work. Watch what you doing, 'cause if you keep on this way, the closest you going to get to the North is in your dreams.[1]

Synopsis

Many African American workers from the South, faced with Jim Crow discrimination, moved North for a better life. Beginning in the 1920s, this particular story follows their lives from the late 1950s through the 1970s, focusing on the women and children living in a worker's neighborhood—All-Bright Court. Despite challenges of poverty and discrimination, these women develop a strong community and a support system that nurtures their children and, although not perfect, offers them a chance for a better life.

Critical Commentary

In her portrayal of African American life in the urban North, Porter moves her story through time and through events of the era, such as the Kennedy assassination, race riots, and changes in 1960s society, with each chapter developing its own unique atmosphere. Porter cleverly and successfully integrates a wide range of viewpoints, authenticating and enriching the story.

What distinguishes this book is Porter's adroit use of language. Her accurate use of the dialect used by the people promotes empathy in the reader. Through their rough but genuine speech, Porter skillfully captures the emotional reactions of people thrust into a modern society while still holding to many of their folkways and traditions.

The novel centers on the Taylor family and especially the challenges that they face when their gifted son, Mikey, gains a scholarship to a private school that sets him on a life path distinctly different from the rest of his family and neighbors. The plot moves along swiftly as various characters—Skip, Henry, Moses, and Venita—in a vignette style, deal with the various vicissitudes of poverty-level life in a Northern industrial town. They must deal with steel mills strikes, crime, race riots, and the influx of other minority groups, such as Jesus and his family from Puerto Rico, with all of this set against the background of the social unrest of the 1960s.

This is a gentle and revealing look at the lives of African Americans in the 1960s and 1970s, during a period of rapid transition. For the people in this novel, life does not go as they hoped it would, but through faith and dignity they surmount adversity, and that gives this book a timeless human quality. This is an insightful and enjoyable book for anyone interested in issues of civil rights or working-class life.

Author Sketch

Porter, a native of Lackawanna, Pennsylvania, earned an undergraduate degree from SUNY–Albany and an MFA from Louisiana State University. She taught creative writing at Southern Illinois University and currently lives in Virginia Beach, Virginia. She is the author of the Addy books in the Pleasant Company's *The All-American Girls Collections* as well as the novel *Imani All Mine*.[2]

Other Works by the Author

Imani All Mine. Boston: Houghton Mifflin, 1999.

Suggestions for Further Reading

Hall, Christopher. *Steel Phoenix: The Fall and Rise of the U.S. Steel Industry*. New York: St. Martin's Press, 1997.

Kirby, Jack Temple. *Rural Worlds Lost: The American South, 1920–1960*. Baton Rouge: Louisiana State University Press, 1987.

Metzgar, Jack. *Striking Steel: Solidarity Remembered, Critical Perspectives on the Past*. Philadelphia: Temple University Press, 2000.

Notes

1. Connie Porter, *All-Bright Court* (New York: HarperPerennial, 1992), p. 7.

2. http://www3.canisius.edu/~cochrane/writer/connie_porter.htm; *Contemporary Authors Online*, Gale, 2002.

Dawn Powell

My Home Is Far Away

South Royalton, VT: Steerforth, 1995

Originally published: 1944

Genre: Historical Fiction

Quote

> This was the month of cherries and peaches, of green apples beyond the grape arbor, of
> little dandelion ghosts in the grass, of sour grass and four leaf clovers, of still dry heat hold-
> ing the smell of nasturtiums and dying lilacs.[1]

Synopsis

In this chronicle of the life of an Ohio family in early-twentieth-century Ohio, young Marcia Willard, along with her two sisters, Flossie and Lena, must develop her own destiny and
character while dealing, along with her family, with a rapidly changing society.

Critical Commentary

Autobiographical novels can be a risk for an author—primarily because most writers usually don't live the types of exciting lives that lend themselves to fiction. In *My Home Is Far
Away,* Dawn Powell uses the very ordinariness of a writer's life to create a shining gem of a
book about life in early twentieth-century Ohio.

The various characters, especially the children Lena and Marcia, are portrayed with sensitivity
and care. The events of their lives are typical ones—such as moving to the larger London Junction
from their smaller hamlet, but this is depicted with interest, as are the other events of their lives,
such as summer carnivals, Sunday school, and the like. Yet there is also an undercurrent of displacement. The lives of the children, despite their comic elements, can also be seen as a gentle indictment
of the adults around them, who are basically neglectful—the father is often absent, their mother
dies, and they are often left to shift for themselves while being cared for by relatives who, with the
exception of their aunt "Jule," are largely indifferent. In many respects, *My Home Is Far Away* can
be seen to echo in tone the work of Dickens, such as in *The Old Curiosity Shop,* where the lives of
children are depicted against the backdrop of a larger unfeeling adult world. This makes for an interesting read because it causes the readers to examine their own conceptions of the world through
the eyes of children—who are attempting to make sense of things with little or no adult guidance.

The book's characters—children, parents, a grandfather with a cork leg, and neighbors—
spend their days doing what most people do: they love, fight, make up, scheme for more money,
and die. Powell portrays them with love and authenticity. Her plotting reveals both her intimate
knowledge of Midwestern small-town life and her refusal to romanticize it. This is not a Midwest
simply filled with corn fields and friendly farm folk. Powell depicts its true and dynamic diversity

of religion and culture, including the contrast between large and small communities, industry and agriculture, Protestants and Catholics, and immigrants and the native-born.

The atmosphere of community and the small-town claustrophobia that result from a small group of people living together in one location for a lifetime is vividly drawn, in part through precise atmospheric detail, down to the Victorian clutter that persists through the years in these living rooms.

Ultimately, this novel goes beyond nostalgia or cheerful World War II home-front propaganda to address universal themes of growing up and growing out. Marcia and the rest of the characters could be any of a million people in American small towns, past or present, who aspire to something better or, at least, to something different. A timeless piece of regional writing, this inspirational novel is written with wit and charm. It should appeal to anyone interested in history or simply in an endearing story of children growing up under difficult circumstances.

Author Sketch

Born August 24, 1896, in Mount Gilead, Ohio, Powell eventually moved to New York, where she married an advertising executive. She wrote a number of novels without a great deal of commercial success or recognition, except from her fellow writers who thought very highly of her talent. She died on November 15, 1965.[2]

Other Works by the Author

She Walks in Beauty. New York: Brentano's, 1928.
Jig Saw, a Comedy. New York: Farrar & Rinehart, 1934.
The Happy Island. New York: Farrar & Rinehart, 1938.
A Time to Be Born. New York: Scribner's, 1942.
The Locusts Have No King. New York: Yarrow Press, 1990.
Dawn Powell at Her Best: Including the Novels "Turn," "Magic Wheel" and "Dance Night" & Selected Stories. Edited by Tim Page. South Royalton, VT: Steerforth Press, 1994.
Sunday, Monday, and Always. South Royalton, VT: Steerforth Press, 1999.
Novels, 1930–1942. New York: Library of America, 2001.
Novels, 1944–1962. New York: Library of America, 2001.
The Story of a Country Boy. South Royalton, VT: Steerforth Press, 2001.
Powell, Dawn, and Tim Page. *The Diaries of Dawn Powell, 1931–1965.* South Royalton, VT: Steerforth Press, 1995.
Powell, Dawn, Tim Page, and Michael Sexton. *Four Plays.* South Royalton, VT: Steerforth Press, 1999.

Suggestions for Further Reading

Page, Tim. *Dawn Powell: A Biography.* New York: Holt, 1998.
Rice, Marcelle Smith. *Dawn Powell.* New York: Twayne, 2000.

Notes

1. Dawn Powell, *My Home Is Far Away* (South Royalton, VT: Steerforth, 1995), p. 1.
2. http://www.steerforth.com/books/display.pperl?isbn=9781883642433; *Contemporary Authors Online,* Gale, 2003; http://www.dawnpowell.org/; Matthew Josephson, "Dawn Powell: A Woman of Esprit," *Southern Review* 9, no. 1 (January 1973): 18–52.

Charles T. Powers

In the Memory of the Forest

New York: Penguin Books, 1997

Originally published: 1997

Genre: Mainstream/Literary Fiction

Quote

> It was natural enough. We had spent our lifetimes in Jadowia, a place where nothing ever
> happened during all that time, and maybe never would, a junction of two main roads, meet-
> ing in an offset cross in the town's center—which happened to be at the doorstep of the
> wretched "fourth-class" restaurant and bar where the town's cast of alcoholics staggered
> out each day looking as if their faces had been boiled.[1]

Synopsis

Leszek Maleszewski is a 20-something farmer in the small Polish village of Jadowia, shortly
after the fall of Communism. When his neighbor, Tomek, who is around the same age and who
is involved in shady business dealings, is found murdered in a local forest, Leszek decides to
look into the matter. He uncovers of a web of deceit, paranoia, and greed—all tied into official
corruption, bribery, the black market, and most disturbingly, the murders 40 years before of
most of the Jewish inhabitants of the village.

Critical Commentary

In this riveting novel, a murder mystery set in the era just after the fall of Communism in
Poland, Powers offers thought-provoking commentary on the nature of history and the power
of memory on human experience. Capturing the essence of this particular time and place,
Powers also conveys important and essential truths about human life.

The story is written from a number of viewpoints, including that of Tomek's grieving father,
Staszek; of the scheming local Communist Party apparatchik, Jablonski; of the troubled priest,
Father Tadeusz; and of Jola, the veterinarian's wife, with whom Leszek, the central character,
is incidentally having an affair. The exploration of a seemingly senseless murder of one man
gradually leads into the discovery of the murder of an entire Jewish population during World
War II. In an examination of memory, Powers reveals the poisonous effects that 40 years of
secrecy have had on the psyche of an entire village—and nation.

Through lively dialogue and colorful descriptions, Powers ably portrays a poverty-stricken
rural Poland facing a painful transition from a harsh totalitarianism to market capitalism that
is, in many ways, even harsher. From decaying farms to silent forests filled with secrets, the
country and its people are drawn with accuracy and style.

The depictions of people—even minor nonrecurring characters—are dead on, written with intense realism. Powers never allows the conventional elements of the mystery to overshadow his larger philosophical purposes. Remarkable in its acute moral vision and in its depiction of an individual and a nation attempting to come to grips with a past of horrific proportions, this novel can be read for enjoyment as a thriller and as a brilliant meditation on the brutal realities of modern history.

Author Sketch

Powers was born in 1943 in Missouri. He began as a newspaper reporter at the *Kansas City Star* before moving on to the *Los Angeles Times,* for which he worked for 20 years; he spent many of these years in Africa and, later, five in Warsaw, Poland. From 1991 until his death in 1996, he lived in Bennington, Vermont, where he wrote fiction, including *In the Memory of the Forest,* his only novel. Powers was a Nieman Fellow at Harvard and also won an award for distinguished journalism from the national Society of Professional Journalists in 1984.[2]

Other Works by the Author

None

Suggestions for Further Reading

Abramsky, Chimen, Maciej Jachimczyk, and Antony Polonsky. *The Jews in Poland.* Oxford and New York: B. Blackwell, 1986.

Huener, Jonathan. *Auschwitz, Poland, and the Politics of Commemoration, 1945–1979.* Athens: Ohio University Press, 2003.

Lukas, Richard C. *Out of the Inferno: Poles Remember the Holocaust.* Lexington: University Press of Kentucky, 1989.

Pinchuk, Ben-Cion. *Shtetl Jews under Soviet Rule: Eastern Poland on the Eve of the Holocaust, Jewish Society and Culture.* Oxford, UK, and Cambridge, MA: B. Blackwell, 1990.

Notes

1. Charles Powers, *In the Memory of the Forest* (New York: Penguin Books, 1997), pp. 26–27.
2. Obituary for Charles T. Powers, *Los Angeles Times,* October 5, 1996.

J. F. Powers

Wheat That Springeth Green

New York: Washington Square Press, 1990

Originally published: 1988

Genre: Mainstream/Literary Fiction

Quote

Joe was passing the Great Badger, "the discount store with a heart," which meant not only that the savings it realized through its wise volume purchases were passed on to you, the customer, in the usual manner of discount houses, but that your dependents in the event of your death would get to keep whatever you had been buying on time without payments or charges of any kind.[1]

Synopsis

Joe Hackett, high school football star, starts his career with high ambitions but by middle age has become a somewhat complacent parish priest in the suburbs of Chicago. The story focuses primarily on a few months during the fall of 1968, when Father Joe has to deal with comic and tragic events that involve his parishioners, his superiors in the Church, and his growing recognition of his own destiny in life—which is actually deeper and more spiritual than he or those around him initially believe.

Critical Commentary

In recent years the Roman Catholic church has had some public image problems. J. F. Powers's *Wheat That Springeth Green* redresses this negative picture in a funny and appealing story of priests and their very human problems. Although ostensibly aimed at Catholic readers, the book has wide appeal to all readers who are interested in an articulate and engaging novel about contemporary life.

In following the life of Joe Hackett, Powell uses a narrative technique that compresses most of the action into the last several months of 1968. This telescoping technique, similar to a cinematic wide shot followed by close-ups, gives an overview of Hackett's life and character while still focusing on a small set of events within a relatively short time frame.

Powers shows priests as human beings with all the problems that any person entering a career has—getting a good position, hiring and managing staff, and attracting "customers" (and getting them to pay), all while learning the politics of the business. Hackett is no saint. He is not a miracle worker. In fact, Hackett and his colleagues come off at times more as tired salesmen than as preachers of the Gospel, but this adds to the authenticity of the work. Hackett's travails, dealing with draft dodgers (and their parents) or managing a parish financial system, are hardly the deeds of saints, but they make for a more accurate depiction of

173

the everyday life of a parish priest than any number of miracles introduced into the text could have.

The story is set in the fictional Chicago suburb of Inglenook. Powers's satirical depiction of American consumerism, in the visage of "the discount store with a heart," the Great Badger, is one of the funnier bits in the novel—along with Hackett's difficulties in buying furniture.

Powers's message is that religion, and specifically Christianity, works. Not always well, not always in the way intended, but the system is valid—flawed people and all. Hackett and his colleagues accomplish their mission, sometimes in spite of the system rather than because of it. By extension, this novel also suggests that contemporary life can work—if people are realistic about what they can do and enter into things with a willing spirit and a sense of humor.

Author Sketch

Born on July 8, 1917, in Jacksonville, Illinois, Powers was educated at Northwestern University. He spent 13 months in jail during World War II as a conscientious objector before taking work in a hospital. In 1951 he moved with his family to Ireland, splitting his time between there and the United States until 1975. He became a university English professor at St. John's University, and at the College of Saint Benedict, he was Regents Professor of English and writer in residence, 1975–93. He died in Collegeville, Minnesota, on June 12, 1999.[2]

Other Works by the Author

Prince of Darkness, and Other Stories. Garden City, NY: Doubleday, 1947.
Morte D'urban. New York: Doubleday, 1962.
Look How the Fish Live. New York: Knopf, 1975.
The Presence of Grace. London: Hogarth Press, 1986.

Suggestions for Further Reading

Glazier, Michael, and Thomas J. Shelley. *The Encyclopedia of American Catholic History.* Collegeville, MN: Liturgical Press, 1997.
Hoge, Dean R., and Jacqueline E. Wenger. *Evolving Visions of the Priesthood: Changes from Vatican II to the Turn of the New Century.* Collegeville, MN: Liturgical Press, 2003.
Varacalli, Joseph A. *The Catholic Experience in America.* Westport, CT: Greenwood Press, 2006.

Notes

1. J. F. Powers, *Wheat That Springeth Green* (New York: Washington Square Press, 1990), p. 104.
2. http://people.mnhs.org/authors/biog_detail.cfm?PersonID=Powe344

Francine Prose

Bigfoot Dreams

New York: Penguin Books, 1987

Originally published: 1986

Genre: Mainstream/Literary Fiction/Comic Fiction

Quote

> Turning down the produce aisle, Vera sees bunches of collards and immediately starts
> wondering what she'll say to the Greens. She notices her palms have started sweating.
> For comfort she thinks back to this morning's dream and wishes she had those dinosaur
> fragments now. She'd hide them behind the gourmet items, the jars of baby corn and bad
> caviar that no one ever buys.[1]

Synopsis

Vera Perl, a feminist and virtually single mother, lives in Brooklyn with her daughter and a
usually absent hippie husband. Vera has a job writing for a sleazy supermarket tabloid—that
is, until by accident one of her fake stories turns out to be true in its particulars, which gets her
fired. As a result, Vera tries for something more in life and ends up as a freelance writer covering a conference on cryptozoology in a conference center at the Grand Canyon—which gives
her a new perspective and makes her realize that she can have a fulfilling life.

Critical Commentary

Novels about young people finding themselves became almost a genre of their own in
the 1980s, Jay McInerney's *Bright Lights, Big City* and Bret Ellis's *Less Than Zero* being two of
the more well-known examples. Francine Prose's *Bigfoot Dreams* also falls into this category,
but unlike some of the titles of this ilk, it's remarkable for its subject treatment, plotting, and
humor.

Vera Perl is one of the more likeable characters one is likely to encounter in fiction. From
the beginning, you'll be rooting for her as she goes through her chaotic life. The surprising
thing—and this gives the novel its strength—is that nothing Prose suggests is unbelievable or
beyond possibility. Coincidences, even really strange ones, do happen, and readers are likely
to respond, "I realize this is fiction, but it could happen—maybe." New York has been depicted
in countless books, television shows, and movies, but rarely with such love or good humor as
here. Prose writes with a real affection for the wonderful, dirty, slightly tacky metropolis, filled
with endearing and affable characters.

She also handles the story and her characters with a light touch. Never falling into stereotypes, the characters retain their originality throughout. For example, Vera's father and
mother, the doctor's neighbors who are hoping for medical miracles from his tap water, seem

175

like people you might meet on your own block. The subplot introduced at the conclusion of the novel, about two attendees at the Arizona cryptozoology conference named Ethel and Carl Poteet and their African safari in search of Mokele-Mbembe, would make a hilarious novel in its own right.

Although lighthearted, *Bigfoot Dreams* is not light reading. Prose asks some serious questions about what constitutes reality and what gives us meaning in life. Vera Perl is a woman on a quest, in the most traditional and ancient literary meaning of the word—a Sir Gawain in skirts.

Prose, perhaps unintentionally, has taken some traditional literary ideas and recast them in an accessible way. Instead of the Knights of the Round Table at Camelot, Vera Perl finds cryptozoologists in an Arizona hotel. More importantly, perhaps, Prose reminds us of the power of wonder. Bigfoot could really be out there, looking for cigarettes, and he may just save us. In our post-9/11 era of somber insecurity, this message is important, and it makes this novel more than an artifact from the frivolous 1980s. It is a long-delayed postcard to ourselves, reminding us that it's all right to have a sense of humor.

Author Sketch

Prose, a native of Brooklyn, was born in 1947 and is a 1968 Radcliffe graduate, where she was a classmate of Hillary Clinton. She has written 14 books and has been widely published in periodicals, such as *GQ, Atlantic Monthly, New Yorker,* and *Paris Review.* She has received many awards, including a Guggenheim and a Fulbright, and she served as a Director's Fellow at the Center for Scholars and Writers at the New York Public Library. She has taught at the Iowa Writers' Workshop, the Sewanee Writers' Conference, and Johns Hopkins University. She lives in New York City.[2]

Other Works by the Author

Judah the Pious. New York: Atheneum, 1973.
Marie Laveau. New York: Berkley Publishing, 1977.
Household Saints. New York: St. Martin's Press, 1981.
Hungry Hearts. New York: Pantheon Books, 1983.
Women and Children First: Stories. New York: Pantheon Books, 1988.
Primitive People. New York: Farrar, Straus and Giroux, 1992.
The Peaceable Kingdom: Stories. New York: Farrar, Straus and Giroux, 1993.
Hunters and Gatherers. New York: Farrar, Straus and Giroux, 1995.
The Lives of the Muses: Nine Women & the Artists They Inspired. New York: HarperCollins, 2002.
Lignel, Benjamin, ed. *Ida Applebroog, 1976–2002: Are You Bleeding Yet?* Introduction by Francine Prose. New York: La Maison Red, 2002.
Lux, Loretta, and Francine Prose. *Loretta Lux.* New York: Aperture, 2005.
Prose, Francine, Karen Finley, Dario Fo, and Charles Simic. *Master Breasts: Objectified, Aesthetisized, Fantasized, Eroticized, Feminized by Photography's Most Titillating Masters.* New York: Aperture, 1998.

Suggestions for Further Reading

Daegling, David J. *Bigfoot Exposed: An Anthropologist Examines America's Enduring Legend.* Walnut Creek, CA: AltaMira Press, 2004.

Eberhart, George M. *Mysterious Creatures: A Guide to Cryptozoology.* 2 vols. Santa Barbara, CA: ABC-CLIO, 2002.

Ellis, Richard. *Sea Dragons: Predators of the Prehistoric Oceans.* Lawrence: University Press of Kansas, 2003.

Notes

1. Francine Prose, *Bigfoot Dreams* (New York: Penguin Books, 1987), p. 97.

2. http://www.bookreporter.com/authors/au-prose-francine.asp; *Dictionary of Literary Biography,* Vol. 234: *American Short-Story Writers since World War II, Third Series,* ed. Patrick Meanor and Richard E. Lee (Detroit: Gale, 2001), pp. 257–265.

Chet Raymo

The Dork of Cork

New York, NY: Warner Books, 1993

Originally published: 1993

Genre: Mainstream/Literary Fiction

Quote

Begin with beauty.
    Clouds part to reveal the moon already contained within the shadow of the earth. Not typical clouds for this part of the world. In Ireland we are used to smothering blankets of gray, or wet sheets of moisture flapping in the wind.[1]

Synopsis

Frank Bois is a 43-inch-high Irish dwarf. This is the story of his life, both as a child living with his mother, Bernadette, a troubled French war bride moved to Dublin, and as an adult who has just written a brilliant book on astronomy. Frank struggles to fit into a society that will never forgive him for being different and fight to come to terms with his reality.

Critical Commentary

In a surprising meditation on the idea of difference, Chet Raymo takes what might be considered an odd central character, a 43-inch-high Irish dwarf, and portrays him as a compelling and fascinating individual whose struggles speak to everyone.

Frank Bois, who has just finished a book based on his observations of the stars, wallows in despair about not fitting into a world that values beauty. Through internal dialogue, he reflects on his life, interspersing past events with wry philosophical meditations and acute observations about the reactions of people to him and his work. Frank is alienated, but he is never truly alien. He tries constantly to create connections.

Raymo's craft and insight never stoop to making the disability of its main character its main emotional and intellectual focus. The empathy of the reader is for Frank Bois as a person, rather than for a physical situation. Raymo has deftly created a compelling story of human interaction. In the end, this is a book about universals—the need to love, the need to belong, and the need to be a member of a community, valued for one's own self. In that lies its strength.

Author Sketch

Raymo was born in 1936 and was educated at the University of Notre Dame (BS 1958, PhD 1964) and the University of California, Los Angeles (MS). A successful academic and writer, he has now retired from Stonehill College in Easton, Massachusetts, where he was a professor of physics. Raymo is also an acclaimed naturalist, having written several well-received books in this field.[2]

Other Works by the Author

365 Starry Nights: An Introduction to Astronomy for Every Night of the Year. Englewood Cliffs, NJ: Prentice-Hall, 1982.

The Crust of Our Earth: An Armchair Traveler's Guide to the New Geology. Englewood Cliffs, NJ: Prentice-Hall, 1983.

The Virgin and the Mousetrap: Essays in Search of the Soul of Science. New York: Viking, 1991.

In the Falcon's Claw: A Novel of the Year 1000. Kerry, Ireland: Brandon, 1995.

Skeptics and True Believers: The Exhilarating Connection between Science and Religion. New York: Walker, 1998.

Climbing Brandon: Science and Faith on Ireland's Holy Mountain. New York: Walker, 2004.

Valentine: A Love Story. Kerry, Ireland: Brandon, 2005.

Walking Zero: Discovering Cosmic Space and Time Along the Prime Meridian. New York: Walker, 2006.

Raymo, Chet, and Maureen E. Raymo. *Written in Stone: A Geological and Natural History of the Northeastern United States.* Chester, CT: Globe Pequot Press, 1989.

Suggestions for Further Reading

Ablon, Joan. *Little People in America: The Social Dimension of Dwarfism.* New York: Praeger, 1984.

Ruggles, C.L.N. *Astronomy in Prehistoric Britain and Ireland.* New Haven, CT: Yale University Press, 1999.

Notes

1. Chet Raymo, *The Dork of Cork* (New York: Warner Books, 1993), p. 1.
2. *Contemporary Authors Online,* Gale, 2005.

Arthur B. Reeve

Guy Garrick: An Adventure with a Scientific Gunman

New York: Grosset and Dunlap, 1914

Originally published: 1914

Genre: Crime Fiction/Mystery

Quote

> "The electric arc," he continued, "isn't always just a silent electric light. You know that. You've heard them make noises. Under the right conditions such a light can be made to talk—the 'speaking arc,' as Professor Duddell calls it. In other words, an arc light can be made to act as a telephone receiver".[1]

Synopsis

When an expensive car is stolen, James McBirney doesn't turn to the ineffectual New York City police. Instead he hires private detective Guy Garrick, who is outfitted with the latest high-tech tools. When the car is located, it's clear it's been used in a murder, especially when a girl's body turns up. Garrick uses his scientific knowledge, along with high-tech scientific gadgets, to ferret out the criminals, smash a gambling ring, and save the reputations of several young people.

Critical Commentary

This novel, which may initially appear to be a simple detective story aimed at the popular reading public, gives today's readers a glimpse into the genesis of the modern fixation on crime fiction—especially that of the scientific variety, which has resulted in *CSI* and the family of *Law & Order* television shows, as well as high-tech espionage fiction. Illustrating the concern of the Progressive Era with social reform—the desire to stamp out crime and vice and to create effective societal change to eliminate poverty—the novel also reveals the anxiety of urban dwellers as they tried to adapt to the new social and economic circumstances created by rapid technological innovation in the early twentieth century, such as the growth in the number of cars and telephones and the threats such inventions held to conventional conceptions of morality.

Reeve has clearly appropriated many of the now-familiar elements of Arthur Conan Doyle's Sherlock for this story—the detective, Guy Garrick, with his sidekick, Marshall, works to solve a string of automobile thefts as well as the murder of a young woman. Besides the murder plot, a subplot revolves around the destruction of a gambling syndicate that threatens public order and morality. This subplot involves a rich man about town, Mortimer Warrington, scion of a real-estate fortune, who is trying to win the hand of debutante Violet Winslow—an objective that may be derailed if Warrington's character is damaged by association with gambling. The story is mediated by a variety of action sequences including car chases, raids on gambling casinos, and gunfights.

Garrick sets about to solve the crime, equipped with scientific devices including a hydraulic ram to open doors, the "detectaphone" (an eavesdropping device he uses to bug the criminal hideout), bulletproof coats, a mortar that fires tear gas, and a portable camera that he uses to photograph crime scenes. The criminals, for their part, are equally well armed, with paralyzing gas guns, hypodermic needles filled with poison, and a variety of other devices—not to mention their use of electricity and magnets to rig the games in their gambling dens. Readers witness a conflict between the uses of technology for good or evil, reflecting early twentieth-century perceptions and anxieties about technology.

As the story progresses, an underlying theme of the conflict between chaos and the forces of order also emerges. On the one hand, Garrick cooperates with various agents, such as the police and the newspapers, to solve the crimes. Yet at the same time, the government is seen as impotent. Garrick is initially drawn into the investigation by an insurance company interested in finding Warrington's missing $9,000 Mercedes automobile—which, incidentally, is about $175,000 in contemporary inflated 2006 dollars—because the police are seen as ineffectual in dealing with this modern kind of crime. The local police are all too eager to accept help from Garrick, who has training and equipment far beyond their own capabilities. In a sense Garrick could be seen as a kind of proto-Batman, sans tights, mask, and secret identity, standing ready to deliver justice where the local police cannot.

To a modern teen raised on a diet of MTV, R-rated movies, and easy access to images of violence and sex, both real and fictional, this story may seem tame to the point of silliness. However, as a historical document illustrating the issues and anxieties of America in the years right before World War I, this book serves as a poignant reminder of how the modern world has lost both its innocence and its belief in progress.

Author Sketch

Born October 15, 1880, in Patchogue, New York, Reeve was educated at Princeton (1903) and the New York Law School. During World War I, he helped establish the anti-espionage Detection Laboratory in Washington, D.C., for the federal government—a precursor to the FBI. He died August 9, 1936, in Trenton, New Jersey.[2]

Other Works by the Author

The Silent Bullet. New York: Harper, 1910.
The Poisoned Pen, Further Adventures of Craig Kennedy. New York: Harper, 1911.
Constance Dunlap. New York: Harper, 1913.
The Dream Doctor. New York: Harper, 1914.
The Exploits of Elaine. New York: Harper, 1915.
The Romance of Elaine. New York: Harper, 1916.
The Ear in the Wall. New York: Grosset & Dunlap, 1921.
The Film Mystery. New York: Grosset & Dunlap, 1921.
Pandora. New York: Harper, 1926.
The Golden Age of Crime. New York: Mohawk Press, 1931.

The Kidnap Club. New York: Macaulay, 1932.

French, Joseph Lewis, and Arthur B. Reeve. *The Best Ghost Stories*. New York: Boni and Liveright, 1919.

Reeve, Arthur B., and Robert H. Davis. *The Fourteen Points: Tales of Craig Kennedy, Master of Mystery*. New York: Harper, 1925.

Suggestions for Further Reading

Merivale, Patricia, and Susan Elizabeth Sweeney. *Detecting Texts: The Metaphysical Detective Story from Poe to Postmodernism*. Philadelphia: University of Pennsylvania Press, 1999.

Panek, LeRoy. *An Introduction to the Detective Story*. Bowling Green, OH: Bowling Green State University Popular Press, 1987.

Symons, Julian. *Bloody Murder: From the Detective Story to the Crime Novel*. 3rd rev. ed. New York: Mysterious Press, 1992.

Wagner, E. J. *The Science of Sherlock Holmes: From Baskerville Hall to the Valley of Fear, the Real Forensics Behind the Great Detective's Greatest Cases*. Hoboken, NJ: Wiley, 2006.

Notes

1. Arthur B. Reeve, *Guy Garrick: An Adventure with a Scientific Gunman* (New York: Grosset and Dunlap, 1914), p. 246.

2. http://www.online-literature.com/arthur-reeve/; http://tarlton.law.utexas.edu/lpop/reeve.html

Conrad Richter

The Sea of Grass

New York: Knopf, 1973

Originally published: 1937

Genre: Western

Quote

And I can feel the long-controlled but now violently overflowing passion of my uncle standing there with his gun belt buckled under his long-tailed gray broadcloth coat, while the man Lutie Brewton had refused to name, but whom we all knew, was coming towards us only a few hundred yards away, somewhere just behind that cloud of emigrant canvas.[1]

Synopsis

After a brief courtship, Jim Brewton marries Lutie of St. Louis. When Lutie arrives at Brewton's ranch in New Mexico, she finds that her husband is considered a brutal man who keeps homesteaders off his large ranch to preserve his cattle empire—his "sea of grass." This is a war zone where cattle rangers and farmers compete, often violently, for land. The disappointed Lutie eventually has an affair with Brewton's arch enemy, Brice Chamberlain. With the ensuing scandal, Brewton forces his wife to leave town—without custody of her children. Many years later, after Brewton's ranch empire has been ruined by drought, and his son Brock is killed, Lutie returns. Their daughter Sarah Beth brings about a reconciliation between her parents—who are now united in their mutual sorrow and regret about how their lives turned out.

Critical Commentary

In *The Sea of Grass,* Conrad Richter employs elements of the traditional Western to create an epic story that evokes deep emotion and reveals universal human truths. Told from the perspective of Jim Brewton's nephew Hal as an old man, this narrative about an unhappy marriage also tells the story of the settling of the West—of greed, boundaries, and dreams. Richter, with his deft characterizations, makes an old story fresh and original. Although *The Sea of Grass* is a book often mentioned in lists of good books, it is, unfortunately, one of those books that many people have never read—which is a pity because it is an important and pioneering book about the effect of man on the American landscape.

Lutie Brewton, an intriguing character, is absent for much of the story, and when she does return, her absence is never fully explained, although it surrounds the other characters in the story the way white space surrounds images in a painting. The primary character, Jim Brewton, is in perpetual conflict with the lawyer Brice Chamberlain, who not only is competing for Lutie, but who is also attempting, favoring the rights of the homesteaders, to bring down Brewton's efforts to build a land empire. Complicating the whole situation is Lutie's son Brock, who ends up on the wrong end of the law (and a rope), but whose death brings about the opportunity for a reconciliation between Brewton and Lutie. The conflict between the characters is played out in a motif reminiscent of classic Greek dramas, where the sins of the fathers are visited on the sons.

Richter's outstanding descriptions of the Western landscape are marvelously full, and he vividly portrays the negative effects of farming during the 1930s Dust Bowl years. Few writers of that time show such an awareness of environmental issues.

Richter successfully contrasts the expectations of different characters who have come into a new land with traditional attitudes in tow. He shows how the land remolds each one not only physically, but in a moral and psychological sense as well. This is a simple story, and Richter tells it in an appropriately minimalist way. Against the grand backdrop of the American Southwest, Colonel Brewton makes a choice for material success, a search that ultimately fails and costs him the love and respect of his wife. By the end of the novel, reduced in circumstances, Brewton has to some extent redeemed himself.

In its reverence for the environment and implicit condemnation of materialism, this novel was ahead of its time—a work that could have been written in the 1960s or even today. Although it was critically acclaimed when published, its status has faded in recent years, perhaps with the general decline of the Western. However, the story is still compelling to readers today, and the message of redemption is one we sorely need.

Author Sketch

Richter was born October 13, 1890, in Pine Grove, Pennsylvania, and became an editor, journalist, and writer. He received various awards, including a National Book Award nomination in 1937 for *The Sea of Grass*; the Pulitzer Prize for Fiction in 1951, for *The Town*; and the National Book Award in 1961 for *The Waters of Kronos*. He died October 30, 1968, in Pottsville Pennsylvania.[2]

Other Works by the Author

Brothers of No Kin, and Other Stories. New York: Hinds, Hayden & Eldredge, 1924.
Early Americana and Other Stories. New York: Knopf, 1936.
The Trees. New York: Knopf, 1940.
Tacey Cromwell. New York: Knopf, 1942.
The Free Man. New York: Knopf, 1943.
The Fields. New York: Knopf, 1946.
The Light in the Forest. New York: Knopf, 1953.
The Mountain on the Desert; A Philosophical Journey. New York: Knopf, 1955.
The Lady. New York: Knopf, 1957.
The Waters of Kronos. New York: Knopf, 1960.
A Simple Honorable Man. New York: Knopf, 1962.
The Grandfathers. New York: Knopf, 1964.
The Awakening Land: I. The Trees, II. The Fields, III. The Town. New York: Knopf, 1966.
A Country of Strangers. New York: Knopf, 1966.
The Aristocrat. New York: Knopf, 1968.
The Rawhide Knot and Other Stories. New York: Knopf, 1978.

Richter, Harvena, and Conrad Richter. *Writing to Survive: The Private Notebooks of Conrad Richter.* Albuquerque: University of New Mexico Press, 1988.

Suggestions for Further Reading

Johnson, David R. *Conrad Richter: A Writer's Life.* University Park: Pennsylvania State University Press, 2001.

Tobias, Henry Jack, and Charles E. Woodhouse. *Santa Fe: A Modern History, 1890–1990.* Albuquerque: University of New Mexico Press, 2001.

Worster, Donald. *An Unsettled Country: Changing Landscapes of the American West.* Albuquerque: University of New Mexico Press, 1994.

Notes

1. Conrad Richter, *The Sea of Grass* (New York: Knopf, 1973), p. 56.

2. "Conrad Richter," in *Dictionary of Literary Biography,* Vol. 212: *Twentieth-Century American Western Writers, Second Series,* ed. Richard H. Cracroft (Detroit: Gale Group, 1999), pp. 226–232; Johnson, David, *Conrad Richter: A Writer's Life* (University Park: The Pennsylvania State University Press, 2001).

Sax Rohmer

The Mask of Fu Manchu

New York: Burt, 1932

Originally published: 1932

Genre: Crime Fiction/Mystery

Quote

> There came a faint pattering sound on the narrow ledge outside and below the shutters. A
> dull impact and a faint creaking of woodwork told of a weight imposed upon the projecting
> window. Something began to move upward—a dim shadow behind the slats—upward and
> inward—towards the opening[1]

Synopsis

This story revolves around the evil Fu Manchu's efforts to obtain the sword and mask of
Genghis Khan. Possession of these items will allow him to start a holy war that will destabilize
Western governments. Scotland Yard becomes aware of this plot and dispatches a team whose
members follow Fu Manchu from Persia to Egypt where they attempt foil the plot of the evil
mastermind.

Critical Commentary

For fans of Indiana Jones and other action-packed adventure stories, *The Mask of Fu Manchu* is equally enjoyable and a similar break from reality. The writer conjures the atmosphere
and air of the Middle East of the late 1920s and early 1930s—as perceived by American readers
with established preconceptions about the nature and behavior of upper-class English aristocrats, imperial administrators, and Asian criminal gangs. Although certainly not a literary
masterpiece, this book, with its nonstop action, constant deaths, explosions, and plot twists,
represents 1930s pulp fantasy at its best and most lurid.

Written from the Western point of view, the novel offers clear evidence of the bias of the
times. The primary characters almost never interact with the local population, except when the
latter are servants, so readers looking for accurate descriptions of daily life should look elsewhere. However, there's something of a P. G. Wodehouse quality to the work, invoking thoughts
of cricket whites and the playing fields of Eton, embellished with entertaining purple prose. At
the same time, Rohmer is a master of suspenseful plotting and pacing, and readers are kept on
their toes, wondering if the evil mastermind Fu Manchu will be victorious or will he be foiled at
the last moment by Anglo-Saxon cleverness. The writer, despite his use of stereotypes, manages
to breathe vitality into the simple plot and create a riveting and entertaining story.

Beyond the roller coast ride of the plot, the story also contains a few other features that
should give contemporary readers pause for thought. Ironically, the primary concerns of the

characters in the novel are the rise of Islamic fundamentalism under a charismatic leader and the effect this will have on the stability of the Middle East. Many of the solutions to the problem promoted in this story are as simplistic, in many respects, as those devised by world leaders today.

This book reveals how our ancestors viewed the world around them and could provide an interesting springboard to discussion about world history, as well as racism and stereotypes. And of course, in spite of its many flaws, the story is still a grabber.

Author Sketch

Born in Birmingham, England, Rohmer was the son of Irish parents, William and Margaret Mary Furey Ward. As a young man he began writing while working in menial clerical and reporting jobs. From 1903 onward, he began publishing stories in magazines and doing other odd writing jobs until the debut in 1913 of *The Mystery of Dr. Fu-Manchu* brought him success. From then until his death from complications of Asiatic flu in 1959, Rohmer had a successful career, not only with the Fu Manchu novels, but also with a number of other books and short stories, mostly in the mystery and horror genre.[2]

Other Works by the Author

The Return of Dr. Fu-Manchu. New York: McKinley Stone & Mackenzie, 1916.

The Golden Scorpion. New York: McKinlay, 1920.

The Green Eyes of Bast. New York: McKinlay, Stone & Mackenzie, 1920.

Bat Wing. New York: Burt, 1921.

Fire-Tongue. London: Cassell, 1921.

Brood of the Witch-Queen. New York: Burt, 1924.

The Devil Doctor; Hitherto Unpublished Adventures in the Career of the Misterious Dr. Fu-Manchu. London: Methuen, 1924.

The Quest of the Sacred Slipper. London: Pearson, 1925.

Tales of Secret Egypt. London: Methuen, 1926.

The Emperor of America. Garden City, NY: Doubleday, Doran, 1929.

Daughter of Fu Manchu. Garden City, NY: Doubleday, Doran, 1931.

The Bride of Fu Manchu. Mattituck, NY: American Reprint, 1933.

The Trail of Fu Manchu. Garden City, NY: Doubleday, Doran, 1934.

The Bat Flies Low. New York: Burt, 1936.

The Drums of Fu Manchu. New York: Doubleday, Doran, 1939.

The Island of Fu Manchu. New York: Doubleday, Doran, 1941.

The Fu-Manchu Omnibus. London: Allison & Busby, 1995.

Ward, Arthur Henry. *Dope, a Story of Chinatown and the Drug Traffic, by Sax Rohmer.* London, 1919.

The Mystery of Dr. Fu-Manchu, by Sax Rohmer. London: Methuen, 1913.

The Sins of Sâeverac Bablon, by Sax Rohmer. London: 1914.

The Yellow Claw, by Sax Rohmer. London: Methuen, 1915.

Suggestions for Further Reading

Chan, Jachinson. *Chinese American Masculinities: From Fu Manchu to Bruce Lee.* New York: Routledge, 2001.

Chen, Tina. *Double Agency: Acts of Impersonation in Asian American Literature and Culture.* Stanford, CA: Stanford University Press, 2005.

Day, Bradford M. *Sax Rohmer: A Bibliography.* Denver: Science-Fiction & Fantasy Publications, 1963.

Notes

1. Sax Rohmer, *The Mask of Fu Manchu* (New York: Burt, 1932), p. 55.

2. *Dictionary of Literary Biography,* Vol. 70: *British Mystery Writers, 1860–1919,* ed. Bernard Benstockand Thomas F. Staley (Detroit: Gale, 1988), pp. 258–268.

Kim Ronyoung

Clay Walls

Seattle: University of Washington Press, 1994

Originally published: 1987

Genre: Mainstream/ Fiction/Immigrants

Quote

> The ride from Bunker Hill to Temple Street was too brief for her. Only a few minutes sepa-
> rated the mansions of the well-to-do Americans from the plain wood-framed houses of
> the ghettos. But it might as well be a hundred years, she thought. Her country's history
> went back thousands of years but no one in America seemed to care. To her dismay, few
> Americans knew where Korea was. This was 1920. The United States was supposed to
> be a modern country. Yet to Americans, Koreans were "oriental," the same as Chinese,
> Japanese, or Filipino.[1]

Synopsis

Three generations of Korean Americans in California from the 1920s onward deal with
their integration and adjustment into a new society. Through the individual narratives of three
individuals, Haesu, Chun, and Faye, a story of success in the face of discrimination, poverty,
and personal struggle is created—against the backdrop of a developing California and political
changes in Korea over several decades.

Critical Commentary

Aside from the stereotype of the workaholic Korean greengrocer, the Korean American
immigrant experience has never received the level of attention given other Asian groups in
American literature. In *Clay Walls*, Kim Ronyoung redresses this inequity with a stunning,
multigenerational novel of a Korean family facing the trials of American immigrant life.

Covering the 1920s through the end of World War II, the story is organized in three parts,
reflecting three generations; but Ronyoung uses the character of Haesu as the linchpin, tracing
her experiences and contrasting them with life in Korea during the same period. This technique effectively illustrates the contrast between Korea and America, and it shows the process
of Americanization affecting all immigrants to some degree. Haesu is, in Korea, a member of
the upper class, but she ends up married to Chun, who is of a lower class and who, because
of his political involvements against Japanese occupation in Korea, is eventually forced to im-
migrate with Haesu to America. So this is a story not only of immigration, but also of how a
woman adjusts herself to a life quite different in status and position from the one she was raised
to expect.

Confronted with racism, the daily humiliations of life on the economic margin, and conflicts with other Koreans who are ambiguous about America, the characters are still emotionally rooted in issues of Korean nationalism during a particularly difficult period of Korean history that included the Japanese occupation and World War II. These events are thoughtfully detailed by an author who lived much of this story.

In Ronyoung's historically sensitive and accurate portrayal of Depression-era California, the reader encounters ordinary people burdened by circumstances, trying to make economic headway while also dealing with the aggravating circumstances of racism and ignorance. Basically, this is the story of a Korean couple that arrives in the 1920s and what happens to them—their struggles to find decent housing, to develop a small business, and to raise a family—all while they are dealing with a pervasive and stressful environment of racism. The story has a vivid documentary quality—evidenced in passages such as the one showing how they had to have a white friend purchase a home for them because the law (and local custom) didn't allow "Orientals" to own real estate. Along the way the couple deals with a variety of other issues—such as their relative Clara's decision to marry a white man and their loss a lucrative business contract because of graft and prejudice.

A sophisticated and subtle commentary on human relationships as well as on the psychological costs of immigration, this book offers a positive message with increased relevance for readers today.

Author Sketch

Kim Ronyoung was born on March 28, 1926, in Los Angeles, California. She attended San Francisco State University and later married Dr. Richard Hahn, a physician, who created a scholarship foundation as a memorial. She died in February, 1987.[2]

Other Works by the Author

None

Suggestions for Further Reading

Charr, Easurk Emsen, and Wayne Patterson. *The Golden Mountain: The Autobiography of a Korean Immigrant, 1895–1960*. 2nd ed. Urbana: University of Illinois Press, 1995.

Jo, Moon H. *Korean Immigrants and the Challenge of Adjustment*. Contributions in Sociology, No. 127. Westport, CT: Greenwood Press, 1999.

Lee, Helie. *Still Life with Rice: A Young American Woman Discovers the Life and Legacy of Her Korean Grandmother*. New York: Scribner, 1996.

Lee, Jennifer. *Civility in the City: Blacks, Jews, and Koreans in Urban America*. Cambridge, MA: Harvard University Press, 2002.

Lee, Mary Paik, and Sucheng Chan. *Quiet Odyssey: A Pioneer Korean Woman in America*. Seattle: University of Washington Press, 1990.

Notes

1. Kim Ronyoung, *Clay Walls* (Seattle: University of Washington Press, 1994), p. 7.
2. http://www.isop.ucla.edu/shenzhen/2002ncta/workman/eaaw/eaaw_korean/ronyoung_kim.htm

James Salter

The Hunters

New York: Vintage International/Random House, 1999

Originally published: 1956

Genre: Military/Adventure

Quote

> For a naked moment, they looked at each other. It had been a genuine confidence, and Cleve knew how good his chances really were. Whatever the advantages of ability, there was something even more important. It was motive. He had come to meet his enemy without reservation.[1]

Synopsis

Air Force Captain Cleve Connell enters the Korean War with the single goal of becoming a jet ace. He goes on mission after mission, but is never able to shoot down a plane; in fact, he rarely even sees the enemy. Connell's young wingman, Pell, seems able to destroy the enemy without effort, as do other pilots—all of which adds to Connell's self-doubt. In addition, his fellow pilots increasingly question his courage and luck. During a successful flight, the gun camera jams. So that his kills will still be counted, Connell gives credit for them to another pilot, Billy Hunter, who died in the action. When Connell is finally killed in combat, it's unclear whether his death is from combat or is a suicide.

Critical Commentary

Contemporary adventure novels don't often go beyond the action and technology. If one, for example, considers the works of Dale Brown, which focus, like Salter, on aerial combat, the stories often seem more about the airplanes and their technology than the people who fly them. Salter pushes past this idea of a superficial action-filled war story to create a timeless and deeply moving and introspective story of men in situations of desperate physical and emotional peril.

Cleve Connell goes to war and faces himself. He enters combat assured of his technical skills as a combat pilot, but in the actual testing of those skills, he finds himself perpetually frustrated.

Although accurately described airplanes and aerial derring-do play a big part in the story, Salter avoids the problem of making them the main focus—which might make the story flat and uninteresting; he instead turns his attention to the real battles that take place on the ground and between and inside the characters. In addition, Salter explores a fundamental paradox of military life. On the one hand, the characters are all brothers in arms, united, supposedly, in a common cause. Yet they are each in competition with one another to prove who is the better pilot.

Salter writes about large issues of men at war—the terrors they face, the frustration, the loneliness of combat, and the essential fact that removes the individual struggle that men face in peacetime, subsuming that into a collective battle. However, he never loses his sense of the importance of the individual perspective, conveyed through the inner dialogues of the characters. This gives an emotional depth to action as it develops, with the reader knowing the characters intimately and deeply caring what happens to them. This is a beautifully written and detailed story about the reality of men in combat that should be of interest not only to military and history buffs, but also to anyone interested in a dramatic psychological portrait of men under stress.

Author Sketch

Born in 1926, Salter grew up in New York City. After graduating from West Point in 1945, he entered the U.S. Army Air Force and served as a fighter pilot, flying more than a hundred combat missions during the Korean War. After publication of his first novel in 1957, Salter resigned his commission. He then earned his living as a writer, was the father of four children, and divided his time between Aspen, Colorado, and Bridgehampton, New York, before his death in 2000.[2]

Other Works by the Author

A Sport and a Pastime. New York: Bantam Books, 1968.
Light Years. New York: Random House, 1975.
Solo Faces. Boston: Little, Brown, 1979.
Dusk and Other Stories. San Francisco: North Point Press, 1988.
Burning the Days: Recollection. New York: Random House, 1997.
Last Night. New York: Knopf, 2005.
Gods of Tin: The Flying Years. Edited by Jessica Benton and William Benton. Washington, D.C.: Shoemaker & Hoard, 2004.
There & Then: The Travel Writing of James Salter. Emeryville, CA: Shoemaker & Hoard, 2005.

Suggestions for Further Reading

Crane, Conrad C. *American Airpower Strategy in Korea, 1950–1953.* Lawrence: University Press of Kansas, 2000.
Sherwood, John Darrell. *Officers in Flight Suits: The Story of American Air Force Fighter Pilots in the Korean War.* New York: New York University Press, 1996.
Werrell, Kenneth P. *Sabres over MiG Alley: The F-86 and the Battle for Air Superiority in Korea.* Annapolis, MD: Naval Institute Press, 2005.
Zhang, Xiaoming, and NetLibrary Inc. *Red Wings over the Yalu China, the Soviet Union, and the Air War in Korea.* Texas A&M University Military History Series, No. 80. College Station: Texas A&M University Press, 2002.

Notes

1. James Salter, *The Hunters* (New York: Vintage International/Random House, 1999), p. 35.
2. "James Salter" in *Dictionary of Literary Biography,* Vol. 130: *American Short-Story Writers since World War II,* ed. Patrick Meanor (Detroit: Gale, 1993), pp. 282–287; http://www.albany.edu/writers-inst/salter.html

Thomas Sanchez

Rabbit Boss

New York: Vintage Contemporaries, 1989

Originally published: 1973

Genre: Mainstream/Literary Fiction/Historical Fiction

Quote

> He looked up from *them* who were on the lake to the power in the Sky, the power of
> *Musege*, his brothers in nature who had secret medicine, strong medicine that many times
> was superior to his own, medicine that he had tried to capture, imitate, kill.[1]

Synopsis

This novel tells the story of the Washo Indians of California over several generations. From
the 1840s onward, when they observed the Donner party, the Washo nation—and in particular
the family of their spiritual leader, the Rabbit—are degraded by the incoming whites who don't
respect their culture and who abuse them in many ways.

Critical Commentary

It has been said that collapsing civilizations often fail from within before they are ultimately
destroyed from without. This principle is examined from a fictional perspective in *Rabbit Boss,*
through the story of the Washo Indians of the California mountains. Sanchez has given readers
a dramatic multigenerational story of a people's destruction, showing both external forces and
personal failures of those on all sides in this cautionary tale about the consequences of choice.

In a distinctive and complex narrative style, a modified steam of consciousness, Sanchez
moves backward and forward in time, showing the gradual erosion of the traditional society,
personified by the Rabbit Boss who goes from being a spiritual leader to displaying total impo-
tence—irrelevant and unable to help his people.

The rich traditional lives of the Washo, with their customs, folklore, and psychology, are
placed in brilliant relief against the poverty and hopelessness of their lives as they move into
modernity. Sanchez's tragic depictions of Washo life in the railroad camps and the modern
squalor of Nevada, with the "honkers" reduced to picking up white women tourists for free
drinks and meals, are gut-wrenching.

Rabbit Boss, portrayed over generations, is the central and most powerful character in the
novel, personifying the various responses to change—from avoidance of the invading whites
to erosion of spirit and culture, to eventual capitulation and destruction, as traditions are replaced with inadequate substitutes such as Christianity and alcohol.

The contrasts are vivid among the white characters in the book—ranchers, the sheriff, the
gas station owner with his hope in his "Snackette" machine, and most disturbingly, the real

estate speculators who are never fully developed as character, but who are truly ominous—anonymous men hidden behind their masks of letters and legal paperwork. In Sanchez's dark irony, those who evicted the Washo—ranchers, businessmen, and whites in general who thought they had a better use for the land, seeing the Washo as primitive—are now themselves evicted by representatives of a newer, more sophisticated society.

The California landscape, vividly described, is an omnipresent character in this novel, its fate paralleling that of the Washo. Rabbits that once ran free end up trapped by mechanical devices, without even the dignity in death allowed them by the Washo.

Sanchez stretches beyond the traditional literary stereotypes of the conflict between whites and Native Americans to show that, ultimately, the Washo share some responsibility for their fate. On one level, they are victims of circumstance, but they also make a number of personal choices, as individuals and as a tribe, that aid in their own destruction. It is this honesty that gives the book its real power. It is certainly a valuable and interesting book for anyone interested in Native American culture or American history generally.

Author Sketch

A California native, born in Oakland on February 26, 1944, Thomas Sanchez has worked on cattle ranches in the Sierra Nevada, ran food to Native Americans during the events at Wounded Knee in 1973 while working for Pacifica Radio, and has traveled widely throughout Europe and Latin America. He currently lives in San Francisco.[2]

Other Works by the Author

Rabbit Boss. New York: A.A. Knopf, 1973.
Zoot-Suit Murders: A Novel. New York: Dutton, 1978.
Angels Burning: Native Notes from the Land of Earthquake and Fire. Bound with Lawrence Clark Powell, *Ocean in View: The Malibu.* Santa Barbara, CA: Capra Press, 1987.
Mile Zero. New York: Alfred A. Knopf, 1989.
Day of the Bees: A Novel. New York: A.A. Knopf: Distributed by Random House, 2000.
King Bongo: A Novel of Havana. New York: Alfred A. Knopf, 2003.
"Saddle up the Rattlesnakes" [Poem]. Tiburon: CA: Cadmus Editions, 1982.

Suggestions for Further Reading

Calabro, Marian. *The Perilous Journey of the Donner Party.* New York: Clarion Books, 1999.
Downs, James F. *Washo Religion.* Berkeley and Los Angeles: University of California Press, 1961.
Walton, Priscilla L. *Our Cannibals, Ourselves.* Urbana: University of Illinois Press, 2004.

Notes

1. Thomas Sanchez, *Rabbit Boss* (New York: Vintage Contemporaries, 1989), p. 3.

2. http://www.thomas-sanchez.com/en/biography/bio_index.html; *Contemporary Authors Online*, Gale, 2005.

George Santayana

The Last Puritan: A Memoir in the Form of a Novel

New York: Scribner's, 1936

Originally published: 1936

Genre: Mainstream/Literary Fiction

Quote

Cities for Oliver were not part of nature. He could hardly feel, he could hardly admit even
when it was pointed out to him, that cities are a second body for the human mind, a second
organism, more rational, permanent and decorative than the animal organism of flesh and
bone: a work of natural yet moral art, where the soul sets up all her trophies of action and
instruments of pleasure.[1]

Synopsis

Oliver Alden is the heir to a fortune. He is also the son of a depraved man who, among other
things, commits a murder at Harvard before going into medicine; Oliver's father eventually
becomes a drug-addicted hedonist wandering the world in his yacht, doomed to suicide. This
is the story of Oliver's quest for meaning.

At age 17 he goes for a cruise on his father's yacht, meeting Jim Darnley. Oliver later visits
the Darnleys in England and falls in love with Jim's sister Rose, who in turn falls in love with
Oliver's European cousin Mario. Thwarted in his romantic pursuit, Oliver then follows Mario's
example, entering the army at the outbreak of World War I.

Critical Commentary

The importance of this novel lies both in its ideas and in its presentation. In ornate and
aphoristic prose, Santayana delivers a story and also a philosophy—a reflection on the growth
of modern society and the psychological cost this has entailed.

Although this novel was a best seller when initially published, today Santayana has fallen
into disregard as an American literary talent. A transitional figure between nineteenth- and
twentieth-century thought, he is better known to historians of philosophy than to the public
at large. *The Last Puritan* can be seen as a criticism of modern society—a society confused
by dimly appreciated and misunderstood views of equity and market economics, which have
eliminated beauty as something held in esteem.

The value of beauty can be seen as the central issue of this novel. Oliver Alden's father
is a materialist who gradually and spiritually declines as his life progresses. His weakness is
inner and moral, hidden in darkness, much like his murder of the Harvard night watchman

early in the novel. As the man ages, his ugliness, like his drug addiction, becomes increasingly pronounced and visible. Oliver Alden, on the other hand, celebrates the creative force and embraces the idea of beauty—with, ultimately, what can be seen as tragic consequences.

Santayana takes a traditional narrative structure and uses it to promote his philosophical ideas. It is a fairly straightforward story carrying the main character from birth through adult life. It is this very simplicity that makes the power of the ideas come through. Readers are not confused, as they might be in a more modernist novel, by constant changes in point of view, interior monologue, and the other technical tricks of the novelist's craft. The ideas are left free to present themselves through the actions and the dialogue of the characters. Santayana has also developed, through the story, beautiful character studies of individuals—some of whom, like Oliver's father, are very ugly people.

The Last Puritan, although technically an "American" novel, more closely resembles European writing, especially in its celebration of creativity and the idea of beauty for beauty's sake. Santayana's writing shares an aesthetic with late nineteenth-century naturalist writers such as Beerbohm and Beardsley, though with more tragic overtones than in early twentieth-century American modernism. In rejecting the ideology of Puritan materialism, he embraces an almost Platonic idealism. He also exhibits an overwhelming European suspicion of progress, especially as expressed in his portrayal of a grasping American industrial development. This sets the novel apart from others of its era and may account, at least in part, for its present unpopularity—which is a pity because Santayana has a great deal to say that is, perhaps, even more relevant to our modern age than to the era in which he was writing.

Author Sketch

Born in Madrid, Spain, on December 16, 1863, Santayana combined the best of the Old World and New. He moved to Boston at age eight, where he was educated both at Harvard, where he pursued undergraduate as well as graduate studies and received his doctorate, and at German universities. Santayana went on to a distinguished career as a Harvard professor. An outstanding intellectual force and philosopher, Santayana was noted for his naturalism and interest in the role of the human imagination. He was also a prolific writer. He wrote widely in the areas of philosophy, religion, fiction, and poetry. Although he spent much of his career in America, he was closely aligned with various elements of the European intellectual tradition, especially in his implicit distrust of modernism. After his retirement from Harvard in 1912, he moved to Europe and spent the last 40 years of his life there, until his death in Rome on September 26, 1952.[2]

Other Works by the Author

The Sense of Beauty, Being the Outline of Aesthetic Theory. New York: Scribner's, 1898.
Soliloquies in England and Later Soliloquies. London: Constable, 1922.
Sonnets and Other Verses. New York: Stone and Kimball, 1896.
Lucifer; A Theological Tragedy. Chicago and New York: Stone, 1899.
The Hermit of Carmel, and Other Poems. New York: Scribner's, 1901.
Three Philosophical Poets: Lucretius, Dante, and Goethe. Cambridge: Harvard University, 1910.
Poems. New York: Scribner's, 1923.

Winds of Doctrine; Studies in Contemporary Opinion. New York: Scribner's, 1926.

Interpretations of Poetry and Religion. New York: Scribner's, 1927.

Platonism and the Spiritual Life. London: Constable, 1927.

The Life of Reason; Or, the Phases of Human Progress. 2nd ed. New York: Scribner's, 1932.

Sense of Beauty. New York: Scribner's, 1936.

The Idea of Christ in the Gospels; Or, God in Man, a Critical Essay. New York: Scribner's, 1946.

The Philosophy of Santayana; Selections from All the Works of George Santayana. New and greatly enlarged edition, edited, with a new pref. and an introductory essay, by Irwin Edman. New York: Scribner, 1953.

Egotism in German Philosophy. New York: Haskell House, 1971.

The Genteel Tradition at Bay. Brooklyn: Haskell House, 1977.

The Works of George Santayana. Cambridge, MA: MIT Press, 1986.

The Sense of Beauty: Being the Outlines of Aesthetic Theory. Critical ed. Cambridge, MA: MIT Press, 1988.

The Sense of Beauty. New Brunswick, NJ: Transaction, 2003.

Suggestions for Further Reading

Kirby-Smith, H. T. *A Philosophical Novelist: George Santayana and "The Last Puritan."* Carbondale: Southern Illinois University Press, 1997.

McCormick, John. *George Santayana: A Biography.* New Brunswick, NJ: Transaction, 2003.

Singer, Irving. *George Santayana, Literary Philosopher.* New Haven: Yale University Press, 2000.

Notes

1. George Santayana, *The Last Puritan* (New York: Scribner's, 1936), p. 140.

2. http://plato.stanford.edu/entries/santayana/; John McCormick, *George Santayana: A Biography* (New Brunswick, NJ: Transaction, 2003).

Lynne Sharon Schwartz

Leaving Brooklyn

New York: Penguin Books, 1989

Originally published: 1989

Genre: Mainstream/Literary Fiction

Quote

> Does being true to one's self mean offering the literal truth or the truth that should have been, the truth of the image of one's self? It hardly matters by this time. By this time the border between seeing straight on and seeing around the corner of solid objects, between the world as smooth and coherent and the world as disassociated skinless particles, is thoroughly blurred.[1]

Synopsis

Audrey, a young Jewish girl growing up in early 1950s Brooklyn, lives a conventional life, circumscribed by her rigid family life, her school, and the confines of her middle- and working-class neighborhood—except for one thing. She has a defect in her right eye that causes her, literally, to see the world differently than others. This is a lifelong problem until, when she is 15 years old, her parents take her to an ophthalmologist in Manhattan for a contact lens. On subsequent office visits, the doctor and Audrey enter into a sexual relationship that, although it ends, causes Audrey to seriously question the staid values of her insular Brooklyn existence. She begins to see the true potential for her life and finally escapes the clutches of her middle-class destiny as a wife and mother to find a creative life.

Critical Commentary

Leaving Brooklyn takes the well-worn theme of leaving home and twists it in a striking and creative way to create a fresh, contemporary story. Schwartz's story of Audrey and her growing up in the insular world of Brooklyn in the early 1950s will likely leave the reader pondering the role of memory in shaping our lives.

Audrey's bad eye is the central motif of the novel. It is what sets her apart, both physically and emotionally, from her family as well as her peers, and it is the driving force that propels events in her life. In first person, Audrey tells us how she adapts to her differences and eventually uses them to become her own person while surrounded by a varied cast of characters—an overbearing Jewish mother, a lesbian teacher, a bourgeois visitor, and perhaps most importantly, a neurotic Manhattan eye doctor with whom Audrey has an affair—a figure who comes off more sad and pathetic than creepy.

This is really a story about the struggle between conformity and the artistic life. Audrey's experiences in Manhattan, sexual and otherwise, differ greatly from the dull noncreative life of

Brooklyn, where the fact that nothing ever happens is considered something of a virtue. The protected, innocent life of Audrey's childhood contrasts with that of an intelligent adult functioning in the world—brave and self-confident enough to take the risks and make the choices that her peers or her parents would not.

Beyond offering readers a well-told and realistic story, Schwartz gives us a dream; and a stimulating dream, it is. In addition, she shows us a lost New York, where it was really possible to have several different lives, with people in one life never intersecting with those in another. She also suggests that under the plainest of exteriors, there can be some intense and even dark things going on—things that can shape lives and the world in dramatic and interesting ways. The result is an intriguing book that should appeal to a wide range of readers.

Author Sketch

Lynne Sharon Schwartz, a native of Brooklyn, is the author of 19 novels, many nominated for awards, including *Leaving Brooklyn* (nominated for a PEN/Faulkner Award); *Rough Strife* (nominated for the PEN/Hemingway First Novel Award); *In the Family Way: An Urban Comedy*; the memoir *Ruined by Reading*; and the poetry collection *In Solitary*. She earned a BA from Barnard College (1959) and an MA from Bryn Mawr (1961) with further graduate study at New York University (1967–1972), after which she left school to write. She lives in New York City.[2]

Other Works by the Author

Rough Strife. New York: Harper & Row, 1980.
Acquainted with the Night, and Other Stories. New York: Harper & Row, 1984.
We Are Talking about Homes: A Great University against Its Neighbors. New York: Harper & Row, 1985.
The Melting Pot and Other Subversive Stories. New York: Harper & Row, 1987.
Balancing Acts. New York: Penguin Books, 1989.
A Lynne Sharon Schwartz Reader: Selected Prose and Poetry. The Bread Loaf Series of Contemporary Writers. Hanover, NH: University Press of New England, 1992.
The Fatigue Artist: A Novel. New York: Scribner, 1995.
Ruined by Reading: A Life in Books. Boston: Beacon Press, 1996.
In the Family Way: An Urban Comedy. New York: Morrow, 1999.
Face to Face: A Reader in the World. Boston: Beacon Press, 2000.
In Solitary: Poems. Riverdale-on-Hudson, NY: Sheep Meadow Press, 2002.
Referred Pain: And Other Stories. New York: Counterpoint, 2004.
The Writing on the Wall: A Novel. New York: Counterpoint, 2005.
Ginzburg, Natalia, and Lynne Sharon Schwartz. *A Place to Live: And Other Selected Essays of Natalia Ginzburg.* New York: Seven Stories Press, 2002.

Suggestions for Further Reading

Abramovitch, Ilana, and Seán Galvin. *Jews of Brooklyn.* Hanover, NH: University Press of New England, 2002.
Cudahy, Brian J. *How We Got to Coney Island: The Development of Mass Transportation in Brooklyn and Kings County.* New York: Fordham University Press, 2002.

Ford, Carole Bell. *The Girls: Jewish Women of Brownsville, Brooklyn, 1940–1995.* SUNY Series in Modern Jewish Literature and Culture. Albany: State University of New York Press, 2000.

Haw, Richard. *The Brooklyn Bridge: A Cultural History.* New Brunswick, NJ: Rutgers University Press, 2005.

Snyder-Grenier, Ellen M., and Brooklyn Historical Society. *Brooklyn! An Illustrated History, Critical Perspectives on the Past.* Philadelphia: Temple University Press, 1996.

Notes

1. Lynne Sharon Schwartz, *Leaving Brooklyn* (New York: Penguin Books, 1989), p. 146.

2. *Dictionary of Literary Biography,* Vol. 218: *American Short-Story Writers since World War II, Second Series,* ed. Patrick Meanor and Gwen Crane (Detroit: Gale, 1999), pp. 265–271; http://www.perseusbooksgroup.com/counterpoint/author_detail.jsp?id=1000016190

Catherine Maria Sedgwick

A New England Tale

New York: E. Bliss and E. White, 1822

Originally published: 1822

Genre: Mainstream/Literary Fiction

Quote

> A robin had built its nest on the vine; and often as she sat watching her sleeping mother, she had been cheered with its sprightly note, and maternal care of its young. She looked to the nest—the birds had flown;—"they too," she exclaimed, "have deserted this house of sorrow."[1]

Synopsis

After a debate among various relatives who all have reasons that taking Jane in would cause problems, Jane Elton, orphaned at an early age, with few resources because of the financial problems of her bankrupt father, ends up with her aunt, Mrs. Wilson. Life in her new home is difficult because Mrs. Wilson is a religious fanatic whose especially narrow Calvinist views are at odds with Jane's good nature and positive view of humanity. As Jane grows up, she searches for a better way to live in the world through both education—her own and her education of others as a teacher—and her interactions with more broad-minded people such as the servant Mary Hull. Eventually, she marries to Mr. Lloyd, whose Quaker religion starkly contrasts with that of Mrs. Wilson. Throughout all of her ups and downs, Jane keeps her good nature and refuses to compromise her honesty or principles for personal gain.

Critical Commentary

The early nineteenth century was beset by a wide range of philosophical discussions about what exactly it meant to be an "American." In truth, although the political issues related to the existence of the nation had been settled by the conclusion of the War of 1812, there was still spirited debate about what precisely had been won. The role of women—and what exactly the "women's sphere" was in the new republic—was a heated topic. In *A New England Tale* Catherine Sedgwick makes one of the earliest and more interesting attempts in American literature to come to grips with this issue.

After orphaned Jane comes to live with her odious relatives, the Wilsons, who scheme and plot at every turn to frustrate Jane in her attempts to have a successful life. Despite this, Jane manages, through becoming a teacher, to develop some modicum of financial and personal independence. The Wilsons, through their narrow Calvinism, see Jane as wayward and evil. Jane, on the other hand, accepts a more gentle and open version of Christianity—culminating in her marriage to the Quaker Mr. Lloyd. Religion is a central concern of the novel's characters. None of them reject religion, but they are definitely at odds in their various interpretations of it.

201

Jane is a not exactly a rebel, although some of her actions, such as sneaking out to a night dance, could be seen that way, but she works within the framework of conventional conceptions of morality—resistant to her aunt and refusing to participate in events that might be morally compromising, such as pilfering small objects from her father's estate even though the chances of her being caught are practically nil.

The conflict within the novel—developed within the framework of a traditional moralistic novel—really represents the conflict between two visions of America: one in which events are dictated by God and another in which, although people acknowledge God, they also accept responsibility for their actions and recognize that they have an obligation to do and achieve and to exercise virtue in the advancement of the community. Implicit in this controversy is the question of what role women have in the development of society.

In Jane, the reader sees a twofold answer. On the one hand, Jane gains employment as a teacher—thus serving to educate the minds of the new republic. On the other hand, Jane eventually retires from teaching, upon her marriage, and in this phase of life, she presumably will work to educate her children in the new values of republicanism. Jane's experience reflects the dualism and ambiguity that early nineteenth-century Americans felt about the role of women—although they had a role in public life, that role was circumscribed by and subservient to their role as mothers and educators of a new generation of Americans.

This traditional novel contains countless references to Christian morality; however, regardless of what could be seen as a didactic tone typical of early nineteenth-century novels, this is a fascinating psychological portrait of people forming a new nation. It is filled with a variety of moral ambiguities and uncertainties about the role of the citizen in a new society—such as the sacrifices that the farmers make to send their children to school when they could be employed on the farm, putting the needs of the new nation for educated citizens above their own economic interest, or such as when Mrs. Wilson asks Jane to take linens and spoons from her dead mother's home at the expense of the estate's creditors. The plotting is tight with enough twists and turns to maintain the reader's interest throughout. *A New England Tale* is well recommended for students of nineteenth-century history as well as for those interested in the history of women in America

Author Sketch

Born in Stockbridge, Massachusetts, on December 28, 1789, Catherine Maria Sedgwick was raised in an environment of culture, tempered by her family's political and social prominence; her father was an active politician and judge on the Massachusetts Supreme Court. Educated both at home and in schools, Sedgwick was an active Unitarian after 1821—a decision that greatly influenced her writing through that sect's interest in issues of social equality and societal reform. Her numerous novels are notable for both their pioneering attempts at a realistic novel and their firm basis in the ideals of morality and domesticity. Never married, Sedgwick traveled extensively throughout the United States and Europe, incorporating her observations into her descriptions of people and landscape. She died on July 31, 1867, in West Roxbury, Massachusetts.[2]

Other Works by the Author

Mary Hollis: An Original Tale. New-York: New-York Unitarian Book Society, 1822.

A New-England Tale; Or, Sketches of New-England Character and Manners. New York: E. Bliss and E. White, 1822.

Redwood; A Tale. New York: E. Bliss and E. White, 1824.

The Deformed Boy. Brookfield, MA: E. and G. Merriam, 1826.

Hope Leslie; Or, Early Times in the Massachusetts. 2 vols. New York: White, Gallaher, and White, 1827.

Clarence: A Tale of Our Own Times. 3 vols. London: Henry Colburn and Richard Bentley, 1830.

The Linwoods; Or, "Sixty Years since" in America. New York: Harper & Brothers, 1835.

Tales and Sketches by Miss Sedgwick. Philadelphia: Carey, Lea, and Blanchard, 1835.

The Poor Rich Man, and the Rich Poor Man. New York: Harper & Brothers, 1836.

The Power of Sympathy: The Autobiography and Journals of Catharine Maria Sedgwick. Ed. Mary Kelley. Boston: Massachusetts Historical Society, 1993.

Letters from Abroad to Kindred at Home. 2 vols. New York: Harper & Brothers, 1841.

The Boy of Mount Rhigi. Boston: C. H. Peirce, 1848.

Tales and Sketches. Second Series. New York: Harper & Brothers, 1858

Howes, Perkins, and Catharine Maria Sedgwick. *The New-England Drama: In Five Acts: Founded on Incidents Contained in the New-England Tale*. [Dedham], MA: M. & W. H. Mann, 1825.

Suggestions for Further Reading

Damon-Bach, Lucinda L., and Victoria Clements. *Catharine Maria Sedgwick: Critical Perspectives*. Boston: Northeastern University Press, 2003.

Welsh, Mary Michael. "Catharine Maria Sedgwick; Her Position in the Literature and Thought of Her Time uqp to 1860." PhD thesis, The Catholic University of America, 1937.

Notes

1. Catherine Maria Sedgwick, *A New England Tale* (New York: E. Bliss and E. White, 1822), p. 37.

2. *Dictionary of Literary Biography*, Vol. 183: *American Travel Writers, 1776–1864*, ed. James Schramer and Donald Ross (Detroit: Gale, 1997), pp. 278–284.

Leslie Marmon Silko

Ceremony

New York: Penguin Books, 1986

Originally Published: 1977

Genre: Mainstream/Literary Fiction/Native American

Quote

> "At one time the ceremonies as they were performed were enough for the way the world was then. But after the white people came, elements in the world began to shift; and it became necessary to create new ceremonies. I have made changes in the rituals. The people mistrust this greatly, but only this growth keeps the ceremonies strong."[1]

Synopsis

Tayo, Rocky, and Emo, Laguna Indians, enlisted in World War II to improve their lives, but found that their service did not allow them an escape from poverty and discrimination.

Rocky is killed in the war, Emo becomes an alcoholic, and Tayo, the central character, has severe psychological problems related to his war service, in particular his guilt over the death of his cousin Rocky in combat—problems not assisted by his heavy drinking. Eventually, Tayo turns to the traditional spiritual practices of his people in an effort to heal himself. Although this is not an easy task, Tayo eventually finds Ts'eh, an herbalist and nature lover, who brings Tayo into better harmony with nature. Ts'eh's work is complemented by that of Betonie, a medicine man who, although he practices traditional healing, incorporates modern ideas into his practice, recognizing that ceremonies must evolve and change to remain relevant. Ultimately, Tayo finds a new way of living, rejecting the pointless violence and abuse of his fellow veterans, and combines the peaceful elements of his traditional culture with an ability to function in the modern world.

Critical Commentary

In *Ceremony* Silko explores the dramatic effects of modernity and war on a traditional society. Descriptions of the life, landscape, and ceremonies of the Laguna Indians are written with careful attention to detail and a full respect for the traditions of the Native Americans. With honesty and unstinting vision, she depicts the experiences of the Native Americans, with their poverty and daily humiliations from the white majority.

Although Silko thoughtfully handles the modern world as well, her intricate descriptions of Native religion and mythology are beautiful and compelling. Native religions are never portrayed as obsolete or quaint, but described as workable and coherent systems that are just as relevant as (and often more effective than) other religions and systems of thought that have been grafted onto the Native culture. This story is placed right after the conclusion of the war when the Laguna veterans—Pueblo Indians of northern New Mexico, a tribe that has lived there since at least the

1300s and that is mostly familiar to Americans from the fact that the famous Route 66 (and now Interstate 40) passed through Pueblo lands—who have seen the outside world, and who were, by virtue of their status in the military, accepted, are dumped back on their reservation, left largely to fend for themselves by a wider society that no longer has need of them.

This is a dramatic and fast-moving story with well-drawn characters and a thoughtfully developed plotline that deals with difficult philosophical issues—in particular, how traditional societies deal with change while keeping their important cultural and spiritual beliefs intact. This novel will be of interest to anyone interested in traditional Native American cultures or traditions, as well as those who simply want a compelling story of how a young man learns to deal with tragedy.

Author Sketch

Born on March 5, 1948, in Albuquerque, New Mexico, Silko was raised at the reservation of Old Laguna in northwestern New Mexico in Cibola County. She graduated with an English degree from the University of New Mexico (1969). Since the early 1970s, Silko has been a full-time writer, supporting herself with a combination of teaching positions and various scholarly grants, including the prestigious MacArthur Foundation Fellowship (1981).[2]

Other Works by the Author

Storyteller. New York: Seaver Books, 1981.
Ordinary Places. Minneapolis: Coffee House Press, 1985.
Almanac of the Dead: A Novel. New York: Penguin Books, 1992.
Sacred Water: Narratives and Pictures. Tucson, AZ: Flood Plain Press, 1993.
Laguna Woman: Poems. 2nd ed. Tucson, AZ: Flood Plain Press, 1994.
Yellow Woman. Edited by Melody Graulich. New Brunswick, NJ: Rutgers University Press, 1993.
Yellow Woman and a Beauty of the Spirit: Essays on Native American Life Today. New York: Simon & Schuster, 1996.
Gardens in the Dunes: A Novel. New York: Simon & Schuster, 1999.
Silko, Leslie Marmon, and Ellen L. Arnold. *Conversations with Leslie Marmon Silko.* Literary Conversations Series. Jackson: University Press of Mississippi, 2000.

Suggestions for Further Reading

Begay, Keats, and Broderick H. Johnson. *Navajos and World War II.* Tsaile, AZ: Navajo Community College Press, 1977.
Felix, Antonia, John Woo, and Jeff Bingaman. *Windtalkers.* New York: Newmarket Press, 2002.
Franco, Jere Bishop. *Crossing the Pond : The Native American Effort in World War II.* Denton: University of North Texas Press, 1999.
Melton, Brad, and Dean Smith. *Arizona Goes to War: The Home Front and the Front Lines during World War II.* Tucson: University of Arizona Press, 2003.

Notes

1. Leslie Marmon Silko, *Ceremony* (New York: Penguin Books, 1986), p. 126.
2. *Dictionary of Literary Biography,* Vol. 275: *Twentieth-Century American Nature Writers: Prose,* ed. Roger Thompson and J. Scott Bryson (Detroit: Gale, 2003), pp. 281–293.

Elizabeth Spencer

The Salt Line

Baton Rouge: Louisiana State University Press, 1995

Originally published: 1984

Genre: Mainstream/Literary Fiction

Quote

> The yard was still the same, though thick now with summer growth, and through it, the flag-
> stone walk still wound whitely past the Great Danes and the urns to the front door. He came
> to the backyard, parked, and walked past the corner of the house, but the Buddha was
> gone. There was only a bare spot in the earth. Even its platform had been taken away.[1]

Synopsis

Arnie Carrington, a former 1960s radical college professor, now resides in southern Mississippi, near Gulfport. As he deals with the death of his wife, he is also trying to rehabilitate some in-
vestment real estate that was, with the rest of the area, devastated by Hurricane Camille in 1969. In
the midst of this descends his old enemy, Lex Graham, from Carrington's former university, who
is also moving to the area. Graham hates Carrington and decides to use his wealth to thwart Carrington's plans. Surrounding these two protagonists are a number of interesting local characters,
including Frank Matteo, a local restaurant owner with connections to the mob, and Mavis Henley,
a waitress and Matteo's sometime girlfriend. As Graham pursues Carrington's destruction like an
avenging angel, these characters begin to find ways to build new and better lives for themselves.

Critical Commentary

The "salt line" is a term for the boundary between ocean and land. This is where things are
in flux, where they change. It could be said that the characters in this novel live at the salt line.
This is a story about the boundaries between people and their reactions—their reactions to
outside changes and to their own inner development. It is a sensitive portrait of people trying
to pick up their lives after storms—storms of weather and of human experience. The landscape
in this novel is one of wreckage; Spencer describes a community living in the aftermath of a
hurricane. But the devastation is portrayed not so much through descriptions of the landscape,
but through the lives of the central characters—particularly longtime adversaries Arnie Carrington and Lex Graham. On the side is Frank Matteo, who, with his schemes and connections
to crime (real and imagined), represents the force of change and modernity, darkness coming
to the coast, and the introduction of alien forces into the fragile environment. Spencer follows
Frank from childhood, using this to illustrate the idea of a man coming from darkness into the
light. In the background, we see the Buddha in the garden and the ducks, reappearing over and
over, symbols of the unknowable and of innocence lost.

The characters are all cut off from each other, although by the end of the novel there appears to be some hope for Matteo, represented by the birth of his child—if not redeemed, he is at least redeemable. There is irony in Spencer's writing about people in the aftermath of a Gulf Coast hurricane, given real-life events after the publication of this novel. In any event, this is a thought-provoking and well-developed novel that should be of great interest to anyone interested in the South.

Author Sketch

Born in Carrollton, Mississippi, on July 21, 1921, Elizabeth Spencer was educated at Bellhaven College in Jackson, Mississippi, and received an MA degree from Vanderbilt (1943). Married to John Rusher of Cornwall, England, in 1956, she taught at several colleges, including Concordia University and the University of North Carolina at Chapel Hill, from which she is now retired. She has received numerous awards and prizes for her work, including the O. Henry Prize for Short Fiction, a National Endowment for the Arts Fellowship (1983), and election to the American Institute of Arts and Letters (1985).[2]

Other Works by the Author

Fire in the Morning. New York: Dodd, Mead, 1948.
This Crooked Way. New York: Dodd, Mead, 1952.
The Voice at the Back Door. New York: McGraw-Hill, 1956.
Knights & Dragons. New York: McGraw-Hill, 1965.
No Place for an Angel; A Novel. New York: McGraw-Hill, 1967.
The Snare; A Novel. New York: McGraw-Hill, 1972.
The Stories of Elizabeth Spencer. Garden City, NY: Doubleday, 1981.
Jack of Diamonds: And Other Stories. New York: Viking, 1988.
The Night Travellers. New York: Viking, 1991.
On the Gulf. Jackson: University Press of Mississippi, 1991.
The Light in the Piazza and Other Italian Tales. Jackson: University Press of Mississippi, 1996.
Landscapes of the Heart: A Memoir. New York: Random House, 1997.
The Southern Woman: New and Selected Fiction. New York: Modern Library, 2001.
Spencer, Elizabeth, and Peggy Whitman Prenshaw. *Conversations with Elizabeth Spencer.* Literary Conversations Series. Jackson: University Press of Mississippi, 1991.

Suggestions for Further Reading

Drye, Willie. *Storm of the Century: The Labor Day Hurricane of 1935.* Washington, D.C.: National Geographic, 2002.
Larson, Erik, and Isaac Monroe Cline. *Isaac's Storm: A Man, a Time, and the Deadliest Hurricane in History.* New York: Crown, 1999.
Lockwood, C. C. *The Gulf Coast: Where Land Meets Sea: Photographs and Text.* Baton Rouge: Louisiana State University Press, 1984.

Notes

1. Spencer, Elizabeth, *The Salt Line.* (Baton Rouge: Louisiana State University Press, 1995), p. 247.
2. *Dictionary of Literary Biography,* Vol. 218: *American Short-Story Writers Since World War II, Second Series,* ed. Patrick Meanor (Detroit: Gale, 1999), pp. 272–280; www.elizabethspencerwriter.com/

Neal Stephenson

The Big U

New York: HarperCollins, 1990

Originally published: 1984

Genre: Speculative Fiction/Science Fiction

Quote

> During the previous five years, a sweatshop of catalogers had begun to transfer the cata-
> log into a computer system, and the Administration hoped that ten percent of the catalog
> could be salvaged in this way. Instead they found that a terrible computer malfunction had
> munched through the catalog recently, erasing call numbers and main entries and replacing
> them with knock-knock jokes, Burma-Shave ditties and tracts on the sexual characteristics
> of the Computer Center senior staff.[1]

Synopsis

This story follows three students at Megaversity through one school year: Casimir Radon, a 30-year-old junior; Sarah, a senior student; and Ephraim Klein, a philosophy major. All have their problems with the bureaucracy, which are paralleled by the gradual disintegration of the university into a war zone. Stephenson describes various student groups, including the Megaversity Association for Reenactments and Simulations (MARS), which is the gaming club, later renamed the Grand Army of Shekondhar the Fearsome, as well as the Stalinist Underground Battalion (SUB) and the Temple of Unlimited Godhead (TUG). When faculty and maintenance workers go on strike, the university begins to implode, and the maintenance workers (Crotobaltslavonian refugees) take over the nuclear-waste disposal site beneath the school. An increasingly serious breakdown of social order ensues, which only ends when the three protagonists effect a mass evacuation, stop the Crotobaltslavonian nuclear blackmail, and bring the story to a conclusion.

Critical Commentary

In his amusing satire of the modern university, Stephenson gives readers a well-characterized, plot-driven novel that, in places, is simply laugh-out-loud funny. Like all satirists, he carries the joke to extremes, but many of the issues that he describes—oversized universities with bloated bureaucracies indifferent to the needs of their students and the larger society—aren't far removed from reality.

Stephenson tells the story of a normal man traveling to a strange place where none of the traditional rules of civilization seem to apply. At first, the Big U seems to be a place of power and order, but as the protagonist travels deeper into it, both literally and philosophically, he finds disorder and, ultimately, anarchy and destruction.

The Big U is a huge university that might be described architecturally as Fascist Georgian—overbuilt and overscale. The university serves as the perfect metaphor for the failure of modern cities, filled with people who fail to connect on any but the most primeval level. The Big U can also be seen, especially through Stephenson's physical description, as another kind of institution—a prison, or perhaps a mental institution where the inmates rule.

Although the book can be enjoyed simply as a satire, like all good satire, it reaches into deeper dimensions—specifically, a criticism of the materialistic statism of late twentieth-century America. Published in 1984, Stephenson's book deliberately incites readers to question a postmodern culture that gives the appearance of liberty while actually quashing it. This is portrayed and even amplified by placing the story within a university that, though ostensibly devoted to the pursuit of knowledge and truth, is more often than not devoted solely to its own perpetuation.

Interesting characters, intriguing plot twists, and Stephenson's insight into the foibles of the modern university make this an engaging read. As an allegory of both the excesses of the university and those of corporate America, *The Big U* stands the test of time as a classic worth revisiting.

Author Sketch

Born on October 30, 1959, in Fort Meade, Maryland, Stephenson grew up in Champaign-Urbana, Illinois, and Ames, Iowa, going to college in Boston. After college he became a professional writer. His first novel, *The Big U*, was published in 1984, followed by a number of other more successful novels. He currently lives in the Seattle area.[2]

Other Works by the Author

The Big U. New York: Vintage Books, 1984.
Snow Crash. New York: Bantam Books, 1993.
The Diamond Age. New York: Bantam Books, 1995.
Zodiac: The Eco-Thriller. New York: Bantam Books, 1995.
Cryptonomicon. New York: Avon Press, 1999.
In the Beginning . . . Was the Command Line. New York: Avon Books, 1999.
Quicksilver. New York: Morrow/HarperCollins, 2003.

Suggestions for Further Reading

Connelly, John, and Michael Grüttner. *Universities under Dictatorship.* University Park: Pennsylvania State University Press, 2005.
Robins, Kevin, and Frank Webster. *The Virtual University? Knowledges, Markets, and Management.* Oxford and New York: Oxford University Press, 2002.
Sterling, Bruce. *Mirrorshades: The Cyberpunk Anthology.* New York: Arbor House, 1986.
Tabbi, Joseph. *Postmodern Sublime: Technology and American Writing from Mailer to Cyberpunk.* Ithaca: Cornell University Press, 1995.
Thelin, John R. *A History of American Higher Education.* Baltimore: Johns Hopkins University Press, 2004.
Vise, David A., and Mark Malseed. *The Google Story.* New York: Delacorte Press, 2005.

Notes

1. Neal Stephenson, *The Big U* (New York: HarperCollins, 1990), p. 169.
2. http://www.electricinca.com/56/stephenson/bio.htm

Elizabeth Drew Stoddard

The Morgesons

New York: Penguin Books, 1997

Originally published: 1862

Genre: Mainstream/Literary Fiction

Quote

My life at Grandfather Warren's was one kind of penance and my life in Miss Black's school another. Both differed from our home life. My filaments found no nourishment, creeping between the two; but the fibers of youth are strong, and they do not perish.[1]

Synopsis

Cassandra Morgeson, a young woman in nineteenth-century New England, is the target of many expectations from her family and society—mainly that she become a docile wife and mother. Cassandra is sent away to her aunt to go to school in Barmouth, which she finds severe and doesn't like. She returns home, but is soon sent away again—this time to school in Rosville, where she lives with distant relations, Charles Morgeson and his wife. Here she begins to flourish. She develops a relationship with Charles Morgeson, who is in love with her. But an accident kills Charles and severely injures Cassandra. After her recovery she returns home and, later, agrees to visit the village of Belem with a man named Ben Somers, whom she thinks is planning to marry her. After this marriage doesn't happen, Cassandra falls in love with Ben's brother Desmond, but they are unable to marry because of his family's opposition. When Cassandra returns home, she finds her mother has died. This death leads to a change in circumstances that, in the end, gives Desmond and Cassandra the freedom to marry.

Critical Commentary

In recent years the work of many prominent historians, such as that of Nancy Cott of Yale, has greatly increased our knowledge and appreciation of the roles of women in nineteenth-century America. Far from being passive victims, as previous research had concluded, women had an active and often controlling interest in their lives and their communities. Elizabeth Stoddard's *The Morgesons* fictionally depicts one of these women, Cassandra Morgeson, in her fight for individuality.

The Morgesons can be read, on one level, as an intriguing piece of regionalism in the same vein as Nathaniel Hawthorne—not especially surprising given that Stoddard both knew and was influenced by Hawthorne. But Stoddard has a more positive and uplifting view of the world than Hawthorne. Her striking descriptions of life in nineteenth-century New England are filled with a wealth of detail. Although the style falls firmly within the tradition of English romantic novels such as those by the Brontë sisters or Trollope, when read at a slightly deeper level, it conveys a social realism that goes beyond the conventions of mere sentimentality to echo the best work of such literary giants as Zola or Balzac.

Stoddard is especially critical, at times almost condemning, of the residual Puritanism of New England and by extension of the parochialism and narrow-mindedness of its residents. Readers may recognize some of Sinclair Lewis's Babbitt in the straitlaced, conventional villagers, especially Grandfather Warren.

Cassandra, on the other hand, is not limited by the convention of separate spheres for women and men, but demands greater equality, implicitly denouncing the fiats of religion that traditionally subjugate women. This condemnation is somewhat surprising, especially in view of mid-Victorian moral sensibilities. Stoddard was not afraid to write a novel that had a great potential to alienate her readers. Indeed, that fact may partly account for her lack of literary recognition.

The author's outstanding command of dialogue is coupled with an adeptness in characterization. Although some of the character types, such as the reformed drunkard, come straight from the tradition of the Gothic novel, Stoddard handles them with originality. Unlike characters in other nineteenth-century novels, Stoddard's characters speak naturally (e.g., "Why don't that lazy Murph light the lamp?").

Cassandra Morgeson takes control of her life, defies the expectations of her society, and becomes her own person: a self-actualized, socially involved—indeed property-owning—member of her community, rather than just a cipher in skirts. Here are the beginnings of a remarkably modern style.

Author Sketch

Elizabeth Stoddard was born Elizabeth Drew Barstow in 1823, in the small coastal town of Mattapoisett, Massachusetts, daughter of a shipbuilder. Educated at Wheaton Female Seminary, in Norton, Massachusetts, she married poet Richard Henry Stoddard in 1852. The couple settled permanently in New York City, where they belonged to New York artistic circles. Elizabeth died in 1902.[2]

Other Works by the Author

Temple House: A Novel. Philadelphia: Coates, 1901.

Two Men; A Novel. Philadelphia: Coates, 1901.

"The Morgesons" and Other Writings, Published and Unpublished. Edited by Lawrence Buell and Sandra A. Zagarell. Philadelphia: University of Pennsylvania Press, 1984.

Elizabeth Stoddard: Stories. Edited by Susanne Opfermann and Yvonne Roth. Boston: Northeastern University Press, 2003.

Suggestions for Further Reading

Cott, Nancy F. *The Bonds of Womanhood: "Woman's Sphere" in New England, 1780–1835.* New Haven: Yale University Press, 1977.

Hansen, Karen V. *A Very Social Time: Crafting Community in Antebellum New England.* Berkeley: University of California Press, 1994.

Lawes, Carolyn J. *Women and Reform in a New England Community, 1815–1860.* Lexington: University Press of Kentucky, 2000.

Notes

1. Elizabeth Stoddard, *The Morgesons* (New York: Penguin Books, 1997), p. 28.
2. *Dictionary of Literary Biography,* Vol. 202: *Nineteenth-Century American Fiction Writers,* ed. Kent P. Ljungquist (Detroit: Gale, 1999), pp. 227–232.

Booth Tarkington

Mary's Neck

Garden City, NY: Doubleday, Doran, and Company, 1932

Originally published: 1932

Genre: Mainstream/Literary Fiction

Quote

> Not being much of a traveler, as I say, I'd taken it for granted that pretty much anywhere
> in the world you'd go you'd find people generally a good deal alike and of a fairly close
> resemblance to those in your own home town. In the fundamentals I still think that's so and
> that all of us human kind operate about the same; but Mary's Neck was beginning to show
> me that different places and conditions have an important effect on the operating.[1]

Synopsis

In the 1920s, the Massey family, from the Midwestern town Logansville, takes a summer
cottage in the quaint New England seaside village of Mary's Neck. Over the course of the
summer, the family has encounters and misadventures with a wide range of local residents,
ranging from the tight-lipped natives to rich Bostonian vacationers, as they try to figure out
how to get in with the "right crowd" of summer visitors. The long-suffering father deals with a
series of comic events, including house renovations, a sinking boat, the mania of his wife and
daughters for antique collecting, and in one hilarious sequence, his agreement to be a country
club manager and deal with unruly nine-year-olds. Through the events of the summer, each
member of the family learns something about themselves as well as the wider world outside
their own.

Critical Commentary

Immensely popular in the period from around 1920 through the 1940s, Booth Tarkington
is rarely read today, and he is remembered, if at all, for his book *The Magnificent Ambersons,*
which was made into an award-winning movie in 1944. The eclipse of his career is regrettable
because he was an accomplished author who used his writing to make insightful comments
about the changing American society of his day. The novel *Mary's Neck* is an excellent example
of Tarkington's wry social commentary.

Mary's Neck can be read as a simple comic novel about Midwesterners going to the sea shore
in Maine for the summer. However, beyond the laughter are some serious issues regarding the
development of the middle class and its place in a rapidly changing society.

The 1920s, when this novel is set, were a time of great social changes, with the development
of automobiles and radios, the creation of modern movements in art and literature, and the
advent of Prohibition. The result, combined with the development of a larger, richer middle

class of white-collar managers, led to social anxieties, especially about class and status—issues that Tarkington makes the focus of the novel.

The story is told through dialogue and conversations, dominated by talk rather than action. One primary source of worry for the adults is the morals of their children, whom they see as increasingly wayward and not following conventional values. Tarkington makes effective use of comedy in the scene where Massey agrees to become (or is rather forced into becoming) the manager of the family club—a scene typical of the most comic in the book.

Regionalism plays an important role in this novel as well. The diverse characters—the Midwesterners, the summer people, Mr. Sweetmus—demonstrate the differences between various geographies. Today, with our ease of travel and communication, it is difficult to appreciate how truly odd people from different regions of the country once appeared to each other. For example, there were regional differences in language use and accent, such as the New England dialect. Tarkington, both through explicit discussion in the story and through his general use of language, explores these language differences and what effect they have on the relationships between people.

Minor characters generally represent different "types"—for example, the Artist, the Football Player, the Young Modern—who contrast with the staid conventions of the Massey family, in particular the father. The issue of social climbing is also addressed, as the daughters, through such things as antique collecting and trying to get into the "right" circle of summer people, attempt to find their place in society—much to the befuddlement of their father.

The issues raised by Tarkington, such as the effect of industrialization and changing technology on young people, are still relevant today. In the 1920s, parents worried about the Model-T and their daughters in the same way that modern parents today worry about the effects of the Internet and violent video games. Tarkington's work has been ignored for decades; perhaps it's time to take another look.

Author Sketch

An Indiana native, born in Indianapolis on July 29, 1869, Booth Tarkington was raised in a middle- to upper-middle-class family, was educated at Princeton, and by the turn of the century had begun to achieve recognition for his writing. By 1922 he had written a number of well-received novels, including *The Gentleman from Indiana* (1899), *Penrod* (1910), *Seventeen* (1917), *The Magnificent Ambersons* (1918), and *Alice Adams* (1921)—the latter two works each winning the Pulitzer Prize. Married twice, the first marriage ending in divorce (1911), Tarkington had one daughter who died before he did. His financial success as an author allowed him to become an expert collector of antique furniture and English paintings. He died on May 19, 1946.[2]

Other Works by the Author

The Gentleman from Indiana. New York: Doubleday & McClure, 1899.
The Two Vanrevels. New York: McClure Phillips, 1902.
Cherry. New York: Harper & Brothers, 1903.
The Conquest of Canaan: A Novel. New York: Harper & Brothers, 1905.
In the Arena: Doubleday, Page, 1905.
His Own People. New York: Doubleday, Page, 1907.
The Guest of Quesnay. New York: Grosset & Dunlap, 1908.

Beasley's Christmas Party. New York: Harper & Brothers, 1909.
Beauty and the Jacobin; An Interlude of the French Revolution. New York: Harper & Brothers, 1912.
The Flirt. New York: Scribner's, 1913.
Monsieur Beaucaire. Garden City, NY: Doubleday, Page, 1913.
Penrod. Garden City, NY: Doubleday, Page, 1914.
Seventeen; A Tale of Youth and Summer Time and the Baxter Family, Especially William. New York: Harper & Brothers, 1916.
The Spring Concert. New York: Ridgway, 1916.
Laughing in German: How Those Americans Almost Disobeyed the Kaiser. New York: Collier, 1917.
The Magnificent Ambersons. Garden City, NY: Doubleday, Page, 1918.
Ramsey Milholland. New York: Grosset & Dunlap, 1919.
Alice Adams. New York: Grosset & Dunlap, 1921.
Clarence; A Comedy in Four Acts. New York: S. French, 1921.
Harlequin and Columbine. Garden City, NY: Doubleday, Page, 1921.
The Fascinating Stranger, and Other Stories. Garden City, NY: Doubleday, Page, 1923.
The Midlander. Garden City, NY: Doubleday, Page, 1923.
Growth. Garden City, NY: Doubleday, Page, 1927.
Looking Forward & Others. London: Heinemann, 1927.
The Plutocrat: A Novel. Garden City, NY: Doubleday, Page, 1927.
Station YYYY. New York: Appleton, 1927.
The Travelers. New York: Appleton, 1927.
Maud and Bill. Indianapolis?: n.p., 1932.
Mirthful Haven. Garden City, NY: Doubleday, Doran, 1932.
Young Mrs. Greeley. Garden City, NY: Doubleday, Doran, 1932.
Little Orvie. Garden City, NY: Doubleday, Doran, 1934.
Rumbin Galleries. Garden City, NY: Doubleday, Doran, 1937.
The Fighting Littles. Garden City, NY: Doubleday, Doran, 1941.
Kate Fennigate. Garden City, NY: Doubleday, Doran, 1943.
Lady Hamilton and Her Nelson. New York: House of Books, 1945.
Your Amiable Uncle: Letters to His Nephews. Indianapolis: Bobbs-Merrill, 1949.
Tarkington, Booth, Blendon Campbell, and William James Jordan. *The Beautiful Lady.* New York: McClure Phillips, 1905.
Tarkington, Booth, John G. Coulter, and Josiah Kirby Lilly. *An Open Letter from Booth Tarkington.* Indianapolis: Indiana Committee for Victory, 1944.
Tarkington, Booth, and Julian Street. *The Country Cousin; A Comedy in Four Acts.* New York: S. French, 1921.
Tarkington, Booth, and Clarence F. Underwood. *The Flirt.* New York: Grosset & Dunlap, 1913.

Suggestions for Further Reading

Torrents, John Edward. *Booth Tarkington: A Man of the Theatre.* Bloomington: Indiana University, 1974.

Notes

1. Booth Tarkington, *Mary's Neck* (Garden City, NY: Doubleday, Doran, and Company, 1932), p. 209.
2. "Booth Tarkington," in *Dictionary of Literary Biography,* Vol. 9: *American Novelists, 1910–1945,* ed. James J. Martine (Detroit: Gale, 1981), pp. 90–96.; http://www.indianahistory.org/library/manuscripts/collection_guides/m0274.html

Jim Thompson

South of Heaven

New York: Vintage Books, 1994

Originally published: 1967

Genre: Crime Fiction/Mystery

Quote

> A stingy moon climbed out of a distant stand of blackjack, and rose slowly in the sky like a sagged-in-the-middle candle. The night wind bustled across the prairie, and the first small stars flickered and winked as though about to blow out. [1]

Synopsis

Tommy Burwell, a young drifter in 1920s Texas, along with his friend Four Trey, gets a job working as a laborer on a remote gas pipeline project. This is brutal work, and the two men live in almost prison-camp conditions with the other laborers, many of whom are ex-cons, drunks, and other societal refuse. Tommy starts a casual affair with a camp follower, Carol. Then one of the job bosses, Bud Lassen, is murdered, and Tommy is accused of the crime. After spending a night in jail, he is released. In a plot by the Long gang to rob the payroll of the gas company, Four Trey and Tommy are blackmailed into helping the gang because the gang is holding Carol prisoner. But there is a shocking ending to the story.

Critical Commentary

Classic Russian novels such as Gogol's *Dead Souls* are characterized by their unsparing and graphic depictions of the human spirit—especially among those people who have been psychologically eviscerated by the trials of life. In Jim Thompson's *South of Heaven* the reader gets a similar experience—gritty and raw. With characters this desperate and nihilistic, you know from the outset that things are going to end badly, probably for everyone involved. But you can't look away.

The plot revolves around attempts to steal the payroll of a gas pipeline company in the wilds of 1920s Texas. Yet Thompson embellishes the story with a range of deftly drawn and sympathetic characters. The young Tommy Burwell is someone who might have a chance in life. Yet he is lost in an endless morass of poverty and violence, aiding and abetting the mysterious Four Trey, who has his own agenda that isn't revealed until the end of the novel. The other characters in the novel exist really as backdrops—the workers at the pipeline camp are largely anonymous—except when they become notable for their brutality, like Bud Lassen. The very anonymity of the characters actually adds to the tension; they exist more or less as a mob, one capable of anything, especially if they don't get paid on time. Carol is the only female character, and even she is somewhat of an enigma—something of a camp follower, but with the sense of untapped potential for something better.

The backdrop of barren and empty west Texas prairies echoes that of the classic Western novel. This is the roaring 1920s, but the contrast between images usually conjured by discussion of that era and the absolute poverty of the characters in this story is striking. The laborers are little more than serfs—held in virtual bondage in company camps in the middle of nowhere. This is fiction, but the circumstances it describes reflect labor history; and the utter misery inflicted on these men to provide the general population with energy should give readers pause for thought.

First and foremost, however, this is a fast-moving crime story. It has an almost cinematic quality, which is unsurprising considering that many of Thompson's novels were adapted for the screen. As the book cover states, this is a "masterpiece of the American dissolute."

Author Sketch

Thompson was born in 1906 in Anadarko, Oklahoma, and educated at the University of Nebraska (BA). He started his publishing career in his thirties, becoming well known for an extensive body of suspense and mystery novels. He died April 7, 1977.[2]

Other Works by the Author

Heed the Thunder, a Novel. New York: Greenberg, 1946.
Nothing More than Murder. New York: Harper, 1949.
A Hell of a Woman. Berkeley: Creative Arts, 1984.
Recoil. Berkeley: Creative Arts, 1985.
A Swell-Looking Babe. Berkeley: Creative Arts, 1986.
Fireworks: The Lost Writings of Jim Thompson. Edited by Robert Polito and Michael J. McCauley. New York: D.I. Fine, 1988.
After Dark, My Sweet. New York: Vintage Books, 1990.
The Grifters. New York: Vintage Books, 1990.
Pop. 1280. New York: Vintage Books, 1990.
The Criminal. New York: Vintage Books, 1993.
The Killer Inside Me. In *Crime Novels: American Noir of the 1950s,* ed. Robert Polito. New York: Library of America, 1997.

Suggestions for Further Reading

Collins, Max Allen, and Ed Gorman, *Jim Thompson: The Killers Inside Him.* Cedar Rapids, IA: Fedora Press, 1983.
Polito, Robert. *Savage Art: A Biography of Jim Thompson.* New York: Knopf, 1995.

Notes

1. Jim Thompson, *South of Heaven* (New York: Vintage Books, 1994), p. 128.
2. *Contemporary Authors Online* (Detroit: Gale, 2002); http://www.geocities.com/SoHo/Lofts/6437/jim.htm

Maurice Thompson

Alice of Old Vincennes

Indianapolis: Bowen-Merrill, 1900

Originally published: 1900

Genre: Historical Fiction

Quote

> From faded letters and dimly remembered talk of those who once clung fondly to the
> legends and traditions of old Vincennes, it is drawn that the Roussillon cherry tree stood
> not very far away from the present site of the Catholic church, on a slight swell of ground
> overlooking a wide marshy flat and the silver current of the Wabash. If the tree grew there,
> then there too stood the Roussillon house with its cosy log rooms, its clay-daubed chimneys
> and its grapevine-mantled verandas, while some distance away and nearer the river the
> rude fort with its huddled officers' quarters seemed to fling out over the wild landscape,
> through its squinting and lopsided port-holes, a gaze of stubborn defiance.[1]

Synopsis

Vincennes, Indiana, in the late 1770s is a sleepy frontier village populated by a colorful group
of pioneers—mostly French—who don't pay much attention to what's going on in the world,
being mostly interested in fur trading and drinking. But with the outbreak of the American Revolution, they must take sides. Led on by the beautiful (and spunky) teenage orphan Alice, they
revolt, in favor of joining the United States. The revolt is initially put down by the British before
the British are, in turn, ousted by the Americans troops of George Rogers Clark, who make an
epic winter trek through freezing waist-deep water to save the town. In the process, Alice falls in
love with one of Clark's men, and everything comes to a happy and romantic conclusion.

Critical Commentary

Alice of Old Vincennes is a delightful yet neglected piece of historical fiction. Combining
compassionately drawn and interesting characters with an exciting story of action and adventure on the American frontier, this is a novel that deserves to be better known—by people
fascinated by history as well as by those interested in regional literature.

The style of this novel could be considered that of a sentimental romance—it may seem
to modern readers almost quaint—but it is this very simplicity that gives the novel its charm.
Unlike modern novels, which are often driven by complicated psychological subplots, *Alice of
Old Vincennes* is a simple story of love and adventure. It's easy to understand, the story moves
quickly, and the outcome is enjoyable.

Innocent Alice lives in the delightfully depicted and rustic village of Vincennes, which is
forced, as a community, to pull itself from its sleepy ways and cast its lot with the development

of a new nation, embodied in the person of heroic George Rogers Clark. Clark leads the villagers in a heroic fight against the British that results in victory and, presumably, in Vincennes and the surrounding region becoming part of the new nation. There is also the romantic subplot involving Alice, which it is difficult to discuss without giving away the ending, but suffice it to say that it will satisfy the reader—especially those whose taste runs to romance novels.

There is the obvious question of whether this is a great novel. Perhaps it isn't—although the image of Alice waving the American flag on the fort ramparts echoes the best of the romanticism found in Dickens's *Tale of Two Cities*. What really makes this story significant for the modern reader is that it reminds us that the middle part of the nation did play an important part in the American Revolution. History, too often, is taught from the edges, and the contributions of more remote areas are not given as much attention. *Alice of Old Vincennes* reminds us of the vibrancy and history of the Midwest and its contribution to the American fabric. It's a well-recommended book for students of history as well as those wanting a well-written piece of Americana.

Author Sketch

Thompson was born in Fairfield, Indiana, in 1844. He was raised and educated in Georgia, where, after the Civil War, he worked as an engineer before moving to Crawfordsville, Indiana, in the late 1860s. Working first as a lawyer, Thompson started a career as a writer and published a number of successful novels before his death in 1901.[2]

Other Works by the Author

Hoosier Mosaics. New York: E. J. Hale, 1875.
A Tallahassee Girl. Boston: Osgood, 1882.
Songs of Fair Weather. Boston: Osgood, 1883.
At Love's Extremes. New York: Cassell, 1885. Microform.
A Fortnight of Folly. New York: J. B. Alden, 1888. Microform.
The Story of Louisiana. Boston: Lothrop, 1888.
The King of Honey Island: A Novel. New York: R. Bonner's Sons, 1893.
The Ocala Boy, a Story of Florida Town and Forest. Boston: Lothrop, 1895.
Stories of Indiana. New York: American Book, 1898.
Milly: At Love's Extremes; a Romance of the Southland. New York: New Amsterdam Book Company, 1901.
Rosalynde's Lovers. New York: New York Book, 1901.

Suggestions for Further Reading

Bigham, Darrel E. *Indiana Territory, 1800–2000: A Bicentennial Perspective.* Indianapolis: Indiana Historical Society, 2001.
Cantor, George. *Old Roads of the Midwest.* Ann Arbor: University of Michigan Press, 1997.
Day, Richard. *Vincennes: A Pictorial History.* St. Louis, MO: G. Bradley, 1988.
Gray, Ralph D. *Indiana History: A Book of Readings.* Bloomington: Indiana University Press, 1994.

Notes

1. Maurice Thompson, *Alice of Old Vincennes* (Indianapolis: Bowen-Merrill, 1900), pp. 2–3.
2. R. E. Banta, *Indiana Authors and Their Books 1816–1916.* Crawfordsville, IN: Wabash College, 1949), pp. 317–319.

Richard Vasquez

Chicano

New York: HarperCollins, 2005

Originally published: 1970

Genre: Mainstream/Literary Fiction/Latino

Quote

> Pete had never before considered moving into an Anglo neighborhood. The more he
> thought about it, the better he liked the idea. He got along fine with Anglos, he knew, and
> there was no reason why he couldn't go buy a nice home. He made a lot more money than
> most of the gringos who worked in factories and offices.[1]

Synopsis

In a multigenerational story of Mexican immigrants in America, Hector moves to California from a small village in Mexico. In the early part of the twentieth century, he and his wife and children illegally cross the border for a better life. Seemingly off to a good start, Hector buys a home and supports his family with a variety of jobs, but gradually drifts into alcoholism. His children—Hortensia, Jilda, and Neftali—drift into petty crime, prostitution, and the like, worn down by prejudice and poverty. Neftali's ambitious son, Pedro, becomes a skilled concrete worker and makes a decent salary, but when he tries to move into an Anglo neighborhood, he finds that even economic success can't insulate him from prejudiced neighbors who drive him out. In the last generation, his two children, Sammy and Mariana, both meet tragic ends.

Critical Commentary

In an epic novel that spans the experiences of an immigrant Mexican family across four generations, Vasquez gracefully traces the series of choices, good and bad, that mark the development of a family over decades as they struggle to come to grips with their culture in the context of a new society and language. The story's backdrop ranges from the violence of the Mexican Revolution to the equally violent underworld of the California drug trade.

The characters—Hector and his wife, Lita; their children Hortensia, Jilda, and Neftali; Neftali's son Pedro; and finally, Pedro's children Mariana and Sammy—are sympathetically drawn, yet each faces his or her own disasters. Hector becomes an alcoholic; his daughters become prostitutes; Pedro, although he seems to have a future as he develops as a skilled tradesman, is still dogged by racism that prevents him from truly moving up in the world; and Pedro's two children come to their own tragic ends.

The events of the novel and the individual acts of the characters are all placed against the developing society of Southern California, where despite claims of progress and the surface appearance of equality, there still loom the old demons of racial intolerance, crime, and poverty.

Each of the characters in the novel is defined by his or her responses to various challenges, and sadly, most of them fail to some extent. Yet the story of their striving gives this novel life. Vasquez, it is clear, writes in large part from his own knowledge of the Chicano experience, and this veracity shines through in his lucid and compelling prose. In the midst of movement and action, Vasquez pauses to make the reader reflect from time to time, yet the story never flags in interest—it is one of those rare novels that one simply cannot put down.

In a society such as the United States where Hispanic Americans are becoming the majority, this novel should be essential reading. Although fictional, it depicts with verve and poignancy the immigrant story, which is a universal one regardless of place of origin, a story that is well worth reading and reflecting upon.

Author Sketch

Born in Southgate, Los Angeles, on June 11, 1928, Vasquez worked at various jobs, including owning a construction company, driving a cab, and working as newspaper reporter for the *Los Angeles Times*. In addition, he was an active writer and novelist. He died in Inglewood, California, on April 23, 1990.[2]

Other Works by the Author

The Giant Killer. Davenport, FL: Coral Reef, 1977.
Another Land. New York: Avon, 1982.

Suggestions for Further Reading

Grajeda, Rafael F. "José Antonio Villarreal and Richard Vásquez: The Novelist against Himself." In *The Identification and Analysis of Chicano Literature*, edited by Francisco Jiménez, 329–357. New York: Bilingual Press, 1979.

Micelson, Joel C. "The Chicano Novel since World War II." Special literary edition, *La Luz* 6 (April 1977).

Serros, Roberto, and Julio A. Martínez. "Richard Vásquez." In *Chicano Literature: A Reference Guide*, edited by Martínez and Lomelí, 404–413. Westport, CT: Greenwood Press, 1985.

Notes

1. Richard Vasquez, *Chicano* (New York: HarperCollins, 2005), p. 221.
2. *Dictionary of Literary Biography*, Vol. 209: *Chicano Writers, Third Series*, ed. Francisco A. Lomelí and Carl R. Shirley (Detroit: Gale, 1999), pp. 275–280.

Susan Warner

The Wide, Wide World

New York: The Feminist Press at the City University of New York, 1987

Originally published: 1850

Genre: Historical Fiction

Quote

> Strong passion—strong pride—both long unbroken; and Ellen had yet to learn that many a
> prayer and many a tear, much watchfulness, much help from on high, must be hers before
> she could be thoroughly dispossessed of these evil spirits. But she knew her sickness; she
> applied to the Physician;—she was in a fair way to be well.[1]

Synopsis

A child, Ellen, is sent out into the world by the death of her mother and an uncaring father. Passed among relatives, she ends up in the care of the spinster Miss Fortune, who has no real idea of how to raise children. Miss Fortune's ineptness is balanced by the kindness and caring of Ellen's other relatives, such as John and Alice Humphreys. Then Ellen is removed from her comfortable urban existence to live on a farm, where she experiences even more difficulties. Yet Ellen submits and endures, and more importantly, her faith never wavers. Eventually, Ellen is shipped off to relatives in Scotland. Although this might seem to have increased her problems, it eventually gets her everything that she desires—marriage, wealth, and a comfortable urban life.

Critical Commentary

In this fascinating example of mid-nineteenth-century domestic feminine literature, Susan Warner tells the story of a young woman's maturation. In so doing, Warner reveals a great deal about the social and moral values of a developing American culture. Much more than a simple piece of sentimental fiction, *The Wide, Wide World* is an important cultural and historical document. Popular at the time, this novel, like Warner's other work, has fallen into something of an eclipse, largely because of changing social and literary tastes. This is regrettable because the book still has much to say to contemporary readers on many levels.

Warner focuses the story on her central character, Ellen Montgomery, and her journey from childhood—during which time she takes an important role in supporting her terminally ill mother—through adulthood. Contemporary readers may see Ellen as too perfect—never seeming to make mistakes and always ready to help others. In reality, what Warner created in Ellen is an idealized vision of American womanhood as understood by people of the mid-nineteenth century. In addition, Warner gives us a series of supporting characters—Mrs. Forbes, Mr. Van Brunt, and Nancy, to name just a few—who add interest and color to the story and who serve to move the plot along at a good clip. They all, in their different ways, try to care for Ellen and mold her into their vision of what a proper young lady is.

The overall pace and tone resemble that found in novels by the Trollopes—the works of both Anthony and his mother—which develop an overall story through a series of small descriptive, supporting elements. For example, there is a delightful description of a shopping trip carried out by Ellen and her mother that not only creates a sense of the closeness between the two, but that also is a lifelike and interesting description of nineteenth-century shopping. In fact, *The Wide, Wide World* might be favorably compared to Trollope's *The Warden*—which was considered by the English critic Max Beerbohm to be the most perfect book ever written.

Never static, the story holds the reader's interest; Ellen's life is constantly filled with movement—both physical and emotional. Underlying themes of homelessness, restlessness, and a reaching for a security of home that is never to be found will echo with today's mobile American reader. In the novel, this theme of dislocation is furthered when Ellen is compelled to relocate to live her European relatives—which also threatens her emerging identity as an American. This represents the ambiguity that many Americans of the time felt about their relations with their trans-Atlantic neighbors and their values.

Warner's detailed descriptions of everyday nineteenth-century objects and activities—from the small teapots and the preparation of evening tea to larger things, such as homes and furniture—make the book historically accurate, not only regarding how people felt, but also regarding how they lived.

Warner's work can also be viewed as one of the first American novels dealing with the conflict between production and consumption. Unlike earlier novels, such as those by Washington Irving, which dealt largely with the idea of production—how does one make a living on the frontier and get ahead?—Warner's book addresses consumerism. Ellen's reaction to problems, like that of many Americans today, is to solve it with a "shopping fix."

The Wide, Wide World retains its appeal to modern readers on a number of levels. It is a sentimental story of a young girl dealing with loss. It is a descriptive and interesting account of life in middle-class America. And finally, it is a thoughtful novel that engages some important intellectual and philosophical questions about what it means to be a woman, what our obligations are to humanity, and what, actually, it means to be an American.

Author Sketch

Born July 11, 1819, in New York City, Warner grew up among the high society of 1830s New York. After her father suffered business reverses, Warner, in reduced circumstances, turned to writing. Her first novel, *The Wide, Wide World*, was very popular and was followed by 30 others as well as by writings in various periodicals. Immensely popular in her time, largely because of Warner's ability to create moving domestic scenes, her work fell into relative obscurity after 1900. Today it is undergoing a small revival, particularly among academics, because of her realism and use of local color. Warner died March 17, 1885, in Highland Falls, New York.[2]

Other Works by the Author

The Wide, Wide World. New York: Putnam, 1851. Microform.
Queechy. 2 vols. London: J. Nisbet, 1852.

Mr. Rutherford's Children. 2 vols. Ellen Montgomery's Book Shelf. New York: Putnam, 1853.

The Hills of the Shatemuc. Philadelphia: J. B. Lippincott, 1856.

Say and Seal. 2 vols. Philadelphia: J. B. Lippincott, 1860.

The Old Helmet. 2 vols. London: J. Nisbet, 1864.

Melbourne House. New York: R. Carter, 1865.

The Little Camp on Eagle Hill. The Say and Do Series. New York: R. Carter, 1874.

Willow Brook. New York: R. Carter, 1874.

Wych Hazel. New York: Putnam, 1876.

My Desire. New York: R. Carter, 1879.

The End of a Coil. New York: R. Carter, 1880.

The Letter of Credit. Boston: De Wolfe, 1881.

Nobody. New York: R. Carter, 1882.

A Red Wallflower. Boston: De Wolfe, 1884.

Daisy Plains. New York: R. Carter, 1885.

Warner, Susan, and Anna Bartlett Warner. *Carl Krinken: His Christmas Stocking.* Ellen Montgomery's Book Shelf. New York: Putnam, 1854.

Suggestions for Further Reading

Foster, Edward Halsey. *Susan and Anna Warner.* Boston: Twayne, 1978.

Noble, Marianne. *The Masochistic Pleasures of Sentimental Literature.* Princeton, NJ: Princeton University Press, 2000.

Seelye, John D. *Jane Eyre's American Daughters: From "The Wide, Wide World" to "Anne of Green Gables," a Study of Marginalized Maidens and What They Mean.* Newark: University of Delaware Press, 2005.

Stokes, Olivia Egleston Phelps. *Letters and Memories of Susan and Anna Bartlett Warner.* New York: Putnam, 1925.

Notes

1. Susan Warner, *The Wide, Wide World* (New York: The Feminist Press at the City University of New York, 1987), p. 181.

2. *Dictionary of Literary Biography,* Vol. 250: *Antebellum Writers in New York, Second Series,* ed. Kent P. Ljungquist (Detroit: Gale, 2001), pp. 338–347; *Dictionary of Literary Biography,* Vol. 3: *Antebellum Writers in New York and the South,* ed. Joel Myerson (Detroit: Gale, 1979), pp. 348–349.

James Welch

Winter in the Blood

New York: Penguin Books, 1986

Originally published: 1974

Genre: Mainstream/Literary Fiction/ Native American

Quote

It could have been the country, the burnt prairie beneath a blazing sun, the pale green of the Milk River valley, the milky waters of the river, the sagebrush and the cottonwoods, the dry, cracked gumbo plats. The country had created a distance as deep as it was empty, and the people accepted and treated each other with distance.[1]

Synopsis

The unnamed narrator of this book lives on a farm near Dodson, Montana, with his mother, grandmother, and stepfather. Haunted by the deaths of both his father, who froze to death, and his brother Mose, who died in an accident, the narrator runs off to town chasing a woman named Agnes. Agnes has been living with him and has left, taking along some of his possessions. The protagonist's adventures in town are a comedy of errors as he gets drunk, keeps finding and losing track of Agnes, and runs into a strange character, the Airplane Man, who has a scheme to have the narrator drive him to Canada. Eventually, the narrator goes back to his ranch, where he finds, to his surprise, that an ancient local recluse is actually his grandfather, and this, in turn, sheds some light on the life of his mysterious grandmother. The novel ends ambiguously with the sum of all these events somehow making the narrator better able to cope with the pain of life and even marry Agnes.

Critical Commentary

As much as a story about modern Native American culture, this is also a story of people trying to survive in rural poverty. In this small and elegant novel, a single young man tries to find his place in the world.

The confused and pointless life of the narrator is that of a man detached from his own culture. Trying to deal with the pointless death of his father, who despite his skills as a mechanic, ended up frozen to death in a drunken stupor, the narrator drifts between life on the reservation and life in the nearby white towns—which mostly consists of his getting drunk and trying various kinds of petty crime.

Although this might seem depressing, the novel is actually filled with humor and surprises. The narrator brings home a Cree girl—whom his ancient grandmother immediately becomes suspicious of—and when the girl takes off with a number of his personal possessions, he begins a comedic quest to find her and recover his stuff. In the meantime, through his interactions with his neighbors, he learns more about his history and the history of his people.

Author Sketch

Born November 18, 1940, in Browning, Wyoming, James Welch was a member of the Black-foot tribe. He attended the University of Minnesota and the University of Montana, where he graduated in 1965. After work in the MFA program at Montana, Welch became a professional writer, producing a wide range of critically acclaimed and recognized work, including both novels and poetry, many dealing with Native American subjects. He died August 4, 2003.[2]

Other Works by the Author

Riding the Earthboy 40; Poems. New York: World Pub., 1971.
The Death of Jim Loney. New York: Harper & Row, 1979.
Fools Crow. New York Viking, 1986.
The Indian Lawyer. New York: Norton, 1990.
The Heartsong of Charging Elk: A Novel. New York: Doubleday, 2000.
Welch, James, and Paul Jeffrey Stekler. *Killing Custer: The Battle of the Little Bighorn and the Fate of the Plains Indians.* New York: Norton, 1994.

Suggestions for Further Reading

Archuleta, Margaret, Brenda Child, K. Tsianina Lomawaima, and Heard Museum, eds. *Away from Home: American Indian Boarding School Experiences, 1879–2000.* Phoenix, AZ: Heard Museum, 2000.
DeMarce, Roxanne, and Blackfeet Heritage Program. *Blackfeet Heritage, 1907–1908: Blackfeet Indian Reservation, Browning, Montana.* Browning, MT: Blackfeet Heritage Program, 1980.
Nasdijj. *The Blood Runs Like a River through My Dreams: A Memoir.* Boston: Houghton Mifflin, 2000.

Notes

1. James Welch, *Winter in the Blood* (New York: Penguin Books, 1986), p. 2.
2. *Dictionary of Literary Biography,* Vol. 175: *Native American Writers of the United States,* ed. Kenneth M. Roemer (Detroit: Gale, 1997), pp. 308–315; *Contemporary Authors Online,* Gale, 2007; *New York Times,* August 9, 2003, p. A12.

Glenway Wescott

The Pilgrim Hawk

In *Great American Short Novels,* ed. William Phillips. New York: The Dial Press, 1946

Originally published: 1940

Genre: Mainstream/Literary Fiction

Quote

In the twenties it was not unusual to meet foreigners in some country as foreign to them as to you, your peregrination just crossing theirs; and you did your best to know them in an afternoon or so; and perhaps you called that little lightning knowledge, friendship.[1]

Synopsis

Taking place in a single afternoon at a house in the French countryside in the 1920s, this is the story of the interactions of two American expatriates who are surprised one afternoon by the unexpected arrival of two Irish visitors, the Cullens, with their pet hawk. The Cullens are stopping by on their way to Budapest. There are interactions on various levels as the two expatriates, Alwyn Tower and Alexandra Henry (whose house is the setting), and the Cullens and their servants of both become involved with each other—all under the watching eye of the captive hawk. The story follows the events of the single afternoon as what appears to be simply a social call becomes an extended discussion and reflection of marriage, faith, hope, and the meaning of human existence.

Critical Commentary

In this small jewel of a novel, Glenway Wescott offers readers a world in miniature that encompasses large and important questions about humankind, freedom, and the choices that people make in life.

Through the voice of the central narrator, Alwyn Tower, Westcott develops the image and symbol of the hawk. In the wrong hands this technique could have doomed the novel, but Westcott effectively uses it to discuss issues of love, marriage, religion, and human freedom. An alternate comparison can be made between the issues relating to the hawk—such as the fact that all captive hawks are born free because they cannot be bred in captivity—and the human experience.

The writing in this novel is clear and elegant—even more than 60 years after publication. The characters are well developed and interesting. At 108 pages, this is a refreshingly short novel, and brevity actually adds to the impact of the work because there is little to get in the way of Westcott's message about freedom and choice.

Author Sketch

Born April 11, 1901, in Kewaskum, Illinois, Wescott briefly attended the University of Chicago before moving to France, where he lived for eight years (1925–33). After returning to the United States, he lived largely in New York City for the rest of his life. As a professional writer, Wescott worked in a variety of forms, including the novel, poetry, librettos, and the short story. He died February 22, 1987, in Rosemont, New Jersey.[2]

Other Works by the Author

The Bitterns: A Book of Twelve Poems. Evanston, IL: M. Wheeler, 1920.
Miss Moore's Observations. New York: M. Wheeler, 1923.
The Apple of the Eye. New York: Harper, 1926.
Like a Lover. Macon, France: Monroe Wheeler, 1926.
A Family Portrait. London: Thornton Butterworth, 1927.
The Grandmothers: A Family Portrait. New York: Harpers & Brothers, 1927.
Good-bye Wisconsin. New York: Harper & Brothers, 1928.
Fear and Trembling. New York: Harper & Brothers, 1932.
Tonny Paintings, Drawings. New York: Julien Levy Gallery, 1936.
The Pilgrim Hawk: A Love Story. New York: Harper & Brothers, 1940.
Apartment in Athens. New York: Harper & Brothers, 1945.
Household in Athens: A Novel. London: Hamish Hamilton, 1947.
Images of Truth; Remembrances and Criticism. New York: Harper & Row, 1962.
Ford, H. D., and G. Wescott. *Four Lives in Paris.* San Francisco: North Point Press, 1987.
Frasconi, A., and G. Wescott. *12 Fables of Aesop.* New York: Museum of Modern Art, 1954.
Maugham, W. S., and G. Wescott. *The Maugham Reader.* Garden City, NY: Doubleday, 1950.
Wescott, G., and P. Bianco. *Natives of Rock: XX Poems.* New York: F. Bianco, 1925.
Wescott, G., Joh. Enschedé en Zonen., et al. *The Babe's Bed.* Paris: Harrison of Paris, 1930.
Wescott, G., and J. Rosco. *A Visit to Priapus.* New York: Jerry Rosco, 1995.

Suggestions for Further Reading

Johnson, I. *Glenway Wescott: The Paradox of Voice.* Port Washington, NY: Kennikat Press, 1971.
Rosco, J. *Glenway Wescott Personally: A Biography.* Madison: University of Wisconsin Press, 2002.
Wescott, G., R. Phelps, et al. *Continual Lessons: The Journals of Glenway Wescott, 1937–1955.* New York: Farrar Straus Giroux, 1990.

Notes

1. Glenway Wescott, *The Pilgrim Hawk*, in *Great American Short Novels*, ed. William Phillips (New York: The Dial Press, 1946), p. 627.

2. *Dictionary of Literary Biography*, Vol. 102: *American Short-Story Writers, 1910–1945, Second Series*, ed. Bobby Ellen Kimbel (Detroit: Gale, 1991), pp. 351–357; *Dictionary of Literary Biography*, Vol. 9: *American Novelists, 1910–1945*, ed. James J. Martine (Detroit: Gale, 1981), pp. 111–116.

Edmund White

Nocturnes for the King of Naples

New York: St. Martin's Press, 1978

Originally published: 1978

Genre: Mainstream/Literary Fiction

Quote

> Congeries of bodies; the slow, blind tread on sloped steps; the faces floating up like
> thoughts out of ink, then trailing away again like thoughts out of memory; entrances and
> exits; the dignified advance and retreat as an approaching car on the highway outside casts
> headlights through the window and plants a faint square on the wall.[1]

Synopsis

Written in the form of eight loosely connected chapters, this story told by an anonymous narrator concerning his relationship with a former lover, tells of a doomed relationship with both its joys and its regrets—especially that his lover has died and any mistakes that were made cannot be undone. It is also a series of meditations on the nature of time that eschew many of the traditional novelistic plot conceptions of time and place.

Critical Commentary

Nocturnes for the King of Naples is less a novel in the traditional sense than a series of loosely connected vignettes that demonstrate the nature of memory. White describes one man's experience in love and his attempt to replace it in some understandable terms.

The book is defined more by its quality of prose than by any idea of narrative flow, and it is the language that captivates readers. Writing in the first person as an anonymous narrator writing to his unnamed lover, White ignores conventions of literary chronology, arranging material by tone and theme, using dual time frames. Lush descriptions of life—from the beautiful to the grotesque—fill these pages with an endless flow of metaphor, producing a wide river of sound, words, and phrases that seems, at times, almost self-indulgent.

In what might be called a surrealist fantasy where past and present are intertwined, White tells a fascinating story of modern bohemian society. He employs an experimentalist style to portray the role of memory in determining human behavior. Following his narrator over a period of years, he shows an evolution and the awakening of a moral conscience and an emotional maturity that allow this character to deal not only with love, but also with its aftermath.

Although it would be easy to label this novel as simply gay fiction, White writes about universal human truths that transcend narrow definitions of sexuality. He handles his theme in a way that is neither gratuitous nor sordid, always showing respect for his characters, from the narrator and the various young men and women to the elderly, sybaritic father. This is a fine book about the nature of the human condition and its ultimate propensity for growth.

Author Sketch

Born in Cincinnati, Ohio, on January 13, 1940, White earned a BA from the University of Michigan (1962). He then worked for Time-Life Books in New York City (1962–1970). In the early 1970s, he began working as a full-time writer with occasional visiting positions in academia at Princeton and elsewhere. White, along with several other writers, was a member of a writing group known as the Violet Quill, which was instrumental in the development and promotion of the genre of gay literature. Recognized as a master prose stylist, White is an insightful commentator and social critic on the gay experience.[2]

Other Works by the Author

Forgetting Elena. New York: Random House, 1973.
States of Desire: Travels in Gay America. New York: Dutton, 1980.
A Boy's Own Story. New York: Dutton, 1982.
The Beautiful Room Is Empty. New York: Knopf, 1988.
Skinned Alive: Stories. New York: Knopf, 1995.
The Farewell Symphony: A Novel. New York: Knopf, 1997.
Marcel Proust. New York: Viking, 1999.
Proust. London: Phoenix, 2000.
The Married Man. London: Vintage, 2001.
Arts and Letters. San Francisco: Cleis Press, 2004.
White, Edmund, and Dale Brown. *The First Men.* New York: Time-Life Books, 1973.
White, Edmund, and Albert Dichy. *Genet.* London: Chatto & Windus, 1993.
White, Edmund, and Adam Mars-Jones. *The Darker Proof: Stories from a Crisis.* New York: New American Library, 1988.
White, Edmund, and Donald Weise. *Fresh Men: New Voices in Gay Fiction.* New York: Carroll & Graf, 2004.

Suggestions for Further Reading

Canning, Richard. *Gay Fiction Speaks: Conversations with Gay Novelists.* Between Men—Between Women Series. New York: Columbia University Press, 2000.
Levin, James. *The Gay Novel in America.* New York: Garland, 1991.
Nelson, Emmanuel S. *Contemporary Gay American Novelists: A Bio-Bibliographical Critical Sourcebook.* Westport, CT: Greenwood Press, 1993.
Summers, Claude J. *Gay Fictions: Wilde to Stonewall: Studies in a Male Homosexual Literary Tradition.* New York: Continuum, 1990.

Notes

1. Edmund White, *Nocturnes for the King of Naples* (New York: St. Martin's Press, 1978), p. 3.
2. http://www.edmundwhite.com; "Edmund White," in *Dictionary of Literary Biography,* Vol. 227: *American Novelists since World War II, Sixth Series,* ed. James H. Giles and Wanda R. Giles (Detroit: Gale, 2000), pp. 335–351.

Marianne Wiggins

John Dollar

New York: Harper & Row, 1989

Originally published: 1989

Genre: Mainstream/Literary Fiction

Quote

> Dying, its progression, is revolt, a rage, a passage, exodus, migration, exclamation, and
> she wasn't dying. She wasn't falling into life, her heat was going, very strange, she watched
> it, watched her endless days, poor thing she sometimes thought about herself as if she'd
> passed a strange girl in the street in early dark, the damp, the cold, she hated London but
> her hatred wasn't anything.[1]

Synopsis

Beginning with the death of Charlotte, who for 60 years has been living a hermit existence on
the shores on Cornwall with her Indian companion, a woman called Monkey, both of them sur-
vivors of some past shared tragedy, this story then flashes back to tell what happened. Charlotte, a
depressed British war widow, decides in 1918 to take a position teaching expatriate British students
in Rangoon. Upon her arrival she begins to shed her inhibitions, developing an interest in art and
nature and having an affair with a sailor named John Dollar. She becomes, if not completely bohemian, at least someone who is seen as an eccentric outsider by the other expatriates. She goes on
a sailing expedition with other members of the local British community who are rather stuffy and
conventional, except John Dollar. They sail to an island off the coast of Burma. The combination
of an earthquake and tidal wave kills almost everyone, except for Charlotte and eight young girls,
who, stripped of social controls and left to their own devices, quickly fall into savagery.

Critical Commentary

John Dollar combines artful descriptions with a compelling horror story. This is a wonderfully readable work that takes a feminine approach to what could be a traditional shipwreck
story to create more imaginative and thought-provoking book.

From its initial paragraph to the end, the narrative flows with power and grace. Wiggins
masterfully describes Charlotte's claustrophobic life in London as well as her journey and life
in Burma and her destiny on an isolated island. Landscapes, full of energy and color, are the
backdrop to life in post–World War I Rangoon. These pictures of urban life later dramatically
contrast with nature imagery—from snakes and dolphins to seashore and shells—that bursts
onto almost every page.

Even more dramatic are the interior landscapes of Charlotte, who rejects her life as a constrained British war widow for a life in Rangoon as a free spirit. Her independence is contrasted,

in a quick episodic style, with the constrained and artificial lives of the British colonists. Likewise, children are presented as individuals with whom the reader can fully engage. When these repressed children are forced to deal with elemental forces of nature, the darkness of their own psychological depths is unleashed, which leads to disturbing and shocking events. The changing perspectives—Charlotte disappears for much of the last chapter, and the focus shifts to the children—add to the drama.

Portraits of people raised in a repressive imperial society, with its emphasis on class and power, who are then suddenly thrust into the wilds with terrible results are not new. Golding's *Lord of the Flies* is an obvious example, along with Defoe's *Robinson Crusoe* and Conrad's *Heart of Darkness*. Wiggins, however, has taken this premise to a new level. This is a riveting story with a profound message about civilization and human nature.

Author Sketch

Born November 8, 1947, in Lancaster Pennsylvania, Wiggins is a professional writer who lived in Europe, including London, for 16 years. Currently, she is on the faculty of English at the University of Southern California. Formerly married to Salman Rushdie, she has received the Margaret Whiting Award, the Janet Heidiger Kafka Prize, and a grant from the National Endowment for the Arts.[2]

Other Works by the Author

Went South: A Novel. New York: Delacorte Press, 1980.
Separate Checks: A Novel. New York: Random House, 1984.
Herself in Love and Other Stories. New York: Viking, 1987.
Bet They'll Miss Us When We're Gone: Stories. New York: HarperCollins, 1991.
Eveless Eden. New York: HarperCollins, 1995.
Almost Heaven. New York: Crown, 1998.
Evidence of Things Unseen: A Novel. New York: Simon & Schuster, 2003.

Suggestions for Further Reading

Fleming, Laurence. *Last Children of the Raj: British Childhoods in India.* London: Radcliffe, 2004.
Hay, Douglas, and Paul Craven. *Masters, Servants, and Magistrates in Britain and the Empire, 1562–1955.* Studies in Legal History. Chapel Hill and London: University of North Carolina Press, 2004.
Morris, Jan. *Pax Britannica: The Climax of an Empire.* New York: Harcourt Brace Jovanovich, 1980.
Vernède, R. V. *British Life in India: An Anthology of Humorous and Other Writings Perpetrated by the British in India, 1750–1947 with Some Latitude for Works Completed after Independence.* Delhi and New York: Oxford University Press, 1995.
Worswick, Clark, Ainslie Thomas Embree, and Asia House Gallery. *The Last Empire: Photography in British India, 1855–1911.* Millerton, NY: Aperture, 1976.

Notes

1. Marianne Wiggins, *John Dollar* (New York: Harper & Row, 1989), pp. 11–12.
2. *Contemporary Authors Online*, Gale, 2002.

Thornton Wilder

The Cabala

New York: Albert and Charles Boni, 1928

Originally published: 1926

Genre: Mainstream/Literary Fiction/Fantasy

Quote

Nothing is eternal save heaven. Romes existed before Rome and when Rome will be a waste there will be Romes after her. Seek out some city that is young. The secret is to make a city, not to rest in it.[1]

Synopsis

A young American visiting Rome in the 1920s is introduced to a strange group of Italian aristocrats, who seem mainly interested in plotting the return of monarchy. This seems both foolish and unrealistic to their guest. Visiting with them in their palaces in Rome, and later on their estates in the Italian countryside, he gradually realizes that these individuals are actually incarnations of the ancient Roman gods, who although displaced from the center of human affairs, have never ceased to be engaged in the world and hopeful of a comeback. During his sea voyage home, the American invokes the spirit of the Roman poet Virgil, who advises him to turn his head from the glory that was Rome and to take pride in the developing new Rome of the Americas, New York City.

Critical Commentary

Thornton Wilder is well known for his novel *The Bridge of San Luis Rey* and his play *Our Town,* both of which explore the connections between human beings However, Wilder started the exploration that he developed in his later work in his first published novel, *The Cabala.*

This fantasy explores the premise of a young man entering the world and becoming enmeshed in the lives and schemes of others. Told in the first person, the story develops the idea of the conflict between ancient beliefs and developing modernity, symbolized by both the American visitor and the modern ideal of New York City.

Wilder's descriptions of life in 1920s Italy and the sleepy Italian landscape have burnished, literary quality. It's clear he is writing from the perspective of many 1920s American expatriates, contrasting the faded Old World with that of modern, jazz-age America. Yet *The Cabala* also exhibits an almost nineteenth-century sense of time and place, with its leisurely pacing and ample time given to character development. Wilder also spends time on long intellectual discourses between the characters, a literary device that may strain the attention span of some contemporary readers.

With mystical themes rooted in classical literature, Wilder has created an allegorical tale that explores serious ideas—the conflict between modernity and antiquity, the differences between the religion of the ancients and modern Christianity. He asks what philosophical solution might be best for human happiness. This intellectual fantasy presumes basic knowledge of classical myths and may not be for all readers, but those who are familiar will find it a rich and rewarding reading experience.

Author Sketch

Thornton Wilder, born in Wisconsin on April 17, 1897, was the son of a diplomat and was educated at Oberlin College and Yale. In the 1920s, he began a brilliant career as a novelist and dramatist, writing many plays that were both commercial and critical successes. In the 1930s he taught at the University of Chicago and later at Harvard. In 1938 and 1943 he won the Pulitzer Prize for drama for his plays *Our Town* and *The Skin of Our Teeth*. He also won several other awards, including the National Book Award and the Presidential Medal of Freedom. Wilder died on December 7, 1975, in Hamden, Connecticut.[2]

Other Works by the Author

The Woman of Andros. New York: A. & C. Boni, 1930.
Queens of France; A Satiric Comedy in One Act. New York: S. French, 1931.
The Bridge of San Luis Rey. Harmondsworth, UK: Penguin, 1941.
Our Century: A Play in Three Scenes. New York: The Century Association, 1947.
The Ides of March. New York: Harper, 1948.
The Happy Journey to Camden and Trenton; Play in One Act. Rev. ed. New York: S. French, 1962.
Heaven's My Destination. Uniform ed. London: Longmans, 1968.
The Eighth Day. New York: Avon Books, 1976.
Theophilus North. New York: Perennial, 2003.
Wilder, Thornton, and Wilhelm Rossi. *The Long Christmas Dinner.* Neusprachliche Textausgaben; 57. Frankfurt am Main, Germany: Hirschgraben-Verlag, 1962.

Suggestions for Further Reading

De Koster, Katie. *Readings on Thornton Wilder.* The Greenhaven Press Literary Companion to American Authors. San Diego, CA: Greenhaven Press, 1998.
Harrison, Gilbert A. *The Enthusiast: A Life of Thornton Wilder.* New Haven, CT: Ticknor & Fields, 1983.
Konkle, Lincoln. *Thornton Wilder and the Puritan Narrative Tradition.* Columbia: University of Missouri Press, 2006.

Notes

1. Thornton Wilder, *The Cabala* (New York: Albert and Charles Boni, 1928), p. 229.
2. "Thornton Wilder," in *Dictionary of Literary Biography,* Vol. 228: *Twentieth-Century American Dramatists, Second Series,* ed. Christopher J. Wheatley (Detroit: Gale, 2000), pp. 267–288.

Sherley Anne Williams

Dessa Rose

New York: Morrow, 1986

Originally published: 1986

Genre: Historical Fiction

Quote

> After a moment, he turned back to her. "You see so many people beat up by slavery,
> Mis'ess," he said wearily, "turned into snakes and animals, poor excuses even for they
> own selfs. And the coffle bring out the worst sometime, either that or kill you. And it didn't
> in Dessa."[1]

Synopsis

In the antebellum South, the lives of two women intersect: Dessa, a runaway slave who is condemned to death for her participation in a slave revolt, and Rufel, a white slave owner. The narrative follows the evolving relationship between the two women, as they work together to gain their freedom, physical in the case of Dessa and emotional in the case of Rufel, causing both of them to confront their most deeply held views about race and slavery.

Critical Commentary

Relationships between slaves and masters in the antebellum South were more complex than is generally acknowledged. These relationships could be further complicated in the interactions of female slaves and white women, who were conjoined in situations where race was compounded by issues of dependence and gender. In *Dessa Rose*, Sherley Anne Williams examines these situations, based on historical events, to produce an elegant novel with a deep intellectual base.

Williams uses as the scribe/narrator of the story the figure of Adam Nehemiah—whose name symbolically represents that of the Old Testament prophet, rebuilder of walls and master of language. Through the course of the novel, the two women are forced to confront their own entrenched attitudes about race, as well as conservative society, represented by Nehemiah, the voice of social norms. Ultimately, both women come to a better, more comprehensive view of themselves as fully realized individuals—defined by their humanity rather than skin color.

Williams accurately depicts the world of the Old South, which contrary to popular conception, was typified by the small farm, where slaveholders held only a few slaves, rather than the atypical large plantation economy associated with the region in the popular mind. This is a novel of life on the margins for both blacks and whites—all trying to resolve the emotional and intellectual contradictions of operating a slave economy within a larger world of emerging capitalist industrialization where the values of a slave society are increasingly irrelevant.

Williams's use of dialogue catches the nuances and tone of Southern dialects without falling into parody. There has been an obvious effort to make the situations realistic. Events are documented with care and empathy as well as a historian's attention to detail.

In *Dessa Rose*, Williams successfully avoids both the pitfall of historical anachronism and that of developing characters who are historical or racial caricatures that diminish the real achievements of the actual figures. The result is a powerful and emotional novel that throws new light on an often misunderstood era of American history.

Author Sketch

Born on August 25, 1944, in Bakersfield, California, Williams was an alumna of California State University, Fresno, where she earned a BA in English in 1966, and of Brown University, where she earned an MA in American literature in 1972. She joined UC–San Diego's literature department in 1973, serving as chair from 1977 to 1980. From 1966 on, Williams was primarily a professional writer who won fame in several genres. Her poetry collection *The Peacock Poems* was nominated for a Pulitzer Prize and a National Book Award. She won an Emmy for a television performance of poems from her second poetry book, *Some One Sweet Angel Chile*. Her *Letters from a New England Negro* was a featured play at the National Black Theatre Festival (1991) and the Chicago International Theatre Festival (1992). On July 6, 1999, she died of cancer.[2]

Other Works by the Author

Give Birth to Brightness; A Thematic Study in Neo-Black Literature. New York: Dial Press, 1972.
The Peacock Poems. Middletown, CT: Wesleyan University Press, 1975.
Some One Sweet Angel Chile. New York: Morrow, 1982.

Suggestions for Further Reading

Blassingame, John W. *The Slave Community: Plantation Life in the Antebellum South.* New York: Oxford University Press, 1972.
Faust, Drew Gilpin. *The Ideology of Slavery: Proslavery Thought in the Antebellum South, 1830–1860.* Baton Rouge: Louisiana State University Press, 1981.
Genovese, Eugene D. *Roll, Jordan, Roll; The World the Slaves Made.* New York: Pantheon Books, 1974.

Notes

1. Sherley Anne Williams, *Dessa Rose* (New York: Morrow, 1986), p. 149.
2. http://voices.cla.umn.edu/vg/Bios/entries/newsreel_sherley_anne.html;   http://ucsdnews.ucsd.edu/newsrel/general/cwilliams.htm

Richard Yates

The Easter Parade

New York: Delacorte Press/Seymour Lawrence, 1976

Originally published: 1976

Genre: Mainstream/Literary Fiction

Quote

> Anyone could be a flashy, irresponsible reporter or a steady drudge of a rewrite man; but the man who wrote the headlines! The man who read through all the complexities of daily news to pick out salient points and who then summed everything up in a few well-chosen words, artfully composed to fit a limited space—there was a consummate journalist and a father worthy of the name.[1]

Synopsis

Sarah and Emily Grimes are the children of divorce. This novel follows their lives over four decades as they drift into two very different lives: Sarah is stable and trapped in a loveless marriage, whereas Emily, more independent, drifts through a series of pointless jobs and even more pointless love affairs—both sisters seeking some kind of redemption and renewal.

Critical Commentary

Yates's *Easter Parade* is a powerful and insightful novel that, through following the lives of two sisters, reveals some universal truths about the human condition. It also adeptly shows the lasting influence that choice can have on the human experience.

Sisters Sarah and Emily are raised in a dysfunctional family that, despite its pretenses to social success, such as the mother being a society sculptress, still leaves them emotionally damaged in various significant ways—especially in their ability to form and maintain lasting healthy relationships.

Yates develops a wonderful set of contrasting character and psychological studies in his examination of these two sisters, set against the turbulence of the late 1950s and 1960s. The plot follows them through their education, their employment, and most importantly, their development and choices of relationships—which, for the most part, are shallow and unfulfilling.

The storyline revolves around a series of vignettes of each sister, developing their lives over time, often with them going for long stretches without interacting with each other and gradually devolving from the comfortable relationship they had with their newspaperman father to increasingly distracted and distant interactions with people who care less and less about them. Sarah settles into what, ultimately, is an unhappy and abusive marriage that leads to her death, and Emily drifts in and out of a series of inadequate relationships—such as a series of

237

one-night stands with the merchant seaman Lars Ericson and others, a brief marriage to another man, and a string of unfulfilling jobs.

Imbued with existential angst and a sense of moral gloom and social failure, this is an honest depiction of the consequence of human choices. Yates has taken the story of two individuals, each of whom has a number of choices and opportunities, and examined in close detail how they either took advantage of or squandered those opportunities. This book deals with the timeless human questions of responsibility and acceptance of consequence.

Yates can be seen as developing—within an American context dominated by materialism— the same kind of powerful human story that writers like Camus and Beckett developed within a European milieu. His writing takes that tradition and adapts it according to an American mindset. Readers who enjoy those existentialist writers and their works—such as Camus's *A Little Death*—will find much in Yates's novel to their liking. Yates was one of the best writers of the twentieth century, and *The Easter Parade* is clear evidence of his genius.

Author Sketch

Yates, born February 3, 1926, in Yonkers, New York, grew up in Manhattan and Westchester. After Army service during World War II, he began a career in writing and journalism that increasingly was filled with visiting professor stints at the New School, Columbia, the University of Iowa, and elsewhere. He developed a substantial body of work that acquired a favorable critical opinion if not the favor of the marketplace. He died November 7, 1992.[2]

Other Works by the Author

Disturbing the Peace: A Novel. New York: Delacorte Press/S. Lawrence, 1975.
A Good School: A Novel. New York: Delacorte Press/S. Lawrence, 1978.
Liars in Love: Stories. New York: Delacorte/S. Lawrence, 1981.
Young Hearts Crying. New York: Delacorte Press/S. Lawrence, 1984.
Cold Spring Harbor. New York: Delacorte Press/S. Lawrence, 1986.
The Collected Stories of Richard Yates. New York: Holt, 2001.
Yates, Richard, and William Styron. *William Styron's Lie Down in Darkness: A Screenplay.* Watertown, MA: Ploughshares Books, 1985.

Suggestions for Further Reading

Bailey, Blake. *A Tragic Honesty: The Life and Work of Richard Yates.* New York: Picador, 2003.
Castronovo, David, and Steven Goldleaf. *Richard Yates.* New York: Twayne, 1996.
Unger, Leonard, A. Walton Litz, Molly Weigel, and Jay Parini. *American Writers: A Collection of Literary Biographies.* New York: Scribner, 1974.

Notes

1. Richard Yates, *The Easter Parade* (New York: Delacorte Press/Seymour Lawrence, 1976), p. 4.
2. *Contemporary Literary Criticism*, Gale, Vol. 7 (1977), pp. 553–556; Vol. 8 (1978), pp. 555–556; Vol. 23 (1983), pp. 479–484.

Anzia Yezierska

Bread Givers: A Struggle between a Father of the Old World and a Daughter of the New

New York: Persea Books, 1975

Originally published: 1925

Genre: Historical Fiction

Quote

A school teacher—I! I saw myself sitting back like a lady at my desk, the children, their eyes on me, watching and waiting for me to call out the difficult ones to the board, to spell a word, or answer me a question. It was like looking up to the top of the highest skyscraper while down in the gutter.[1]

Synopsis

Sara Smolinsky is the youngest of four daughters of an immigrant Polish rabbi on the Lower East Side of New York City in the early 1900s. Her father is an unpleasant and cruel man who sabotages his three older daughters' attempts at love and happiness to ensure that they will stay home and support him. Sara rejects this traditional role of marrying and supporting her parents, especially her father, in favor of living her own Americanized life—living independently, getting a college education and a city job as a teacher, and ultimately choosing her own husband.

Critical Commentary

In this vivid description of early twentieth-century American Jewish immigrant life, Anzia Yezierska offers readers a poignant portrait of a dysfunctional family torn apart by the conflicting needs of father and daughters. Although it describes a particular era and place, the universal theme of the father–child relationship makes this story relevant to contemporary readers, particularly in the light of recent immigration. The title, *Bread Givers,* refers to the paradox of how the men in the story, who are supposed to be the providers, are actually supported by the sacrifices of the women in the family.

Sara's father is dominated by his religious devotion—so much so that he blights the lives of each of his daughters to some degree. He justifies the time he spends on religious study with theological arguments. But his behavior does not reflect the refined spirituality he aspires to.

His wife acts as a mediator between the father and daughters while also dealing with the practical problems of everyday life. Thus, the characters can be seen as representing three different viewpoints: Old World and tradition (father), immigration and survival (mother), and assimilation and change (daughters).

The three viewpoints are repeated by Yezierska in three parts of the story. First, one daughter, Bessie, is thrown into marriage and a life of poverty without opportunity, which leads to misery and oppression, both material and spiritual. The second daughter, Fania, gains material success through her marriage to a Los Angeles businessman, but at the cost of experiencing love and personal growth. The third daughter, Mashah, like her sisters, is also forced into an unsuitable marriage. The fourth daughter, Sara, who is the focus of the novel, gains economic stability and becomes a full person with both intellectual achievement and the hope, at the novel's conclusion, of real love and happiness. At the end of the book, Yezierska ties up the plot a little too neatly. However, the book remains a moving and realistic portrayal of immigrant life and of the challenges faced by countless new Americans.

Author Sketch

Born in Plinsk, Poland, on October 19, 1885, Yezierska immigrated to the United States in 1901. Growing up in similar circumstances to those of the heroine of *Bread Givers,* the daughter of a Talmud scholar and a homemaker, Yezierska worked in a sweatshop and other menial jobs while studying at Columbia University. From 1915 onward, Yezierska worked as a full-time writer, until her death on November 21, 1970, in Ontario, California.[2]

Other Works by the Author

Children of Loneliness; Stories of Immigrant Life in America. New York and London: Funk & Wagnalls, 1923.
Arrogant Beggar. Garden City, NY: Doubleday, Page, 1927.
Hungry Hearts and Other Stories. London: Virago Press, 1987.
Red Ribbon on a White Horse: My Story. London: Virago Press, 1987.
How I Found America: Collected Stories of Anzia Yezierska. New York: Persea Books, 1991.
Yezierska, Anzia, Harold Denison, and Boni & Liveright. *Salome of the Tenements.* New York: Boni & Liveright, 1923.

Suggestions for Further Reading

Bloom, Harold. *Jewish Women Fiction Writers.* Philadelphia: Chelsea House Publishers, 1998.
Dearborn, Mary V. *Love in the Promised Land: The Story of Anzia Yezierska and John Dewey.* New York: Free Press, 1988.
Henriksen, Louise Levitas, and Jo Ann Boydston. *Anzia Yezierska: A Writer's Life.* New Brunswick, Rutgers University Press, 1988.
Konzett, Delia Caparoso. *Ethnic Modernisms: Anzia Yezierska, Zora Neale Hurston, Jean Rhys, and the Aesthetics of Dislocation.* New York: Palgrave Macmillan, 2002.
Rosen, Norma. *John and Anzia: An American Romance.* Syracuse, NY: Syracuse University Press, 1997.

Notes

1. Anzia Yezierska, *Bread Givers: A Struggle between a Father of the Old World and a Daughter of the New* (New York: Persea Books, 1975), p. 155.

2. *Dictionary of Literary Biography,* Vol. 70: *British Mystery Writers, 1860–1919,* ed. Bernard Benstock (Detroit: Gale, 1988), pp. 258–268.

George Zebrowski

Macrolife: A Mobile Utopia

New York: Harper & Row, 1979

Originally published: 1979

Genre: Speculative Fiction/Science Fiction

Quote

> An infinity of universes swim in superspace, all passing through their own cycles of birth
> and death: some are novel, others repetitious; some produce macrolife, others do not;
> still others are lifeless. In time, macrolife will attempt to reach out from its cycles to other
> space-time bubbles, perhaps even to past cycles, which leave their echoes in superspace,
> and might be reached.[1]

Synopsis

In the early twenty-first century, Earth has become dependent on the use of an amazing
structural material invented by the Bulero family. Unfortunately, this material eventually becomes dangerously unstable and explodes—in the process bringing about the destruction of
the Earth and death to billions of its inhabitants. The surviving humans, including the Bule-
ros, must start civilization anew in great asteroid habitats. Following human evolution over
the course of eons, the novel tells the story of "macrolife" and human evolution—all the way
through to the end of the universe.

Critical Commentary

It's a brave and skillful author who can take on the subjects of the end of the earth and the
end of the universe in the same novel—and pull it off successfully. Zebrowski is such an author.
This is a novel that appeals to people who like hard science fiction, filled with gadgets, scientific
theory, and space adventure, as well as to those who prefer a more cerebral approach, dealing
with deep philosophical issues of life and death, cosmology, and the meaning behind it all.

Colorful characters, including members of the Bulero family, populate the novel from beginning to end. Zebrowski takes on the realities of space travel—discussing the specifics of the
engineering and adaptation that it takes for humans to occupy space on a permanent basis.
His speculations will please any science buff, especially given that most of his ideas seem to
be rooted in real science rather than based on some arcane yet-to-be-discovered theories of
physics.

As in many science fiction novels, the heart of this story is adventure. The plot develops
quickly, especially early in the novel, when the failure of the Bulero family's Bulerite com-
pound leads to the immediate and dramatic destruction of the earth. As the story continues,
Zebrowski gets into deeper philosophical issues—the nature of human evolution over millions

241

of years, the ethics of survival, and what the ultimate fate of the human species might be. He aptly illustrates the conflict that might arise between space-dwelling civilizations and world-based ones—each with different attitudes and values. Zebrowski has taken the ancient theme of apocalypse and given it a clean new twist with a clear expository style.

Author Sketch

Born in Austria in 1945, Zebrowski has been recognized by the science fiction community for his writings. He currently lives in upstate New York.[2]

Other Works by the Author

Brute Orbits. New York: HarperPrism, 1998.

Cave of Stars. New York: HarperPrism, 1999.

Swift Thoughts. Urbana, IL: Golden Gryphon Press, 2002.

Asimov, Isaac, George Zebrowski, and Martin Harry Greenberg, eds. *Creations: The Quest for Origins in Story and Science.* New York: Crown, 1983.

Benford, Gregory, and George Zebrowski, eds. *Skylife: Space Habitats in Story and Science.* New York: Harcourt, 2000.

Dann, Jack, and George Zebrowski, eds. *Faster Than Light: An Original Anthology About Interstellar Travel.* New York: Harper & Row, 1976.

Pellegrino, Charles R., and George Zebrowski. *The Killing Star.* New York: William Morrow and Co., 1995.

Scortia, Thomas N. *The Best of Thomas N. Scortia.* Edited by George Zebrowski. Garden City, NY: Doubleday, 1981.

Suggestions for Further Reading

Finney, Ben R., and Eric M. Jones. *Interstellar Migration and the Human Experience.* Berkeley: University of California Press, 1985.

Gould, Stephen Jay. *Wonderful Life: The Burgess Shale and Nature of History.* New York: Norton, 1989.

Steele, Allen M. *Coyote Frontier: A Novel of Interstellar Exploration.* New York: Ace Books, 2005.

Notes

1. George Zebrowski, *Macrolife: A Mobile Utopia* (New York: Harper & Row, 1979), p. 278.
2. http://www.isfdb.org/cgi-bin/ea.cgi?George_Zebrowski

Index

About the Author

KARL BRIDGES is Associate Professor, Reference Librarian/Bibliographic Instructor and Coordinator of Electronic Resources at the Bailey/Howe Library, Department of Information and Instruction, University of Vermont, Burlington.